D0427244

PRAISE FOR
Proclaiming the Message of Life

"Clergy and laity alike are called to root their pro-life commitment in the Word of God. Fr. Pavone's new book gives all of us an effective way to do that, and I recommend it to those in the pulpit and those in the pews as well!"

—MOST REV. MICHAEL J. SHERIDAN, S.Th.D., bishop of Colorado Springs

"People frequently ask me why their priests do not preach more about life and against abortion. Now I can recommend Fr. Frank Pavone's book as a resource that lays out the message of life, responds to the common objections to preaching this message in the pulpit, and integrates the life message to the rich selection of Scripture texts that are proclaimed through each of the Sundays of all three cycles of the lectionary. Not only can priests learn from this book, but all Christ's faithful laity can learn how to bring the message of life in a way that is more integrated with God's sacred Word."

—FR. MITCH PACWA, SJ, author, host of *EWTN Live*

"Written by one of the Christian heroes of our age, Fr. Frank Pavone, this timely book will help bishops, priests and deacons fulfill their gospel duty to preach and teach about the great moral evil of our age, the denial of the fundamental human right to life of our youngest neighbors in their first home…their mother's womb."

—DEACON KEITH FOURNIER, editor in chief at Catholic Online

"*Proclaiming the Message of Life* is a welcome guide to clear and compassionate preaching on abortion. Ministers are often afraid to preach on the 'difficult issues,' fearing how people will receive the message. Fr. Pavone provides clergy with biblically based tools for preaching the truth in love. This book is a much needed resource and a tremendous gift for the entire Church, one that will empower, inspire, and encourage preachers to build a culture of life."

—DEACON HAROLD BURKE-SIVERS, author, *Behold the Man: A Catholic Vision of Male Spirituality*

"*Proclaiming the Message of Life* is a powerful resource not only for preachers, but for those of us who, as lay faithful, want to prepare each week to hear the Gospel of Life in the Sunday readings."

—ALAN NAPLETON, president, Catholic Marketing Network

"*Proclaiming the Message of Life* is a rich and practical resource for priests, deacons, and anyone responsible for preaching or teaching on the dignity of human life. Do not mistake this book for a mere collection of homilies on life. It is much more: It is a resource that stimulates and inspires the preacher to confront the most critical issue of our time in a manner that is pastoral, effective, compassionate, and intellectually sound. Your pastor or deacon will thank you for the gift of this book!"

—FR. ROBERT SIRICO, president, the Acton Institute

"*Proclaiming the Message of Life* by Father Frank Pavone is an excellent book for any priest or deacon who wishes to consistently preach pro-life throughout the liturgical year.... The second part of the book can be used by the average layperson as a scriptural, pro-life meditation on the weekly Mass readings. I recommend it for every seminarian, deacon, and priest, as well as anyone wanting to continue the spiritual battle for defending the unborn."

—FR. JOHN TRIGILIO, JR., Ph.D., president, Confraternity of Catholic Clergy

PROCLAIMING THE MESSAGE OF LIFE

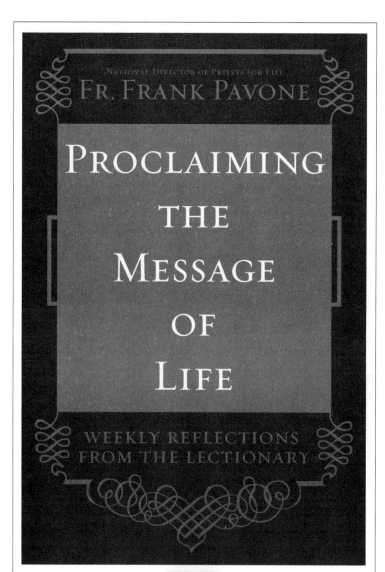

NATIONAL DIRECTOR OF PRIESTS FOR LIFE

FR. FRANK PAVONE

PROCLAIMING THE MESSAGE OF LIFE

WEEKLY REFLECTIONS FROM THE LECTIONARY

servant
AN IMPRINT OF
FRANCISCAN MEDIA
Cincinnati, Ohio

Unless otherwise noted, Scripture texts in this work are taken from the *Lectionary for Mass for Use in the Dioceses of the United States of America*, second typical edition © 2001, 1998, 1997, 1986, 1970 Confraternity of Christian Doctrine, Inc., Washington, D.C. Used with permission. All rights reserved. No portion of this text may be reproduced by any means without permission in writing from the copyright owner. Scripture texts marked *NAB* are taken from *New American Bible*, revised edition © 2010, 1991, 1986, 1970 Confraternity of Christian Doctrine, Washington, D.C., and are used by permission of the copyright owner. All Rights Reserved. No part of the *New American Bible* may be reproduced in any form without permission in writing from the copyright owner. Quotes are taken from the English translation of the *Catechism of the Catholic Church* for the United States of America (indicated as *CCC*), 2nd ed. Copyright 1997 by United States Catholic Conference—Libreria Editrice Vaticana.

Cover and book design by Mark Sullivan

LIBRARY OF CONGRESS CATALOGING-IN-PUBLICATION DATA
Names: Pavone, Frank A., author.
Title: Proclaiming the message of life : weekly reflections from the
lectionary / Fr. Frank Pavone.
Description: Cincinnati, Ohio : Servant, 2016. | Includes bibliographical
references and index.
Identifiers: LCCN 2015050144 | ISBN 9781616369309 (alk. paper)
Subjects: LCSH: Church year meditations. | Catholic Church. Lectionary for
Mass (U.S.). | Life—Religious aspects—Catholic Church—Meditations. |
Abortion—Religious aspects—Catholic Church—Meditations.
Classification: LCC BX2170.C55 P38 2016 | DDC 242/.3—dc23
LC record available at http://lccn.loc.gov/2015050144

ISBN 978-1-61636-930-9

Copyright ©2016, Frank Pavone. All rights reserved.
Published by Servant, an imprint of Franciscan Media
28 W. Liberty St.
Cincinnati, OH 45202
www.FranciscanMedia.org

Printed in the United States of America.
Printed on acid-free paper.
16 17 18 19 20 5 4 3 2 1

· · · · · · · · · ·
CONTENTS

My Prayer for You

There is a lot of pain in our midst regarding the tragedy of abortion. Some of the pain comes from having been involved in an abortion. Some of the pain, on the other hand, comes from simply knowing it happens. We Christians share in that pain. We are also called to address it.

For priests, deacons, and other preachers, dealing with abortion is an essential aspect of our call to serve the needs of people. Most people in our churches understand that abortion is wrong but don't make much of an effort to learn more about it. Many of them know that doing something to stop abortion will involve sacrifices they would rather not make. And facing abortion directly will make them feel worse about *not* having done something about it.

In the midst of this dilemma, we are called to promote respect for the lives of our unborn brothers and sisters, to encourage and equip people to protect those lives, and to bring hope, reconciliation, and healing to those who have procured or cooperated in abortions. God calls us to be ministers of truth and compassion, two realities that, far from being contrary to each other, are essential aspects of each other. God, after all, is both truth and compassion, and he is one.

To fail in compassion for the weakness and suffering of people is to fail to reflect the truth about their lives and the truth about God's love. To fail to bear witness to the truth, in all its clarity and vigor, is to fail in compassion, because truth is as necessary for the growth of the spirit as food is for the body.

I wrote these pages to help priests and deacons preach, in truth and compassion, about what the United States bishops have called "the fundamental human rights issue of our day," that is, abortion.[1] I hope this book will also be helpful for Christian ministers of other denominations and for all who want to speak about life issues from a Christian perspective. My hope is that these reflections will provide a springboard, a stimulus to prayerful thought, from which you will be able to build a fruitful pro-life ministry adapted to the concrete situation in which you serve.

As national director of Priests for Life, I have preached about abortion in different parts of the country every week since 1993. I have been in all fifty states multiple times. I can summarize the reaction I receive from people in two words: "Thank you!" People are grateful to hear the truth spoken in compassion. They are grateful when their clergy can help them deal intelligently and courageously with the pain that abortion brings to all of us.

I pray that these pages will help all preachers do precisely that. I also pray that all Christians will be strengthened by Scripture and the teachings of the Church to share God's mercy with those wounded by abortion and to help save those being threatened by it.

PART ONE

An Urgent Message

CHAPTER ONE

Are You Ready to Talk about Abortion?

· ·

Father, I came into this church this morning totally pro-abortion, and the homily changed my views completely.

Father, I had an abortion, and sometimes it hurts to hear about it, but please keep up the preaching! I gladly endure whatever pain I have, because I know the homilies will keep some other woman from ever going through what I have gone through.

Hi! I'd like to begin this letter by thanking you for last week's homily. I was deeply moved, and so was my younger brother. I'm seventeen, and he's twelve. We did not fully understand what goes on in abortion till your homily. We both would like to get on the mailing lists of pro-life organizations.

These are three of the thousands of reactions I have received after preaching about abortion over the years. They are characteristic of the content and tone of the others. They offer evidence that people are open to hearing about this immense evil. More than that, many are eager to join the pro-life effort.

WHERE ARE CHRISTIANS ON ABORTION?

Sometimes we hear that "most Americans are pro-choice." The statement is meaningless until the term *pro-choice* is defined. A more helpful way to understand what most people think is to ask them the specific circumstances in which they think abortion should be legal.

A detailed analysis of Gallup polling reveals that most Americans believe abortion should be either illegal in all circumstances or legal only in a few circumstances.[2] A Gallup poll in May of 2013, for instance, showed that only 26 percent of the public thought abortion should be legal in all circumstances, which is the policy advocated by the abortion lobby, while 58 percent opposed legal abortion in all or most circumstances.[3]

An analysis of statistics from multiple sources suggests that abortions done for the circumstances of rape, incest, or risk to maternal life constitute less than 1 percent of total abortions.[4] The testimony of many medical experts asserts that abortion is *never* necessary to save a mother's life. Thus a majority of Americans oppose 99 percent of the abortions taking place in our country.

We have also seen for decades a curious phenomenon: Among the majority of Americans who oppose most abortions but permit some, there is a significant number of people who admit that the abortions they consider justified are murder. In a June 2000 poll conducted by the *Los Angeles Times,* 57 percent of respondents called abortion "murder." In a 1989 *Los Angeles Times* poll, 57 percent called abortion "murder," including one-fourth of those who also said that they "generally favored abortion." In 1998, a CBS–*New York Times* poll indicated that some 50 percent of respondents were willing to call abortion "murder," yet one-third of those people said it is sometimes the best course of action for a woman to take.

What is going on here? Why are there so many abortions when most people oppose them and even admit what they are?

First of all, people have gotten the message from the pro-life movement that abortion kills a baby. They have also gotten the message from the abortion-rights side that sometimes abortion benefits women. Having accepted both messages, the majority of Americans belong to the conflicted middle. Where this group ultimately goes is where America will ultimately go on abortion.

The other phenomenon at work is denial fueled by pain. There are more people each day who are directly involved in an abortion decision and are therefore, at least initially, not eager to get involved in an effort to either expose what it is or stop it. There are an even larger number of people whose pain over abortion is not because of direct personal involvement but because of a dilemma. These people know enough to realize that to learn a little more will involve some risk. They know that if they look at abortion too directly, they will not be at peace with themselves unless they do something to stop it. Yet they know that if they try to stop it, there will be a price to pay. They may lose friends or face other kinds of opposition. They don't want to make the sacrifice necessary to confront injustice.

What, then, is their solution to this dilemma? They ignore the problem altogether. Denial protects them from the pain of the situation. This is why some people become angry when the topic of abortion is raised. They were succeeding in ignoring it until someone brought it to the surface.

WHAT CAN WE TELL PEOPLE?

Given the attitudes people have about abortion and the pro-life effort, we can trace several themes we need to communicate as we speak on this topic.

We Are on Their Side

A discussion of abortion, whether in private or public, should acknowledge the pain that most of us feel about it, whether we describe ourselves as pro-life or not. The psychological attitude to take and to convey is, "You are not my enemy. We are in this painful situation together, and we need to help each other out of it."

We can approach the individual who reacts angrily to a pro-life discussion as we do others affected by personal disasters. We are dealing with good people who have pain, not with enemies. We can gently ask questions so as to draw out the cause for their anger and help them think about it.

In all my preaching on abortion, I can count on one hand the number of people who came to me angry afterward. They were all in some kind of comfortable denial until this meddlesome preacher brought it up. I invite such people to sit down in an out-of-the-way place to talk calmly. Some will do that, and others will leave. But it is much harder to criticize or to be angry with someone who wants to *listen* to you rather than lecture you or get angry in turn. Let people know that you are listening, that you know their pain, and that the message of respect for life that you steadfastly preach also says that their lives are precious, no matter how strongly they disagree with you.

To Be Pro-Life Is to Be Pro-Woman

The difference between pro-life and pro-choice is not that pro-lifers love the baby and pro-choicers love the woman. The pro-choice message says you can separate the two, and the pro-life message says you cannot. Pro-lifers are criticized for being "fetus lovers" who are insensitive to women. But one cannot love the child without loving the mother.

Abortion defenders claim that they are loving women even as they admit that they are killing women's children. But one cannot love the woman without loving the child. Nor can one harm the child without harming the mother.

The message must be clear: To be pro-life is to be pro-woman. The challenge the pro-life movement gives to society is, "Love them both!" It is a message of equality. It is a challenge to *expand* the circle of our love, welcome, and protection. There is no conflict in being pro-life and caring about women.

Opposing Abortion Does Not Mean Opposing Those Who Have Them

An aspect of the pro-woman theme of our pro-life preaching is the healing and forgiveness the Church and the pro-life movement offer to those who have been involved in abortion. I have ministered to people who have had as many as twenty-five abortions. When I mention this in my homilies, I also proclaim that, even for those women, the doors of the Church are open!

The Church has the perfect spiritual and psychological balance necessary for those who have been involved in an abortion. The last thing such a person needs to hear is, "What you did is no big deal." The individual who is enduring post-abortion grief has begun to realize precisely what a big deal her abortion was! Now this person needs someone to tell her that she should not feel silly for feeling sad, that there is indeed a reason for the grief in her heart, and that what her heart is telling her is true: Her child was killed.

Obviously, someone already did this woman (and her child) the great disservice of telling her that the abortion would be no big deal. Accepting that line was a major act of denial. Healing now begins when the woman breaks out of denial and calls the evil what it is. The clear preaching of the Church about abortion helps her to do this.

At the same time, the post-abortive woman does not need to hear, "You are rejected; there is no hope." As she realizes the evil that has occurred, she may be tempted to say this to herself. The Church, however, contradicts that despair with the clear message of forgiveness, expressed by St. John Paul II in his encyclical The Gospel of Life:

> I would now like to say a special word to women who have had an abortion. The Church is aware of the many factors which may have influenced your decision, and she does not doubt that in many cases it was a painful and even shattering decision. The wound in your heart may not yet have healed. Certainly what happened was and remains terribly wrong. But do not give in to discouragement and do not lose hope. Try rather to understand what happened and face it honestly. If you have not already done so, give yourselves over with humility and trust to repentance. The Father of mercies is ready to give you his forgiveness and his peace in the Sacrament of Reconciliation. To the same Father and to his mercy

you can with sure hope entrust your child. With the friendly and expert help and advice of other people, and as a result of your own painful experience, you can be among the most eloquent defenders of everyone's right to life. Through your commitment to life, whether by accepting the birth of other children or by welcoming and caring for those most in need of someone to be close to them, you will become promoters of a new way of looking at human life.[5]

The Church accompanies all who have been involved in abortion—the mother, the father, the grandparents, and even the abortion provider—to the forgiveness and healing Christ offers.

Some pastors refrain from preaching about abortion with the sincere motive of not hurting women who have had abortions. Yet that silence does not interpret itself. The person grieving over abortion can infer that the pastor does not know her pain or that he does not care or that there is no hope. Silence does not help those in the pain of abortion. Clear and compassionate homilies can break through the silence that leads to disastrous choices in the first place.

Abortion Is Their Business

The key challenge in presenting people with the abortion issue is not to convince them that it is wrong, but rather to overcome their conviction that someone else's abortion is "none of my business." Abortion defenders will say, "If you are against abortion, fine. Don't have one. But leave the rest of us alone to exercise our own beliefs and make our own choices." Many people who oppose abortion will therefore feel out of place trying to stop it. They see it as wrong but as a private wrong, making it none of their business to interfere.

One of the key tasks necessary here is to de-isolate the issue. People understand that we have to intervene to help the poor, the AIDS victims, the drug addicts, the victims of crime, and the victims of wars. Even if we do not know their names and have never seen the faces of these victims, we know it is our business to help them.

We do not hear people say, "I would never abuse my child, but if the other person wants to do so, that's her choice." People do not say that, because they realize that some choices have victims. When somebody's choice destroys or threatens somebody else's life, that's everyone's business. It is, after all, the business of love, which intervenes to save our brothers and sisters in need. That is why it is both our business and our privilege to work to stop abortions.

There Is Something They Can Do to Stop Abortion
Many oppose abortion but do not think anything can be done. Some think of the pro-life movement as an extreme and fanatical movement characterized by activities they want nothing to do with. If we awaken people to the evil but do not guide their response, they will either end up depressed or perhaps act irresponsibly.

The problem is not that there is nothing that can be done but that there are not enough people doing the perfectly legal, peaceful, and effective activities that can end abortion. Presenting such options will overcome this obstacle to the involvement of many in this cause.

THREE ELEMENTS OF A PRO-LIFE HOMILY
Speaking to preachers now, what of all this can we convey in ten or fifteen minutes?

In the preaching seminars that Priests for Life presents to clergy in dioceses around the country, we explain three key points that need to be integrated, in the following order, into a homily that seeks to draw pro-life themes from the readings of the day.

There are alternatives to abortion.
Many people are pro-choice not because they like abortion but because they wonder, "How can women live without it?" The good news is that the

Church and the pro-life movement provide better choices than abortion. In fact, those who procure abortions often do so not because of freedom of choice but because they feel they have no freedom and no choice. Yet a wide range of help is available for anyone who needs it.

It is amazing to see how many people who know that the Church opposes abortion are unaware of the Church's willingness to provide alternatives. Thousands of pregnancy resource centers, agencies, private individuals, and families provide financial assistance, medical services, legal advice, counseling, places to live, jobs, education, and assistance to help women keep their children or place their children for adoption. People at Mass can be offered a handout with phone numbers and websites connecting them to these resources, and they can pass on this information to those who need this help.

Informing parishioners of the vast network of pregnancy supports makes them feel good about being Catholics and about helping the pro-life movement. By mentioning the point about alternatives first, a major objection is tackled before it arises: "What are those of you who oppose abortion going to do to help the woman who needs it?"

There is forgiveness and healing after abortion.
This point is critical, because many people feel they cannot be forgiven. If all abortions end tomorrow, the mission of healing will remain. The gospel of life is a gospel of mercy. The hope of mercy, furthermore, prevents the additional abortions to which despair often leads. (According to the Centers for Disease Control and Prevention, some 44 percent of abortions in the United States are repeat abortions.[6])

Many hesitate to become active in the pro-life movement because they think that to oppose abortion means to oppose those who have had them, and they do not want to compromise a relationship with a sister, cousin, or friend. If they see that being pro-life means embracing these women with forgiveness, they may be more inclined to join the effort. A convenient way to point people to resources for healing after abortion is the website we at Priests for Life have set up called AbortionForgiveness.com.

Help people see through the slogans that make tolerance of abortion seem so reasonable.

The term pro-choice, for example, fails to point to what is chosen. It would never be applied to child abuse or violent crime. Some choices have victims, including the choice of abortion.

"Safe and legal abortion" is a slogan that misleads people. If it is legal, it must be safe, they think, and to keep it safe, we need to keep it legal. Yet the abortion industry is the most unregulated surgical industry in the nation. It regularly destroys the health and lives of the women who procure abortions in legal facilities.

Also focus on some basic facts that most people do not know: There is an abortion every twenty-nine seconds in America; abortions happen through all nine months of pregnancy; less than 1 percent occur following rape or incest.

The practical follow-up to the homily is a handout about alternatives. It is a Priests for Life brochure entitled *You Can Save Someone's Life Today!* It tells of practical things people can do to help stop abortions. It directs them to key pro-life websites. It gives them toll-free numbers (like 1-800-712-HELP) that can be dialed from anywhere in the nation twenty-four hours a day for counseling with a live person and other assistance. These resources serve those who are tempted to have abortions and those who have already had them.

I suggest you have brochures at all the exits of the church and that you ask everyone to take one home, read it, keep it, and use it. These brochures, combined with the courage of those willing to speak up, have saved lives throughout the country.

CHAPTER TWO

A Message for Young and Old

Some people are afraid to use the word *abortion* with children. As someone once told me, "They don't understand all the aspects of it." Some express the concern that children will be traumatized if we tell them that abortion kills babies. But the pro-life message will not harm our children. What will harm them is the pro-choice mentality, which will train them to think that human life is a disposable item and which, if unchallenged, may lead them to an abortion mill someday.

Teaching children about abortion is not as difficult as many think. Children are particularly receptive to the message of equality of all people and to the truth that might does not make right. They have a keen sense of justice and fairness. They know what it means to need protection from dangers they can neither withstand nor understand. They know what a baby is, and they know it is wrong to kill a baby.

HUMAN DIGNITY

At the start of one homily, I asked for a volunteer from among the youngest members of the congregation. Sharon, who was about six, came forward. I had her stand next to me, facing the people, and I asked her, "Sharon, are there people out there who are bigger than you?"

"Yes!" Sharon exclaimed.

"Are there people out there who are older than you?"

"Yes!"

"Are there people out there who are stronger than you?"

"Yes!"

"Are there people out there who are more important than you?"

"No!" she declared, with even more conviction in her voice.

All the other children understood the same thing. And thus they understood the key problem in the abortion tragedy. Abortion builds on the lie that the smallest and weakest among us have less value and can even be discarded. Fortunately, children have not been around long enough to practice the mental gymnastics and exercises in denial that are necessary for developing and maintaining a pro-choice position.

It is not necessary to teach children the details of reproduction before they learn that abortion is a bad thing. The basis for teaching about abortion is not the reproductive system but the dignity and worth of every human person—whether that person is big or small, young or old, healthy or sick, wanted or unwanted, convenient or inconvenient. It is the basis from which we teach that the commandment "You shall not kill" applies to every category of people.

We do not aim to teach children all the aspects of abortion. Let's face it: Nobody understands all its aspects. The key point with children is that when they hear the word *abortion*, they know it is something bad, something that kills, something to be avoided.

Education is not just concepts. We influence children not only to think clearly about abortion but also to feel a proper aversion toward it. They should be trained to reject it and to see it as a part of the list of injustices and evils in the world rather than part of a list of rights, freedoms, and choices. The Vatican's Pontifical Council for the Family has written, "Before adolescence, the immoral nature of *abortion*, surgical or chemical, can be gradually explained in terms of Catholic morality and reverence for human life."[7]

I once sat in on a staff meeting at which a proposal was made to set up a sign on parish property that said, "Abortion Kills Children." The staff voted down the proposal on the grounds that it would give nightmares to the school children who would see it. A few days later, I was in that school, and in the corridor of the first and second grade, I saw posters made by the students. There were skeletons coming up from the grave, people falling off an abyss, and various other nightmare scenes, with the messages "Drugs kill" and "Saying yes to drugs is like saying yes to Mr. Death."

Isn't it curious how selective we can be about which messages will frighten our children? The Partnership for a Drug-Free America has a television commercial that says, "The perfect time to talk to your child about using marijuana is when you think he's too young to talk about using marijuana. Talk to your child before someone else does." Abortion is a clear parallel.

To a parent who once objected to my pro-life preaching because her children were present, I gently pointed out that I share her concern for her children's welfare. I then told her that it is better that they hear about abortion from me, in the presence of their parents, than from pro-choice people. Parents can discuss children's questions and calm their fears, while pro-choice people will tell them the dangerous lie that abortion is no big deal. Worse yet is that children might hear about abortion from the so-called counselor who is trying to sell them one.

LIES HURT MORE THAN THE TRUTH

Parents are the primary educators of their children. Priests and other educators must cooperate closely with them. This does not mean, however, that parents have the right to keep their children from the truth.

In one instance when I spoke to seventh graders about how abortion harms women, a girl's parents objected because I had not received their permission to bring up the topic in class. I assured them that I had no intention of bypassing their parental authority and that, in fact, I welcomed their input. I pointed out that people differ in their judgment of which matters require special parental approval and which do not.

I then invited these parents to be at least equally upset over the fact that their daughter can actually obtain an abortion without their knowledge or consent. According to the Guttmacher Institute, over 4,200 abortions a year in the United States are performed on girls younger than fifteen years of age.[8]

I know of another case in which parental permission was obtained for all the students in the class, except one, to see a photo of an aborted baby. After school, the student whose parents had denied permission insisted that her friend let her see the picture. On returning home, she passionately challenged her mom, "Why did you not want me to see what is really happening to these babies? Why was I not allowed to see the truth?"

It is particularly appropriate that children share our concern about abortion. After all, they are closer in age to those who are being killed. Furthermore, they were considered nonpersons by law during the first nine months of their existence! If I were born after the *Roe v. Wade* decision, I would take that as a personal insult!

What loss today's children have sustained from abortion! Those aborted would have been their classmates, their friends, their husbands and wives! Psychological research is being done on the impact of this tragedy on those whose lives might have been taken had they been "unwanted." The International Institute for Pregnancy Loss and Child Abuse Research and Recovery has identified various types of "abortion survivors" and has published evidence of how damaging it is for a child to grow up in a society in which he or she could have been aborted.[9]

I once spoke at a gravesite containing the aborted bodies of several hundred babies. At the end of the burial service, each person present placed a rose on the grave and departed. Most people missed the scene at the very end. A very young girl, just able to walk, took a rose to the grave by herself and placed it there. She was at that time the closest she could be to her brothers and sisters in that grave. She had compassion on her peers, who would never see the sun as she did that day.

YOUNG WITNESSES FOR LIFE

"Children too have an apostolate of their own. In their own measure they are true living witnesses of Christ among their companions."[10] I have often seen the truth in these words from the Second Vatican Council. Children can and will respond actively to the pro-life message.

Earlier I quoted a letter I received from a seventeen-year-old who, along with his younger brother, "did not fully understand what goes on in abortion till [my] homily" and subsequently wanted "to get on the mailing lists of pro-life organizations." Children particularly like to wear the Precious Feet pin, showing the exact size and shape of a baby's feet at ten weeks after conception. It was a child's idea to put those feet on top of pink and blue ribbons. A major pro-life organization then made the combination into a pin!

I once met a seven-year old named Nick among a group of young people peacefully demonstrating outside an abortion mill. "This must be your first time taking part in something like this," I said to him.

"Oh, no, Father," he exclaimed. "I've protested abortion in New York, Chicago, Atlanta, and other places."

Preaching and teaching will lead the young to action. A group of summer campers I once served, ages eight to ten, sent a joint letter to the local paper to speak up for preborn children. The following letter was written by a fourth-grade girl:

> Dear Christians,
>
> I was so excited about what my life in this world would be. I thought about all the things I would like to do, like playing with toys, riding a bike, going to the zoo, and having a dog. I wanted to see movies, go to school, make friends, and go to the park and the circus. I wanted to celebrate Christmas and receive Jesus in Holy Communion. I looked forward to listening to music, dancing, swimming in a pool, playing soccer, and having dolls.

I am very sad that I never got to do any of these things. My mother did not let me be born. I just don't understand one thing. Why didn't any of you help me? I wish you had. No one heard my crying voice.

—from an unborn baby

"Let the children come to me," the Lord declares (Matthew 19:14). Let them come to his Church; let them come to us, that we may love them and teach them the dignity and greatness of all human life.

Never Too Old to Save a Life

At the other end of the age spectrum, people beyond their childbearing years sometimes tell us, "Abortion is not my problem. I'm too old for that!"

While people may be too old to have a child, they are never too old to love one and never too old to save one. They are therefore never too old to be concerned about abortion. By our active concern, any one of us can save the life of a baby scheduled to die. To try to save our youngest brothers and sisters is an expression of the love that is supposed to grow in us all the days of our lives, and indeed into eternity.

Parents and grandparents, furthermore, have a crucial, sometimes decisive role in forming the attitudes of their children and grandchildren toward abortion. Do they pass on a concern for life? Do they convey compassion so that if their daughter or granddaughter were to become pregnant, she would know she could turn to them for understanding rather than turn to the abortionist?

No matter what their age, people can continue to make their voices heard in the arenas of public opinion and in the political process. Let nobody say they are too old to be concerned about abortion. As long as we possess life, we have the duty and privilege to defend life.

CHAPTER THREE

At the Heart of the Priesthood

· ·

Priesthood and pro-life ministry are essentially linked, for the reason that the Holy Father points out in *Evangelium Vitae*: "The Gospel of God's love for man, the Gospel of the dignity of the person and the Gospel of life are a single and indivisible Gospel."[11] Defending the dignity of the human person is not a task added on to our ministry but rather one inseparable from it and flowing from its very heart.

Pro-life ministry flows from our priesthood by way of many angles. Considering these will help us situate pro-life issues in our preaching.

CONFIGURED TO CHRIST THE HEAD

The priest is "another Christ," and as such he is a man of salvation, bringing others the benefits of the Redemption. Yet the priest is also a man of creation, for Christ not only saved the world but also made it.

The earliest New Testament reference to this is 1 Corinthians 8:6.

> For us there is…
> …one Lord, Jesus Christ,
> through whom all things are and through whom we exist.

Colossians reiterates the theme:

> For in him were created all things in heaven and on earth,
> the visible and the invisible,
> whether thrones or dominions or principalities or powers;
> all things were created through him and for him.

> He is before all things,
> and in him all things hold together. (Colossians 1:16–17)

It is the message of John's prologue.

> In the beginning was the Word....
> All things came to be through him,
> and without him nothing came to be.
> What came to be through him was life.
> (John 1:1, 3; see also Hebrews 1:2; Proverbs 8:30)

Christ is "the Alpha and the Omega" (Revelations 22:13); he is the beginning of life and the purpose of life. He is the answer to the child's question, "Mommy, why are there stars and mountains and people?"

To stand for Christ is to stand for creation and for life; to minister Christ to the world is to minister life. The preborn child exists through Christ and for him. To be silent about that child's destruction is to betray both the child and Christ. To bring salvation to God's people is first of all to defend their very existence.

Do Justice!

The Old Testament prophecies pertaining to Christ are heavily linked with the word *justice*. Psalm 72 declares:

> Justice shall flower in his days,
> and profound peace till the moon be no more.

The psalm goes on to specify what that justice entails:

> He shall rescue the poor man when he cries out,
> and the afflicted when he has no one to help him.
> ...
> From fraud and violence he shall redeem them,

and precious shall their blood be in his sight.
(Psalm 72:7, 12, 14).

Justice refers to an act of intervention for the defenseless. God does justice for his people, and his people must do it for one another. If they don't, worship of God is pointless. God states this forcefully through the prophet Amos:

> I hate, I despise your feasts,
> I take no pleasure in your solemnities.
> …
> Take away from me
> your noisy songs;
> The melodies of your harps,
> I will not listen to them.
> Rather let justice surge like waters,
> and righteousness like an unfailing stream.
> (Amos 5:21, 23–24; see also Isaiah 1:10–17)

Christ preaches and acts in the name of justice, declaring that the Spirit of the Lord has anointed him to free the oppressed (see Luke 4:18, quoting Isaiah 61). In his ministry, Christ seeks those whom society oppresses and rejects: the poor, lepers, lunatics, tax collectors, sinners, and children, whom even his apostles considered troublesome (see Matthew 19:14). His justice, ultimately, is "to destroy the works of the devil" (1 John 3:8). Those works, Christ declares, are lies and murder (see John 8:44; Psalm 72 speaks of "fraud and violence").

The alliance between lying and murder is clear in the abortion industry. Women are told that their child is a blob of tissue. They are told that the abortion procedure is safe, whereas in truth it carries untold burdens of physical and mental anguish. The pro-abortion lies are echoes of the original lie told to the first woman, "You certainly will not die" (Genesis 3:4b).

Nowhere are there more defenseless people crying out for our intervention than in our country's abortion mills today. A man of Christ must intervene; a priest must make justice his aim (see Isaiah 1:17).

In the days of the Nazi atrocities, trains carrying Jews to execution passed a church on Sunday mornings. The helpless prisoners would cry out in the hope that the worshipers would hear and rescue them. The noise of the wailing prompted members of the congregation to ask the pastor, "What are we to do about this disturbance to our worship?" The pastor paused and then said, "Tell the people to sing a little louder."[12]

This sad temptation to avoid the distraction of human lives in danger surfaces again today. Christians may think they are too busy to worry about the abortion issue, too busy to worry about justice. Faithful priests must tell them otherwise.

THE BREAD OF LIFE

A priest is a man of the Eucharist, and it is in the Mass that we touch the definitive victory of life over death: "Dying you destroyed our death, rising you restored our life."[13] Jesus said, "I am the Bread of Life" (John 6:35). The Eucharist is the sacrifice of life and the banquet of life, and because the priest officiates at this sacrificial banquet, he is truly "Father," imparting life to all who come.

Christ gives himself away on the cross and in the Eucharist, and in him we find the meaning of love: "I sacrifice myself for the good of the other person." This is the perfect reversal of abortion, which says, "I sacrifice the other person for the good of myself." The same words, in fact, that the Lord and his priests use to proclaim love are used by the defenders of abortion: "This is my body." These people say they control their bodies, and so others must die; Christ says he gives his body away so others may live.

"This is my body, which will be *given for you*" (Luke 22:19; emphasis added). In the power of these words, the culture of death will be transformed into the culture of life.

The priest guards the Eucharist, which is both a human and a divine life, for it is Christ himself. The priest leads his people to adore the Eucharist and to see, beyond the appearances, the reality of life. Thus he must stand powerfully in defense of human life, which in its initial stages is also hidden from human sight yet no less sacred. Just as the Sacred Host is defenseless, so is the preborn child. Just as the Sacred Host is sacred because it is God, so is the preborn child the sacred image of God. If the priest is the defender of the sacred, then he is such wherever and whenever the sacred is attacked.

"This is my body." These words are at the heart of priesthood. They are the words of Christ. Are they not also the words of the preborn child?

The Greatest Power of Heaven

Dr. Bernard Nathanson was one of the engineers of the abortion-rights movement in this country. He later became a leading spokesperson for life. I remember attending a talk he gave to priests in the archdiocese of New York in 1990. After recounting to us how he and his colleagues launched the abortion industry, he looked at us and said, "We would never have gotten away with what we did if you had been united, purposeful, and strong."[14] He knew then what abortion-rights activists still know today: Their greatest obstacle is the Church.

The Church is the only institution that has a divine guarantee that it will prevail over the culture of death. "The gates of the netherworld shall not prevail against it," the Lord said (Matthew 16:18) When we hear these words, we tend to think, "The Church will survive all the attacks launched against her," and certainly that is part of the meaning. However, a gate does not run onto the battlefield to attack the enemy. Rather, the gate stands still and defends the city against the enemy attacking it! When the Lord says that the gates of hell will not prevail against the Church, he means that the Church takes the initiative and storms the gates!

Those gates of hell cannot withstand the power of heaven. Gates of sin melt in the presence of saving grace; gates of death fall in the presence of eternal life; gates of falsehood collapse in the presence of living truth; gates of violence are flattened in the presence of divine love. These are the tools with which Christ has equipped his Church. These are the tools at our disposal as priests.

A System of Communication

With over seventeen thousand parishes and nearly seven thousand schools of every educational level in the United States, the Catholic community has a unique structure through which we can reach people with the truth regarding abortion and what they can do about it. Progress in the pro-life effort does not so much require new structures but rather the full activation of the structures we already have.

Pastoral experience indicates that a person's position will tend to be more pro-life the more regularly that person engages in Sunday worship, no matter what the denomination is. This might suggest that we don't need to "preach to the choir." But we do not preach about abortion because people do not know about it but rather because they *do*. The fact that they do makes them the most likely group to do something about it.

A woman in the large parish I served in the city of New York said to me one Sunday, "About all this preaching on abortion, Father, we're not the ones who need to hear it. It's all the people out there; they need to hear it!" "Well then," I told her, "go tell them!"

When we say, "Go in peace," we give people a commission, as the Lord gave the apostles, to take the grace and truth they have received at Mass into the world, which needs it so much. Priests and other preachers are called to inspire and equip the laity to exercise their role in the family, the world of business, the realm of politics, the domain of the media, and countless other arenas.

Choirs need choir practice. Outside the church building, people encounter a constant barrage of pro-choice propaganda. The faithful need to be constantly nourished with the gospel of life. We should not hesitate, therefore, to preach to the choir. Such preaching equips them to sing their song to the rest of the world.

A Consistent Ethic of Life

The Catholic Church endorses a consistent ethic of life, and it is essential that we preach within that context. Human life is sacred under each and every circumstance and at all stages of its development. Pro-life issues and social justice concerns are intimately tied together. Social justice is required precisely because of the dignity of human life, and an act that deprives one of life is a tremendous social injustice.

As Cardinal Joseph Bernardin used to point out, progress in any area of the defense of human life promotes progress in all other areas, while setbacks in one area slow progress in others. Nobody should feel exempt from concern for human life across a broad spectrum of issues.

At the same time, Cardinal Bernardin made it clear that not all issues are the same. "Each of the life issues—while related to all the others—is distinct and calls for its own specific moral analysis."[15] The cardinal likewise pointed out, on numerous occasions, that the consistent ethic of life does not preclude individuals or groups from focusing on specific issues:

> Does this mean that everyone must do everything? No! There are limits of time, energy, and competency. There is a shape to every individual vocation. People must specialize, groups must focus their energies. The consistent ethic does not deny this.[16]

The Pastoral Plan for Pro-life Activities of the United States Catholic Bishops states:

Among important issues involving the dignity of human life with which the Church is concerned, abortion necessarily plays a central role. Abortion, the direct killing of an innocent human being, is *always* gravely immoral (The Gospel of Life, 57); its victims are the most vulnerable and defenseless members of the human family. It is imperative that those who are called to serve the least among us give urgent attention and priority to this issue of justice.

This focus and the Church's commitment to a consistent ethic of life complement one another. A consistent ethic of life, which explains the Church's teaching at the level of moral principle—far from diminishing concern for abortion and euthanasia or equating all issues touching on the dignity of human life—recognizes instead the distinctive character of each issue while giving each its proper place within a coherent moral vision.[17]

Both *Evangelium Vitae* and The Gospel of Life point out similar reasons why abortion deserves priority.

WHERE ELSE WILL PEOPLE HEAR THE TRUTH?

It is important also to understand how difficult it is for people to find the truth about abortion. Dr. Nathanson, for example, admitted that the efforts he and his colleagues made to promote abortion consisted of lies.[18] Carol Everett and many other former abortionists admit how abortion facilities lie to women.[19] Studies have shown the pro-abortion bias of the media.[20]

Many politicians refuse to address abortion because they say it is a religious issue. Many schools do not want to impose morality or deal with issues that are too controversial. And although abortion is among the most frequently performed surgeries in America, it's hard to find someone who has actually viewed one. The teaching and preaching of the Church are today one of the only avenues through which this tragedy is likely to be addressed adequately and honestly.

Some clergy ask how often they should preach on abortion. One way to approach this question would be to ask yourself, "What would I do if some force in our country were claiming the lives of close to three thousand two-year-olds every day?" How often would you bring it up in your preaching? Whatever your answer, consider the fact that abortion has the same effect. The victims are simply younger.

A NOTE ON LITURGICAL NORMS FOR HOMILIES

A significant number of Catholic clergy find it difficult to preach on abortion because the topic does not seem to harmonize with the readings assigned for a given liturgy. I'd like to address this concern from at least two perspectives: First, the homilist is not absolutely constrained by the readings. Second, the Scriptures provide countless links with the abortion issue.

The liturgical norm found in the *General Instruction of the Roman Missal* (*GIRM*, which is printed at the beginning of every Sacramentary), paragraph 65, reads,

> The Homily is part of the Liturgy and…should be an explanation of some aspect of the readings from Sacred Scripture or of another text from the Ordinary or the Proper of the Mass of the day and should take into account both the mystery being celebrated and the particular needs of the listeners.[21]

Notice that the homilist is given a choice. He can preach on the readings *or* "another text" of the liturgy. These "other texts" include the prayers of the Mass, which are constant, such as the Profession of Faith, the prayers at the Presentation of the Gifts, the Eucharistic Prayers, and the Our Father. They also include the "presidential prayers," which vary from day to day.

In relation to abortion, the Profession of Faith has three powerful points of departure:

I believe in one God...*Maker of heaven and earth*, of all things visible and invisible....

I believe in one Lord, Jesus Christ.... *Through him all things were made*....

I believe in the Holy Spirit, the *Lord, the Giver of life.*

Paragraph 65 of the *GIRM* also indicates that "the particular needs of the listeners" are to be kept in mind in shaping the homily. Abortion continues within our own Catholic communities, and many people are subject to the constant stream of propaganda from so-called respectable segments of society that tries to justify abortion. It is quite clear that the community has a paramount need to hear the truth about abortion.

When the homilist does preach more directly on the readings, he should note that there are countless ways to bring in the abortion issue. The *GIRM* says that he should give "an explanation of some aspect of the readings." This indicates that the readings are a springboard rather than a straitjacket. What is preached does not have to be explicitly mentioned in the passages.

A theme may be suggested in any one or several of the readings. The homilist is not limited to the Gospel. The other readings, including the psalm, provide powerful themes. The abortion issue is right in the firing line of such basic scriptural themes as the dominion of God over human life, justice, the defense of the weak and helpless, the creation of man and woman in God's image and likeness, the covenant, the prohibition of murder, sin, love of neighbor, truth, service, Christ as the Resurrection and the Life, responsibility and solidarity, God's victory over death, and many others.

"The Homily is part of the Liturgy," the *GIRM* states. Liturgy is, ultimately, a life-giving encounter with God. There can be no more appropriate setting in which to proclaim and defend the gift of life. The liturgical laws of the Church certainly leave the door wide open for such a proclamation and defense!

. . . .

CHAPTER FOUR

Scriptural Starting Points

. . . .

There are many "points of entry" into the abortion issue. One may speak directly of the children in the womb as the least among us and of their rights and our responsibilities toward them. One may, on the other hand, begin by speaking about the rights of women to better choices than abortion, for abortion hurts women in many ways. We can also address abortion in the context of justice and peace, stressing the need to reject violence and promote the unity of the human family. The point of entry can also be God, who is the source of life and the giver of the right to life.

For us priests and preachers, sometimes an entire homily can be devoted to the abortion tragedy. At other times, one can simply make reference to abortion when speaking, for example, of the evils in the world or the requirements of loving our neighbor. The Golden Rule, for example—"Do to others as you would have them do to you" (Luke 6:31)—provides a short, effective argument against abortion. Just let people put themselves in the baby's place. (We were, in fact, there at one time.)

In this chapter, I'd like to focus on the life message that Scripture consistently gives us. We'll look at some overall themes and how they pertain to the life issue. In the next chapter, we'll examine some key passages that speak to our issue, and I'll give you a list of specific Scripture references that will be helpful in preparing for and delivering a pro-life message—to a relative, to a friend, or in the case of us preachers, to our congregations.

The Bible clearly teaches that abortion is wrong. Some people point out that the word *abortion* is not in the Bible, and that is true. Nevertheless, the teaching about abortion is there.

This is the case with many teachings. The word *Trinity* is not in the Bible, but the teaching about the Trinity runs throughout:

> God said: Let *us* make human beings in *our* image, after *our* likeness. (Genesis 1:26, emphasis added)

> It was not you who chose me, but I who chose you and appointed you to go and bear fruit that will remain, so that whatever you ask the Father in my name he may give you. (John 15:16)

> It is not for you to know the times or seasons that the Father has established by his own authority. But you will receive power when the holy Spirit comes upon you, and you will be my witnesses…to the ends of the earth. (Acts 1:7–8)

In the case for life, I suspect that a person who wants to deny Christian teaching about abortion would deny it even if the word were in the Bible. But let's look at some of the biblical reasons why abortion, the deliberate destruction of a child in the womb, is very wrong.

GOD HAS ABSOLUTE DOMINION OVER HUMAN LIFE

This theme is reflected in the creation accounts and in all the passages declaring God to be Lord of the universe. Because God has made us, our lives and bodies are not our own, nor are our choices absolute. "None of us lives for oneself, and no one dies for oneself. For if we live, we live for the Lord, and if we die, we die for the Lord" (Romans 14:7–8). "You are not your own?… For you have been purchased at a price" (1 Corinthians 6:19–20).

HUMAN LIFE IS DIFFERENT FROM OTHER TYPES OF LIFE, BECAUSE HUMAN BEINGS ARE MADE IN THE VERY IMAGE OF GOD

The accounts of the creation of man and woman in Genesis tell us this:

God created mankind in his image;

in the divine image he created them;

male and female he created them. (Genesis 1:27)

The word *create* is used three times here, emphasizing a special crowning moment in the whole process of God's making the world and everything in it. The man and woman are given "dominion" over everything else in the visible world (see Genesis 1:28).

Original sin does not take away the image of God in human beings. St. James refers to this image in his exhortation against unkind speech: "With [the tongue] we bless the Lord and Father, and with it we curse human beings who are made in the likeness of God.… This need not be so, my brothers" (James 3:9, 10).

The image of God! This is what it means to be human! We are not just a bunch of cells randomly thrown together by some impersonal force. Rather, we reflect an eternal God who knew us from before we were made and purposely called us into being.

At the heart of the life issue is the question raised in Psalm 8:

What are humans that you are mindful of them,

mere mortals that you care for them?

Yet you have made them little less than a god,

crowned them with glory and honor,

You have given them rule over the works of your hands.

(Psalm 8:5–7)

Not only did God make us, but he values us. The Bible tells us of a God who is madly in love with us, so much so that he became one of us and even died for us while we were still offending him (see Romans 5:6–8). All of this clearly contradicts the statement abortion makes, that human life is disposable.

CHILDREN ARE A BLESSING

God commanded our first parents to "be fertile and multiply" (Genesis 1:28). Why? God himself is fertile. Love always overflows into life. When the first mother brought forth the first child, she exclaimed, "I have produced a male child with the help of the Lord" (Genesis 4:1). The help of the Lord is essential, for he has dominion over human life and is its origin.

Parents cooperate with God in bringing forth life. Because this whole process is under God's dominion, it is sinful to interrupt it. The prophet Amos condemned the Ammonites "because they ripped open pregnant women in Gilead" (Amos 1:13).

> Certainly sons are a gift from the Lord;
> the fruit of the womb, a reward. (Psalm 127:3)

THE CHILD IN THE WOMB IS TRULY A HUMAN CHILD, WHO EVEN HAS A RELATIONSHIP WITH THE LORD

The phrase "conceived and bore" or "conceived and gave birth" is used repeatedly in Scripture (see Genesis 4:1, 17, for example), and the individual indicated has the same identity before as after birth. "In sin my mother conceived me," the repentant psalmist says in Psalm 51:7. The word *brephos*, that is, "infant," is used in Luke 1:41 and Luke 18:15—the same word referring to a child before birth and a child after birth.

God knows the preborn child:

> You knit me in my mother's womb....
> My bones are not hidden from you,
> When I was being made in secret. (Psalm 139:13, 15)

God also helps and calls the preborn child:

> For you drew me forth from the womb,
> made me safe at my mother's breasts.

Upon you I was thrust from the womb;

since my mother bore me you are my God. (Psalm 22:10–11)

St. Paul stated to the Galatians, "God…from my mother's womb had set me apart and called me through his grace" (Galatians 1:15).

SCRIPTURE REPEATEDLY CONDEMNS THE KILLING OF THE INNOCENT
God's own finger writes in stone the commandment "You shall not kill" (Exodus 20:13; Deuteronomy 5:17). Christ reaffirms it, mentioning it first in a list in Matthew 19:18. The book of Revelation states that unrepentant murderers cannot enter the kingdom of heaven (see Revelation 22:15).

The killing of children is especially condemned by God through the prophets. In the land God gave his people to occupy, foreign nations had the custom of sacrificing some of their children in fire. God told his people that they were not to share in this sin. They disobeyed, however, as Psalm 106 relates:

[They] mingled with the nations

and imitated their ways.

They served their idols

and were ensnared by them.

They sacrificed to demons

their own sons and daughters,

Shedding innocent blood,

the blood of their own sons and daughters,

Whom they sacrificed to the idols of Canaan,

desecrating the land with bloodshed.

(Psalm 106:35, 37–38, *NAB*)

This sin of child sacrifice is mentioned as one of the major reasons that the kingdom of Israel was destroyed by the Assyrians and that the people were taken into exile: "They immolated their sons and daughters by fire…till the Lord, in his great anger against Israel, put them away out of his sight" (2 Kings 17:17–18).

Notice that this practice was a religious ritual. Not even for religious freedom can the killing of children be tolerated.

GOD IS A GOD OF JUSTICE

An act of justice is an act of intervention for the helpless, an act of defense for those who are too weak to defend themselves. In foretelling the Messiah, Psalm 72 says,

> For he rescues the poor when they cry out,
> the oppressed who have no one to help. (Psalms 72:12)

Jesus Christ is our justice (see 1 Corinthians 1:30). He rescued us from sin and death when we had none to help us (see Romans 5:6; Ephesians 2:4–7).

If God does justice for his people, he expects his people to do justice for one another. Jesus said, "Be merciful, just as your heavenly Father is merciful" (Luke 6:36). And at the end of the parable of the Good Samaritan, he commanded, "Go and do likewise" (Luke 10:37). "Do to others whatever you would have them do to you" (Matthew 7:12). "Love one another" (John 15:17).

Abortion is the opposite of these teachings. It is a reversal of justice. It is a destruction of the helpless rather than their rescue. If God's people do not intervene to save those whose lives are attacked, then we do not please or worship him.

God says through Isaiah,

> Trample my courts no more!
>   To bring offerings is useless...
> Your...festivals I detest...
>   When you spread out your hands,
>   I will close my eyes to you;

Though you pray the more,
　I will not listen.
Your hands are full of blood!

　Wash yourselves clean!…
　Learn to do good.
Make justice your aim: redress the wronged,
　hear the orphan's plea, defend the widow. (Isaiah 1:13–17)

Indeed, those who worship God but promote abortion are falling into the same contradiction as God's people of old. They need to hear the message.

JESUS CHRIST PAID SPECIAL ATTENTION TO THE POOR, THE DESPISED, AND THOSE WHOM THE REST OF SOCIETY CONSIDERED INSIGNIFICANT
Jesus broke down the false barriers that people set up among themselves. He acknowledged the equal human dignity of every individual, despite what common opinion might have said. Hence we see him reach out to children, despite the efforts of the apostles to keep them away (see Matthew 19:13–15); to tax collectors and sinners, despite the objections of the scribes (Mark 2:16); to the blind, despite the impatience of the crowd (Matthew 20:29–34); to a foreign woman, despite the utter surprise of the disciples and of the woman herself (John 4:9, 27); to gentiles, despite the anger of the Jews (Matthew 21:41–46); and to lepers, despite their isolation from the rest of society (Luke 17:11–19).

When it comes to human dignity, Christ erases distinctions. St. Paul declares, "There is neither Jew nor Greek, there is neither slave nor free person, there is not male and female; for you are all one in Christ Jesus" (Galatians 3:28).

We can likewise say, "There is neither born nor unborn." The unborn are the segment of our society who are most neglected and discriminated against today. Christ surely has a special love for them.

Scripture Teaches Us to Love

St. John says, "This is the message you have heard from the beginning: we should love one another, unlike Cain who belonged to the evil one and slaughtered his brother" (1 John 3:11–12). Love is directly contrasted with slaughter. To take the life of another is to break the command of love. To fail to help those in need and danger is also to fail to love.

Christ teaches this clearly in the parable of the Good Samaritan (Luke 10:25–37), in the story of the rich man and Lazarus (Luke 16:19–31), and in many other places.

"If someone…sees a brother in need and refuses him compassion, how can the love of God remain in him?" (1 John 3:17). No group of people is in more serious danger than the boys and girls in the womb. Love is what fuels the pro-life movement, impelling us to save the lives of children and provide life-giving alternatives to their parents. Love likewise demands that we reach out with compassion and healing to all who are wounded by abortion. If the pro-life movement is not a movement of love, it is nothing. But if it is a movement of love, nothing can stop it, for "Love is strong as Death" (Song of Songs 8:6).

Abortion, in short, is the opposite of love. Love says, "I sacrifice myself for the good of the other person." Abortion says, "I sacrifice the other person for the good of myself."

Life Is Victorious over Death

This is one of Scripture's most basic themes. The victory of life is foretold in the promise that the head of the serpent, through whom death entered the world, would be crushed (see Genesis 3:15). Isaiah promised that God "will destroy death forever" (Isaiah 25:8).

At the scene of the first murder, the soil "opened its mouth" to swallow Abel's blood (see Genesis 4:11). At the scene of the final victory of life, it is death itself that will be:

"...swallowed up in victory.

Where, O death, is your victory?

Where, O death, is your sting?"

...

Thanks be to God who gives us the victory through our Lord Jesus Christ. (1 Corinthians 15:54–55, 57)

Abortion is death. Christ came to conquer death, and therefore he conquers abortion. "I came so that they may have life and have it more abundantly" (John 10:10).

The final outcome of the battle for life has already been decided by the resurrection of Christ. We are not just working *for* victory; we are working *from* victory. We joyfully take this victory that has already been won, and we proclaim, celebrate, and serve it until he comes again to bring it to its fullness. "There shall be no more death" (Revelation 21:4). "Amen! Come, Lord Jesus!" (Revelation 22:20).

CHAPTER FIVE

Some Specific Scripture Passages about Life

GENESIS 4:8–16: AM I MY BROTHER'S KEEPER?

"Let us go out into the field," Cain said to his younger brother, Abel. When they were in the field, Cain killed Abel. The Lord then asked Cain, "Where is your brother?"

This was the most uncomfortable question Cain had yet faced in his life. How could he stand up to God and explain the murder of his own brother? It was an issue he wished would go away; it was a truth too hard to deal with. So in a desperate attempt to dodge the issue, he claimed ignorance. "I do not know," was his response to God.

It is interesting to note that the United States Supreme Court, in its 1973 abortion decision *Roe v. Wade*, faced the same question, "Where is your brother?" and gave the same answer:

> We need not resolve the difficult question of when life begins. When those trained in the respective disciplines of medicine, philosophy, and theology are unable to arrive at any consensus, the judiciary, at this point in the development of man's knowledge, is not in a position to speculate as to the answer.[22]

In other words, "I don't know."

Cain went on to challenge God for asking the question in the first place: "Am I my brother's keeper?" (Genesis 4:9). With these words, he tried to absolve himself of responsibility for his brother. Abel's whereabouts, his safety, his very life were not the responsibility of Cain! This response is mirrored today by those who claim they would rather mind their own business than get involved in the effort to end abortion.

God, however, called Cain back at once to take responsibility for his actions against his brother. "What have you done?" God demanded (Genesis 4:10). Cain wanted the issue to go away, but it wouldn't go away. The issue was as close to Cain as Cain himself. It was his own action that took his brother's life. Yes, he was his brother's keeper by the very fact that Abel was his brother. His brother had rights that Cain should have *kept*, that is, respected and, if necessary, defended.

Cain did the opposite. He held his brother's rights in contempt. He had no regard for his brother's very right to life. He tried to conceal his action by taking his brother into the field, where nobody else would see them. Yet God confirmed that the deed could not be covered over. "Your brother's blood cries out to me from the ground!" (Genesis 4:10). The issue would not go away.

We are our brothers' keepers; this is not an option. The responsibility flows from our very existence as sons and daughters of one God in one human family. We do not only have responsibilities toward those we *choose*; we have responsibilities toward one another even *before* we choose. Our lives have been entrusted to one another. Pope St. John Paul II wrote, "The God of the Covenant has entrusted the life of every individual to his or her fellow human beings, brothers and sisters, according to the law of reciprocity in giving and receiving, of self-giving and of the acceptance of others."[23] We have responsibility especially for the weakest and most defenseless ones in our society, the unborn, who are daily ripped apart in their mothers' wombs by abortion.

Our Lord Jesus Christ is ultimately the one who answers Cain's argument, "Am I my brother's keeper?" and our arguments about minding our own business and privacy. Christ is the one who teaches us in clear terms that we do have responsibility for each other and that we cannot make the issue of injustice to our neighbor go away. For Christ declares to us, "Love one another as I love you" (John 15:12).

How did he love us? St. Paul tells us, "God proves his love for us in that while we were still sinners Christ died for us" (Romans 5:8). In other words, Christ took the initiative. He came to us and died for us before we asked him and without our deserving him. We were totally helpless. He acted out of pure love when he saw our need. He made our plight his business. He didn't hesitate for one minute. He didn't ask his Father, "Am I my brother's keeper?"

As Christ loved us, so must we love our preborn brothers and sisters. We do not love them because they ask it or merit it. We love them because they are our brothers and sisters in need.

Abortion is an issue that is solved not by wishing it away or ignoring it. It is solved only by active love. We are our brothers' keepers. Amen!

Exodus 20:16: The Eighth Commandment

We usually think of abortion as a violation of the fifth commandment, "You shall not kill," and that is true. But abortion is wrong for many reasons. It breaks all the commandments.

The eighth commandment says, "You shall not bear false witness against your neighbor." This is not only a matter of falsely testifying that somebody did something wrong, as we see, for example, in the Old Testament story of Susanna (see Daniel 13). This commandment also forbids false testimony about who our neighbor is, about what value and dignity our neighbor possesses, and about what our obligations to our neighbor are.

The question in abortion is not only "When does life begin?" but more deeply, "What does life mean?" What are the implications of being human? Is human life disposable when it is unwanted or inconvenient or not recognized by a government? Does human existence cry out for any recognition and protection apart from what society decides to bestow?

What is the truth about humanity? What is the human person's destiny? Are we made for the grave or for the skies?

Abortion not only takes a life; it makes a statement about life, and not only about the life it takes but about the lives of us all. Abortion says we are disposable. Abortion says our value is determined by others. Abortion says there is no intrinsic dignity in human life that requires its absolute protection and no destiny that reaches beyond this world or even beyond this Supreme Court.

We at Priests for Life, working with the healing ministry of Rachel's Vineyard and the Silent No More Awareness Campaign, gather testimonies of women who have had abortions. They describe what led them to abortion and what consequences followed. Case after case shows how they were victimized by lies and half-truths.

Carol Everett, a victim of abortion and once an abortion provider, wrote:

> Like many others, I bought the big lie: "It is only a glob of tissue, not a baby." I was a victim of all the other lies: Abortion is all right. After all, I do them all the time. It will be so simple. It's only a glob of tissue. There's really nothing to the procedure; it will only take a little while and then everything will be fine. You can have the abortion on Friday morning and be back to work on Monday.[24]

The efforts made to initiate widespread abortion in America were marked by lies, as Dr. Bernard Nathanson, former abortionist and one of the founders of NARAL and the abortion industry in America, readily admits. After he turned away from his strong advocacy of abortion, he wrote of the back-alley abortions used to justify legalization of the killing, "How many deaths were we talking about when abortion was illegal?... It was always '5,000 to 10,000 a year.' I confess that I knew the figures were totally false."[25]

A growing number of former abortion providers in our country are coming forward to tell how they lied to women before abortions and covered up the tracks of botched abortions by falsifying medical records. Workers at abortion centers were trained to give as little information as possible so that women would not know the truth.

Do not bear false witness against your neighbor! Do not call the unborn anything less than beautiful creations of our God.

Christ reveals the truth about human life. "It is only in the mystery of the Word made flesh that the mystery of man truly becomes clear."[26] Particularly by his ascension, Christ shows that we are made for the heights of heaven, not for the medical waste bag.

"What is man that you are mindful of him?" (Psalm 8:5). The psalmist asked the question, and God himself answered it in Christ. May our treatment of human life faithfully echo that answer!

MATTHEW 7:12: THE GOLDEN RULE

When we come close to Christ, he makes it very clear how we are to respond to our neighbor. In fact, the first two commandments, he tells us, are to love God above all and to love your neighbor as yourself (see Matthew 22:34–40). Two sayings of Our Lord make it clear how we must love our neighbor. One is the Golden Rule: "Do to others whatever you would have them do to you" (Matthew 7:12). The other is "Whatever you did for one of these least brothers of mine, you did for me" (Matthew 25:40).

Let us apply the Golden Rule to the tiny, helpless child in the womb and to his or her mother. Put yourself in the child's place. (We were, in fact, all in the womb at one point ourselves.) Would you want to be cared for and nourished and brought safely to birth, or would you want to be aborted?

The Golden Rule also applies to the mother. If you were afraid because you felt you could not handle a pregnancy, what would you want? Help! We need to commit ourselves to help mothers raise their children, not kill them. There are over three thousand helping centers throughout the country, and they need our assistance!

Our Lord also tells us, "Whatsoever you do to the least of my brothers, you do to me." After we put ourselves in the position of the preborn child and the mother, we then put Christ there! Surely the preborn child is the least of his brothers and sisters! The preborn have the least power, the least protection, the least voice! They cannot speak, vote, protest, or even pray! The mothers also are often alone, cast aside by those who don't understand their problems. Christ makes it clear: By helping both mother and child, we are helping him! But if we reject the mother and the child, we reject him!

To love one another as Christ taught us demands that we reject abortion completely and work for better, life-giving choices! Amen!

LUKE 16:19–31: THE POOR LAZARUSES OF TODAY

We learn many lessons from those who go to heaven. In the story of the rich man and Lazarus, we learn a lesson from one who went to hell.

Why was the rich man condemned? Was it because he had so much? Was there something inherently sinful about the purple and linen in which he dressed or the feasts in which he indulged? No. The rich man went to hell not for what he did but for what he did *not* do. He let the beggar's cries go unheeded.

The story causes us to wonder what we would do if we were at the rich man's table. But, brothers and sisters, we *are* there. You and I have an appointment with Lazarus today, and we will be judged on how we respond. Lazarus is in our midst.

This was a point that Pope St. John Paul II made in his homily at Yankee Stadium in New York on October 2, 1979:

> The parable of the rich man and Lazarus must always be present in our memory; it must form our conscience. Christ demands openness to our brothers and sisters in need—openness from the rich, the affluent, the economically advanced; openness to the poor, the

underdeveloped and the disadvantaged. Christ demands an openness that is more than benign attention, more than token actions or half-hearted efforts that leave the poor as destitute as before or even more so.[27]

Lazarus is in our midst in the poor, the troublesome, the annoying, the person who is smaller and weaker than we are, and the person who seems different and less valuable. In particular, Lazarus rests today in our preborn brothers and sisters. These are the persons rejected by society, who beg for help to live but whose cries are rejected some three thousand times a day in our country. These are the persons torn apart and thrown away by abortion.

The rich man was condemned for not treating Lazarus as his brother. We also will be condemned if we do not treat the preborn as our brother or sister. Many oppose abortion and would never have one, but they then ask, "Who am I to interfere with a woman's choice to abort?" Today I will tell you who you are: You are a brother or a sister of that child in the womb!

"Who am I to interfere with her choice?" You are a human being who has enough decency to stand up and say *No!* when you see another human being about to be killed.

"Who am I to interfere with her choice?" You are a person who has enough wisdom to realize that injustice to one human being is injustice to every human being, and that your life is only as safe as the life of the preborn child.

"Who am I to interfere with her choice?" You are a follower of the one who said, "Whatsoever you do to the least of my brothers, you do to me."

Do we not believe that if we allow a person to die of starvation, we are allowing Christ to die of starvation? Do we not believe that if we leave the sick untended, we are leaving Christ untended? Must we not then also believe that whenever a child in the womb is ripped apart, burned, crushed, and then thrown away, Christ is ripped apart, burned, crushed, and thrown away? It is Christ in the womb! When we stand up for life, we stand up for him!

If abortion is not wrong, then nothing is wrong. If we cannot be stirred to respond as individuals, as a Church, and as a nation to the plight of preborn children, then we have lost our souls. Indeed, the Lazarus of the twenty-first century is knocking at our door. May God have mercy on us and help us to respond!

John 14:6: The Way, the Truth, and the Life

There are many ways to express the purpose of Christ's mission in the world. St. John, in his first letter, sums it up by saying, "The Son of God was revealed to destroy the works of the devil" (1 John 3:8). What "works of the devil" does Christ destroy?

Christ himself tells us that the devil "was a murderer from the beginning and does not stand in truth, because there is no truth in him. When he tells a lie, he speaks in character, because he is a liar and the father of lies" (John 8:44). In one and the same breath, our Lord calls the devil a liar and a murderer. Lies and murder go together. The only way abortion can continue on such a horrible scale is for it to be covered in lies, sugarcoated with denials and distortions of truth.

Christ has come to destroy the works of the devil. "I am the way and the truth and the life" (John 14:6). He is the way to salvation precisely because he is the truth, shattering the devil's lies, and because he is the life, undoing the devil's work of death.

We see the devil act in character—with lies and murder—from the first pages of the Bible. Adam and Eve had been told they could eat of any tree in the garden except "the tree of knowledge of good and evil." "When you eat from it," God warned them, "you shall die" (Genesis 2:17).

What is wrong with knowing good from evil? Aren't we supposed to know the difference? Isn't that part of our religious and moral education?

When people do not know good from evil, don't problems follow? Why then is this the one tree of which our first parents were not to eat?

The answer lies in the fact that the "knowledge of good and evil" does not simply mean "knowing." It means that Adam and Eve would think they could *decide* the difference between good and evil, that they would be the ones to determine what was right and wrong, that they would be the norm of morality. This is the original temptation.

In his encyclical *Veritatis Splendor*, Pope St. John Paul II comments on Genesis 2:16–17:

> With this imagery, Revelation teaches that the power to decide what is good and what is evil does not belong to man, but to God alone. The man is certainly free.... But his freedom is not unlimited: it must halt before the "tree of the knowledge of good and evil," for it is called to accept the moral law given by God.[28]

The original sin is to put choice above goodness and truth, to abuse freedom by trying to create what is right rather than submit to what is truly right.

We hear it today: "What's right and wrong for me is up to me. What's right and wrong for you is up to you. Do not impose your morality on me. I will create my own values. I am accountable to nobody but myself." In other words, "it's all up to my personal choice."

The devil had to lie to Adam and Eve in order to introduce death into the world. The original liar approached the original woman and offered the original lie: "You certainly will not die! For God knows well that when you eat of it your eyes will be opened and you will be like gods, who know good and evil" (Genesis 3:4–5). Eve bought the lie, as did Adam, and they committed the original sin. Death then entered the world, on the heels of a lie.

The lie continued at the Tower of Babel, in Babylon. It is noteworthy that *bab-ili* means "gate of the gods." Here again, humans tried to exalt themselves to the status of God. "Come, let us build ourselves a city and a tower with its top in the sky, and so make a name for ourselves" (Genesis 11:4). "Let us make," they said, forgetting that God is the one who said, "Let us make human beings" (Genesis 1:26).

Seeing their forgetfulness and pride, God said, "If now, while they are one people and all have the same language, they have started to do this, nothing they presume to do will be out of their reach" (Genesis 11:6). God was not saying here that he felt threatened. He was saying that people who have bought the lie of the evil one will think they can do anything and, in trying to do so, will destroy themselves. The lie perpetuated will perpetuate death.

It is God's infinite mercy and love that move him to say, "Come, let us go down and there confuse their language, so that no one will understand the speech of another" (Genesis 11:7). Better for them to be scattered by God's intervention than dashed on the rocks of their own pride! God confused the language only after the people had confused it first by speaking the lie that they could make a name for themselves, rather than submitting to the name (the truth) of God.

This lie continues in our day. In fact, it has become the official policy of America, according to the Supreme Court. In its 1992 *Planned Parenthood v. Casey* decision, in which the error of *Roe v. Wade* was upheld, the court stated, "At the heart of liberty is the right to define one's own concept of existence, of meaning, of the universe, and of the mystery of human life."[29]

This line is incredible! We cannot even decide the weather, and yet we can claim to define existence itself! We live in a universe we did not create, and yet we declare ourselves the creators of that universe's meaning! We did not call ourselves into life, yet we have the liberty to define the meaning of life! Not only is this absurd, but it is frightfully familiar: "You shall be like God, knowing good and evil." "Let us make a name for ourselves." Perhaps the court's decision should be renamed "Eden and Babel Revisited" or "The Gate of the Gods."

The original lie leads to the ongoing slaughter of babies by abortion. The mother is told, "It's your choice. It's your freedom. It's your body. Nobody can impose their morality on you." It is the lie that choice prevails over life itself.

Truth is on the side of life. Truth and life go together. Let us proclaim the truth that the preborn child is a human person from the moment of conception, that love for the woman demands love for her child, that there are concrete, life-giving alternatives to abortion, that there are negative physical, psychological, and spiritual consequences of abortion, that choice never takes priority over life itself, and that freedom is found by submitting to the moral truth that comes from God, rather than by trying to be God ourselves. We find the bedrock foundation of moral sanity and salvation in documents such as The Splendor of Truth and The Gospel of Life. Christ provides us the only way of salvation, namely, himself, for he is truth and life.

Ultimately we will save the world from the bondage of abortion and every other sin by lifting Christ high. "If you remain in my Word, you will truly be my disciples, and you will know the truth, and the truth will set you free" (John 8:31–32).

1 John 4:7–10; John 15:9–17: Love Leads to Life

The basis of Christianity is the resurrection of Jesus Christ from the dead. Christians rejoice in the resurrection, because it is the victory of life not only for Christ but for each person who believes in him. Christ's rising from the grave means that we too will rise from the grave!

The victory of life is also the victory of love. From the first page of Scripture to the last, it is clear that love leads to life. Love and life cannot be separated, because they are rooted in the one God, who cannot be divided. "God is love" (1 John 4:8), and God is life (see John 14:6). Love and life always go together.

We see this in creation. Where were you a hundred years ago? You were nowhere; you did not exist. So why are you here today? How were you rescued from that nothingness? Certainly you did not ask to be born; you weren't there to do the asking. Certainly you did not earn birth; you weren't able to do anything that could earn it. What accounts for the fact that you are here?

We can say that your parents came together and you were conceived and born, and that is true. But that doesn't fully answer the question of why *you* are here. When your parents came together, there could have been millions of possible people conceived and born. It didn't have to be you!

The only ultimate explanation of why you are here is that God loves you. He chose *you* to be! In fact, at each moment, he is literally loving you into existence. If he stopped loving you for one instant, you would fall back into the nothingness you were a hundred years ago. Love leads to life.

This is clear also in the mystery of salvation. St. John tells us, "In this way the love of God was revealed to us: God sent his only Son into the world so that we might have life through him" (1 John 4:9). Christ's love for us brought him to the cross, and this led to the victory of life.

The crucifix is the best symbol of love. Love is self-giving for the good of another person. Christ gives his life for us without complaining and without counting the cost. His concern is that we have life.

Having shown his love for us in this way, he does not say, "Love one another in whatever way you want." Rather he instructs us, "Love one another as I love you" (John 15:12). We are called to love in a way that brings forth new life. We are called to give ourselves, without counting the cost, that others may live.

Parents cooperate with the work of God when their love for each other becomes a new human being. The child they bear belongs to God first. Only God can create. Parents do not own their children; God does. In fact, parents do not own themselves. Many people today say, "This is *my* life, *my* body, *my* choice." But we are *not* our own masters. We belong to God. "None of us lives for oneself, and no one dies for oneself" (Romans 14:7). "You are not your own" (1 Corinthians 6:19).

The choice to be a mother or father is not merely a human choice. It is God's choice first. Our Lord tells us, "It is not you who chose me, but I who chose you and appointed you to go and bear fruit that will remain" (John 15:16). A parent becomes a parent before he or she knows it. One is a father or mother as soon as his or her child begins to exist, at the moment of conception. (This is not a matter of opinion or religious belief but a matter of verifiable and established scientific fact.) Parents discover that they have become parents several weeks after the fact. A pregnant woman should not say, "I'm expecting a child." The child already exists. Nor should she say, "I'm going to be a mother." She already is. And the man is already a father.

There is nothing comparable to having a child. Even if someone owns a multimillion dollar corporation, all that money is ultimately a pile of rocks. Even gold will eventually fade away into nothing. But a child, given an immortal soul and the call to eternal life, will never go out of existence. For all eternity, the child, the person, will exist. Were one to take all of the galaxies in the universe, with their hundreds of billions of stars and incalculable beauty and power, they would not add up to a fraction of the worth of one tiny human child.

Children are equal to their parents, not in age, nor in knowledge (though they often think so), nor in experience, but they *are* equal in dignity, in value, in worth as a person created in God's image and redeemed by Christ. Every person is equal in this way, whether in the womb or outside the womb, no matter how young or old, healthy or sick, big or small, famous or obscure. Parents are called to love their children as Christ has loved us. "No one has greater love than this, to lay down one's life for one's friends" (John 15:13).

A mother who demonstrated this in a particularly striking way is St. Gianna Beretta Molla, who died in 1962 and was canonized by Pope St.

John Paul II in 2004. She was a doctor and the mother of three children. When she became pregnant with her fourth, it was discovered that she had a tumor near her uterus. She made it very clear to her doctor and her family that she wanted everything done to save the life of her baby. The baby was born healthy, but Gianna, despite efforts to save her, died several days later, at the age of thirty-nine.

"This is absurd," some may say. But look again at the words of Our Lord Jesus Christ: "No one has greater love than this, to lay down one's life for one's friends" (John 15:13).

Most parents will not be called to face what Gianna Molla faced, but all parents, and all Christians, are called to lay down their lives for the sake of others in many ways every day. Let us pray especially for mothers who are afraid of motherhood and who are tempted to abort their children. Let us pray that they accept the grace to love as Christ has loved us.

God will never place an obligation before us without also giving us every ounce of strength we need to carry it through. Let us praise him for his grace, for his love, and for the victory of life!

Partial List of Helpful Scripture References to Life

Genesis 1:1–2, 26–28	Creation of man.
Genesis 2:7–8, 18, 21–24	Creation of man and woman.
Genesis 4:8–16	The first killing of the innocent.
Exodus 20:1–17	The Decalogue.
Leviticus 19:15–18	Love of your neighbor's life.
Deuteronomy 30:15–20	Choose life!
2 Kings 24:1–4	The exile occurred because innocent blood was shed.
Psalm 72	He will save the weak from violence.
Psalm 82	Rescue the lowly.
Psalm 139	You knit me together in the womb.

Proverbs 6:16–19	The Lord hates six things.
Proverbs 24:8–12	Did you fail to rescue those being dragged off to death?
Wisdom 1:12–15	God did not make death.
Wisdom 7:1–6	I was formed in the womb.
Isaiah 1:10–17	Do justice!
Isaiah 49:1–6	The Lord called me from the womb.
Isaiah 49:14–16	Can a mother forget her infant?
Jeremiah 1:4–8	I called you from the womb.
Jeremiah 7:28–34	Rebuke of child sacrifice.
Ezekiel 23:36–39	Child sacrifice.
Amos 5:21–24	Let justice surge like waters!
Matthew 18:1–6	The greatest in the kingdom of heaven.
Matthew 18:10–14	Do not despise the little ones.
Matthew 19:13–15	Let the children come to me.
Matthew 25:31–46	Whatever you did for one of these least…
Mark 10:13–16	Jesus blessed children.
Luke 1:39–45	The babe leapt in the womb.
Luke 6:20–26	Beatitudes and woes.
Luke 10:29–37	The Good Samaritan is neighbor to anyone in need.
Luke 16:19–31	The Lazarus of the twenty-first century: the unborn child.
John 1:1–5	All things, all life, come through Christ.
John 10:1–16	The Good Shepherd came to give us life.
John 11:17–27	Christ is the resurrection and the life.
John 14:1–6	Christ is the way, the truth, and the life.
1 Corinthians 15:51–58	The victory belongs to life; you do not labor in vain.
Ephesians 6:10–20	Be strong in this battle!

James 1:22–27	Religion requires us to help the helpless.
1 John 3:11–18	Love rather than kill.
Revelation 4:8–11	God has created all things.
Revelation 21:1–5	Death shall be no more!

CHAPTER SIX

Doctrinal Starting Points

The Catholic Church is unabashedly pro-life in her teaching and practice.

> Since the first century the Church has affirmed the moral evil of every procured abortion. This teaching has not changed and remains unchangeable. Direct abortion, that is to say, abortion willed either as an end or a means, is gravely contrary to the moral law:
>
> You shall not kill the embryo by abortion and shall not cause the newborn to perish. [*Didache* 2, 2]
>
> God, the Lord of life, has entrusted to men the noble mission of safeguarding life, and men must carry it out in a manner worthy of themselves. Life must be protected with the utmost care from the moment of conception: abortion and infanticide are abominable crimes [*Gaudium et Spes*, 51 § 3]. (*CCC* 2271)

In this chapter, we'll look at several doctrines of particular importance to Catholics—our understanding of the Eucharist, our reliance on the Holy Spirit, and several Marian doctrines—and show how they support and enrich the Church's pro-life stance.

THE EUCHARIST

Our commitment to defend our preborn brothers and sisters receives its form and sustenance from the Eucharist as a sacrament of faith, unity, life, worship, and love.

The Eucharist Is a Sacrament of Faith.
The Host looks no different after the Consecration than it does before. It looks, smells, feels, and tastes like bread. Only one of the five senses gets to the truth. The ears hear the words, "This is my Body; this is my Blood," and faith takes us beyond the veil of appearances. As St. Thomas's *Adoro Te Devote* expresses,

> Seeing, touching, tasting are in Thee deceived.
> What says trusty hearing, that shall be believed?

Christians are used to looking beyond appearances. The baby in the manger does not look like God, nor for that matter does the man on the cross. Yet by faith we know he is no mere man. The Bible does not have a particular glow setting it off from other books, nor does it levitate above the shelf. Yet by faith we know it is uniquely the Word of God. The Eucharist seems to be bread and wine, and yet by faith we say, "My Lord and my God!" as we kneel in adoration.

The same dynamic of faith that enables us to see beyond appearances in these mysteries enables us to see beyond appearances in our neighbor. We can look at the persons around us, at the annoying person or the ugly person or the person who is unconscious in a hospital bed, and we can say, "Christ is there as well. There is my brother, my sister, made in the very image of God!" By the same dynamic, we can look at the preborn child and say, "There too is my brother, my sister, equal in dignity and just as worthy of protection as anyone else!"

Some people will say that the child in the womb, especially in the earliest stages, is too small to be the subject of Constitutional rights. Is the Sacred Host too small to be God, too unlike him in appearance to be worshipped? The slightest particle of the Host is fully Christ. Eucharistic faith is a powerful antidote to the dangerous notion that value depends on size.

The Eucharist Is a Sacrament of Unity.

"When I am lifted up from the earth," the Lord said, "I will draw everyone to myself" (John 12:32). He fulfills this promise in the Eucharist, which builds up the Church. The Church is the sign and cause of the unity of the human family.

Imagine all the people, in every part of the world, who will receive Communion today. Do they receive their own personalized, customized Christ? Absolutely not. Each receives the one and only Christ. Through this Sacrament, Christ the Lord, gloriously enthroned in heaven, is drawing all people to himself. If he is drawing us to himself, then he is drawing us to one another. St. Paul comments on this, "We, though many, are one body, for we all partake of the one loaf" (1 Corinthians 10:17).

When we call each other "brothers and sisters," we are not merely using a metaphor that dimly reflects the unity between children of the same parents. The unity we have in Christ is even stronger than the unity of blood brothers and sisters, because our common blood is the Blood of Christ! The result of the Eucharist is that we become one, and this obliges us to be as concerned for each other as we are for our own bodies.

Imagine a person who accepts the Host when the priest says, "The Body of Christ," says "Amen," and then breaks off a piece, hands it back, and says, "Except this piece, Father!" This is what the person who rejects other people may as well do. In receiving Christ, we are to receive the whole Christ, in all his members, our brothers and sisters, whether convenient or inconvenient, wanted or unwanted.

As St. John remarks, Christ was to die "to gather into one all the scattered children of God." Sin scatters; Christ unites. The word *diabolical* means "to split asunder." Christ came "to destroy the works of the devil" (1 John 3:8). The Eucharist builds up the human family in Christ, who says, "Come to me, feed on my Body, become my Body."

Abortion, in a reverse dynamic, says, "Go away! We have no room for you, no time for you, no desire for you, no responsibility for you. Get out of our way!" Abortion attacks the unity of the human family by splitting asunder the most fundamental relationship between any two persons: mother and child. The Eucharist is its opposite, a sacrament of unity.

The Eucharist Is the Sacrament of Life.
"I am the Bread of Life.... Whoever eats this bread will live forever.... I will raise him on the last day" (John 6:48, 51, 54). The eucharistic sacrifice is the very action of Christ by which he destroyed our death and restored our life. Whenever we gather for this sacrifice, we celebrate the victory of life over death and therefore over abortion.

The pro-life movement is not simply working *for* victory; we are working *from* victory. As Pope St. John Paul II said in Denver in 1993, "Have no fear. The outcome of the battle for Life is already decided."[30] Our work is to apply the already established victory to every facet of our society.

The Eucharist Is the Supreme Act of Worship of God.
Two lessons each person needs to learn are (1) there is a God, and (2) it isn't me! The Eucharist, as the perfect sacrifice, "the source and summit of the Christian life,"[31] acknowledges that God is God. We pray, "It is right that all your creatures serve you."[32]

Abortion, on the contrary, proclaims that a mother's choice is supreme. "Freedom of choice" is considered enough to justify even the dismemberment of a baby. Choice divorced from truth is idolatry. It is the opposite of true worship. It pretends that the creature is God. Real freedom is found only in submission to the truth and will of God. Real freedom is not the ability to do whatever one pleases but the power to do what is right.

The Eucharist Is, Finally, the Sacrament of Love.
St. John explains, "The way we came to know love was that he laid down his life for us" (1 John 3:16). In the Eucharist, we see the meaning of love and receive the power to live it. Christ teaches, "No one has greater love than this, to lay down one's life for one's friends" (John 15:13). The best symbol

of love is not the heart but rather the crucifix.

Abortion is the exact opposite of love. Love says, "I sacrifice myself for the good of the other person." Abortion says, "I sacrifice the other person for the good of myself." The very same words, furthermore, that the Lord uses to teach us the meaning of love are also used by those who promote abortion: "This is my body." These four little words are spoken from opposite ends of the universe, with totally opposite results. Christ gives his body so others might live; abortion supporters cling to their bodies and let others die. Christ says, "This is my body given up for you; this is my blood shed for you." These are the words of sacrifice; these are the words of love.

The French philosopher Simone Weil (1909–1943) said that the true God transforms violence into suffering, while the false god transforms suffering into violence.[33] The woman tempted to have an abortion will transform her suffering into violence unless she allows love to transform her, to make her willing to give herself away. The Eucharist gives both the lesson and the power. Mom is to say, "This is my body, my blood, my life, given up for you, my child."

Everyone who wants to fight abortion needs to say the same. We need to exercise the same generosity we ask mothers to exercise. We need to imitate the mysteries we celebrate. "Do this in memory of me" applies to all of us: We are to lovingly suffer with Christ so others may live. We are to be like lightning rods in the midst of this terrible storm of violence and destruction. We need to say, "Yes, Lord, I am willing to absorb some of this violence and transform it by love into personal suffering, so that others may live."

Indeed, the Eucharist gives the pro-life movement its marching orders. It also provides the source of its energy, which is love. Indeed, if the pro-life movement is not a movement of love, then it is nothing at all. But if it is a movement of love, then nothing will stop it,

For Love is strong as Death,

longing is fierce as Sheol. (Song of Songs 8:6)

THE HOLY SPIRIT

The Holy Spirit is God, and all he does and speaks to us is consistent with what God the Father and God the Son have done and spoken.

He will not speak on his own, but he will speak what he hears.... He will take from what is mine and declare it to you. (John 16:13, 14)

The Holy Spirit...will...remind you of all that I told you." (John 14:26)

No disciple can claim the "freedom of the Spirit" to contradict the commandments, including that which forbids the killing of the innocent.

The creation account in Genesis 1 tells us that "a mighty wind," the "breath" or "spirit" of God hovered over the waters and brought life and light out of chaos and darkness (Genesis 1:2). The Holy Spirit is proclaimed in the Creed to be "the giver of life," and this is true both on a natural and on a supernatural level. To worship the Holy Spirit, then, demands that we stand against all that destroys life.

On the first Easter night, Jesus breathes his Spirit upon the apostles (see John 20:22), that they too might bring new life out of the chaos and darkness of sin. A second creation account is taking place here. God indeed "has sent the Holy Spirit among us for the forgiveness of sins."[34] The same Spirit who causes sin to flee will cause death to flee as well. "If the Spirit of the one who raised Jesus from the dead dwells in you, the one who raised Christ from the dead will give life to your mortal bodies also, through his Spirit that dwells in you" (Romans 8:11).

Jesus refers to the Holy Spirit as "the Spirit of truth" (John 15:26). The Spirit's gifts enable us to understand created realities, their value, and their relationship to the Creator and to our own happiness. We can therefore ask the Holy Spirit to give us an understanding of the value of the human person.

The Spirit enables us to cry out, "Abba! Father!" (Romans 8:15). "The Spirit itself bears witness with our spirit that we are children of God" (Romans 8:16). The Spirit of truth likewise shows us the truth about our sins (see John 16:8). In him we come to understand the difference between good and evil.

The Holy Spirit works directly against the abortion movement, which sees the human person as a disposable object and identifies a moral evil as a right.

> Ah! Those who call evil good, and good evil,
> who change darkness to light, and light into darkness,
> who change bitter to sweet, and sweet into bitter! (Isaiah 5:20)

Devotion to the Holy Spirit is a key element in praying for the conversion of mind and heart necessary for those who defend and perform abortions.

St. John declares, "If anyone does sin, we have an Advocate with the Father, Jesus Christ the righteous one" (1 John 2:1). Our Lord referred to the Holy Spirit as *another* advocate (John 14:16), and St. Paul writes that the Spirit "intercedes for the holy ones according to God's will" (Romans 8:27). Because we cannot save ourselves, we need an advocate to speak on our behalf and plead for our forgiveness and salvation.

What then does the Holy Spirit do to his people when he comes to them? He makes *them* advocates! He gives speech to the tongue, not only that we may tell who God is but that we may defend those among us who need advocates. The Pentecost Sequence invokes the Spirit as "Father of the Poor." Just as the Messiah will defend the poor and helpless (see Isaiah 11), so do the people of the Messiah, filled with his Spirit.

Jesus Christ made the sacrifice of himself "through the eternal spirit" (Hebrews 9:14). It is in the Holy Spirit that we too have the power to love, which consists in giving ourselves away for the good of the other. "There is no greater love than this: to lay down one's life for one's friends" (John 15:13; see also 1 John 3:16). Such is to be our response to the unborn.

The Spirit is the bond of love between the Father and the Son. He unites the human family, whereas abortion divides it.

THE VIRGIN MARY

Some Christians question why we Catholics give so much devotion to the Blessed Virgin Mary. Some claim that it compromises the unique worship that Christ alone deserves.

Catholics do not, of course, worship Mary. She is a creature, and all her importance flows from the uniqueness of Christ. Christ is the "one mediator between God and the human race" (1 Timothy 2:5). But how did he become that?

A mediator is a bridge between two parties—in this case, God and humanity. Christ is God from all eternity. It is precisely in taking upon himself a *human nature* that he became the mediator. This human nature is taken from Mary. The very fact that Christ is the one mediator demonstrates the critical role of the one mother from whom he became human. All the importance of Mary flows from her Son, and worship of the Son naturally leads to honoring the mother. From this fundamental point, Marian devotion teaches us something about our pro-life commitment: mother and child belong together.

The difference between the pro-abortion side and the pro-life side is *not* that they favor women's rights and we love the baby. The real difference is that they think you can separate the two, and we say you can't. The pro-abortion mentality claims you can love the mother while killing the child. The pro-life mentality asserts that you can't harm one without harming the other, and you can't love one without loving the other. The pro-life position is always and only "Let's love them both."

The Immaculate Conception

Mary was conceived without original sin. This favor was granted to her in anticipation of her role as the Mother of God. A fundamental truth that appears here, and that is reflected in various Scriptures, is the relationship of God with the child in the womb and the manner in which he prepares for the child's mission. God created a sinless mother to hold his sinless Son.

The doctrine of the Immaculate Conception likewise proclaims to us the broader truth about victory over sin. Mary was not exempt from the need of a Savior. Jesus shared with her, in a unique way, the victory over sin that he offers all of us.

In the struggle against temptation and sin, including the temptation to abort, there is always sufficient grace to do what is right. God keeps his promise. "God is faithful and will not let you be tested beyond your strength; but with the trial he will also provide a way out, so that you may be able to bear it" (1 Corinthians 10:13).

The Annunciation

Mary faces an unplanned pregnancy. Her response is, "May it be done to me according to your word." She freely chooses to accept the child, and in doing so, she acknowledges the primacy of the Word. The truth of God's Word exists before her choosing. She submits to a word, a truth that she did not create (see Luke 1:26–38).

At the heart of the pro-choice mentality is the idea that we create our own truth. For example, the value of the unborn child, that child's very right to exist, depends upon the choice of the mother. In the pro-life mentality, on the other hand, the choice of the mother must respect the inherent value of the child, which does not in any way flow from or depend upon her. As she submits to that truth, God does not rob her of freedom but instead lifts that freedom up to himself.

Mary was firmly rooted in the truth and in charity. When she learned she would be the Mother of God, she did not lose sight of the pressing needs of her kinswoman Elizabeth (see Luke 1:39–56). Mary was in touch with both heavenly and earthly reality. Her new status did not distract her from Elizabeth's needs, and she responded to those needs in a very practical way.

We see a similar situation at Cana. The celebration there, in company with Christ and the apostles, did not blind Mary to the real needs of the newlyweds. And she responded.

Union with God does not turn us in on ourselves. Authentic holiness makes us more aware of and responsive to the real needs of others. The pro-life movement responds to the real needs of real children and their mothers. We provide mothers with the concrete medical, financial, psychological, and spiritual help they need. Nothing distracts us. This is Marian pro-life ministry.

There is an axiom in psychiatry, "Believe behavior." The pro-choice movement, for all its rhetoric, leaves women only three things: a scarred mind, a wounded body, and a dead baby. The pro-life movement, through more than three thousand helping centers across the nation, offers women real help and the gift of life. We learned this from a very special mother. She is Jesus's mother and our mother too.

THE ASSUMPTION

At the end of her life, Mary was assumed into heaven, body and soul. The Assumption speaks of the victory of life over death. The Preface on this feast states, "Today the virgin Mother of God was taken up into heaven to be the beginning and the pattern of the Church in its perfection." The Assumption is not only about Mary; it's about us.

Mary has a unique privilege. The Mother of God was taken at once into glory upon the completion of her earthly life. Yet the entire Church is the body of Christ. We pray on the Feast of the Ascension, "Where he has gone, we hope to follow." We too are called to share an everlasting life, in body and soul, in the company of Christ and all who are saved. "I will raise him on the last day" (John 6:54).

The assumption of Mary into heaven renews our conviction that the destiny of the human person is the heights of heaven. What a sharp contrast to the mentality that allows human persons to be thrown in the garbage.

CHAPTER SEVEN

Common Obstacles to Preaching on Abortion

This chapter is directed toward priests, deacons, and ministers who have the privilege and responsibility of presenting the truth to their congregations. Preaching should foster the ongoing conversion and growth in holiness of the people entrusted to our pastoral care. A pastor is a shepherd. To shepherd people, preachers must be clear and courageous in confronting evil and likewise calm and compassionate. Our desire is to instruct people, inspire them, and equip them to take action. This is a challenging art and an urgent need. By the grace of God, it is a mission for which we will never lack the necessary tools and graces.

Since 1991, Priests for Life has worked closely with clergy around the world to assist them in addressing the abortion problem. Based on our extensive contact with priests through our seminars and individual consultations, and on professional polling that we commissioned, we have compiled a list of the most common fears and hesitations that clergy have about addressing abortion. We hope the questions below will help you discern where your concerns lie. Then you can move to the corresponding reflections, which I hope will build your confidence in addressing the pressing moral problem of abortion.

PREACHING ON ABORTION: WHY NOT?

1. Do I see the issue as too emotional and sensitive?
2. Am I afraid I won't be loved?
3. Am I afraid of being perceived as right wing, fanatical, traditionalist, or out of step with my people?

4. Am I afraid I may alienate some of my parishioners?

5. Am I afraid of dividing my parish?

6. Am I afraid of being a single-issue priest?

7. Do I see the "consistent ethic of life" as incompatible with a focus on abortion?

8. Do I believe there are simply too many issues to address to allow me to focus on abortion?

9. Am I just too busy to get more involved?

10. Will preaching on life issues increase the sense of guilt and pain of women who have had abortions?

11. Do I simply feel inadequate to the task of addressing abortion?

12. Do I feel I have no right to address this issue because I am a man, and celibate at that?

13. Do I believe abortion is too complex an issue to address in a homily?

14. Does the complexity of a large and varied congregation deter me from addressing abortion?

15. Do I have trouble relating abortion to Scripture?

16. Am I afraid that, in addressing abortion, I might allow a personal agenda to intrude into the liturgy?

17. Do I need more resources?

18. Am I disillusioned by the lack of support I have in addressing abortion?

19. Am I turned off by the eccentricity of some pro-lifers?

20. Am I afraid of political issues?

21. Will I endanger our tax exemption by speaking on abortion?

22. Do I see no connection between abortion and the salvation of the people I serve?

23. Do I think that abortions are rare in my congregation?

24. Do I feel that my people just don't care about the issue?

25. Do I feel that people already hear and know enough about abortion?

26. Do I consider my congregation too elderly to be concerned about abortion?

27. Am I afraid of being confrontational?

28. Do I think my preaching on this issue won't do any good?

29. Do I think the fight against abortion is a lost cause and a waste of time?

30. Am I afraid that, in addressing abortion, I may be forced to address contraception too?

31. Am I uncertain about the credibility of the teaching against abortion?

32. Do I simply not know why I don't address abortion?

MY RESPONSES

1. Do I see the issue as too emotional and sensitive?

Many aspects of abortion *are* very sensitive. That means that they have to be dealt with in a sensitive way; it does not mean that they should be ignored. The impact of abortion on the lives of people—physically, spiritually, and emotionally—is ample reason for a shepherd to pay attention to these wounds and to help people avoid them in the first place.

Ministry necessarily involves confronting problems that provoke emotions within us and among people. Ministry regarding abortion involves nothing less than life and death.

2. Am I afraid I won't be loved?

Sometimes our fear about addressing abortion, or other controversial issues, is as simple as the fear of rejection—and as profound. A strong relationship with Christ, who is the source of all love, and a conviction that fidelity to him is the foundation for love between human beings are the key remedy for this fear. Moreover, fidelity to our mission of proclaiming the Gospel—especially when that means taking on hard issues—will earn us the love and respect of those we serve.

To the extent that we are disliked for what we say about abortion, we might ask whether efforts to save the life of a child are worth that sacrifice. The answer is self-evident.

3. Am I afraid of being perceived as right wing, fanatical, traditionalist, or out of step with my people?

Unfortunately, some use these labels to describe the pro-life movement. Yet we were not ordained to belong to any one faction of the Church but rather to faithfully articulate the Church's teachings, among the most fundamental of which is the right to life. That teaching should find expression at each and every point along the spectrum of legitimate theological pluralism in the Church. No person or group in the Church is exempt from the privileged duty to defend life, nor does any group within the Church have a monopoly on the defense of life.

An important aspect of our leadership is to reframe the issue. There should not be a gap between social-justice concerns and right-to-life concerns. The starting point and heart of social justice is the dignity of the human person.

4. Am I afraid I may alienate some of my parishioners?

We do not want to unnecessarily offend or alienate anyone from the parish. We are reconcilers. At the same time, the one to whom we reconcile people is God. To have people come to the parish is one aspect of our mission; another aspect is to make sure that when they come, they hear the full message of God through his Church. This is not a favor to them; they have a right, in strict justice, to hear the full truth of Church teaching.

Our experience through Priests for Life is that people throughout the nation appreciate hearing clear teaching from the pulpit about abortion. Yet to believe we can do this faithfully and at the same time *never* alienate *anyone* is to ignore the fact that even Christ alienated some people. (See, for example, the conclusion of his Eucharistic discourse in John 6.) Can we do better than he did? Such alienation is not intentional on our part but is, in some cases, inevitable.

COMMON OBSTACLES TO PREACHING ON ABORTION

This is so because of the mystery of freedom. Some people have alienated themselves from the truth about abortion. If then we faithfully expose that truth, they may choose to alienate themselves from us too. This is not the same as driving them away by carelessness or unkindness.

5. Am I afraid of dividing my parish?

I suspect your parish is already divided, with people on different sides of the abortion issue. If you never speak of the issue, you may cover over the division for a while, but that is not the same thing as unity. Unity is founded on truth, and it is fostered by a clear exposition of truth.

"When I am lifted up from the earth, I will draw everyone to myself" (John 12:32). We do not build unity by our own human plans, efforts, and programs. We build it by lifting up Christ for all to see and hear. We build it by proclaiming his Word, without ambiguity or apology.

Sure, there will be some divisions for the same reasons that there will be some alienation. But the Word itself causes that. "Do you think that I have come to establish peace on the earth?" Jesus asked. "No, I tell you, but rather division" (Luke 12:51). It is the division between truth and error, grace and sin, life and death. This division must come before unity is possible; otherwise the unity will be superficial and illusory.

6. Am I afraid of being a single-issue priest?

As priests, we necessarily address a multitude of issues. Numerically, abortion is one issue, but it is one issue as the foundation of a house is one part of the house. There is a hierarchy of moral values, and according to numerous documents of the Church, the dignity of life is the fundamental one. Catholics are to be committed to a consistent ethic of life.

Every other issue comes from a human being's right to life. We address abortion not because we are unconcerned about other issues but precisely because we are concerned about them. We realize that we cannot make progress on them unless the foundation itself is secure.

7. Do I see the "consistent ethic of life" as incompatible with a focus on abortion?

The U.S. Bishops' Pastoral Plan for Pro-life Activities states, "This focus [on abortion] and the Church's commitment to a consistent ethic of life complement one another."[35] Cardinal Joseph Bernardin made this point clearly in his speeches. "The fundamental human right is to life—from the moment of conception until death. It is the source of all other rights."[36]

8. Do I believe there are simply too many issues to address to allow me to focus on abortion?

The fact that we have to address innumerable problems puts us in the same position in regard to all of them. We judge which ones to devote more time to, depending on their urgency. Which do the most harm to the human family? Which present the greatest threat to the spiritual well-being of people? How does the Church's preferential option for the poor and weak inform each specific issue?

Abortion, which claims more victims than any other act of violence, and whose victims are the weakest and most defenseless, ranks quite high in the answers to these and similar questions.

9. Am I just too busy to get more involved?

Much of what we are called to do for the pro-life cause does not take additional time. Rather, it takes more spirit. It doesn't take more time to preach on abortion than it does to preach on any other topic. It doesn't take any more time to put a pro-life announcement in the bulletin than it does to put in any other kind of announcement. It doesn't take any more time to let a pro-life group know they have your encouragement than to let any other group know that.

Beyond this, we must bear in mind the fact that innocent lives are at stake. If we would take the time to try to save a child who was struck by a car on the road near our church, can we not also take time to do something about the more than three thousand being deliberately torn limb from limb every day? All our time is God's anyway. Let's use more of it to save his children!

10. Will preaching on life issues increase the sense of guilt and pain of women who have had abortions?

An understanding of the dynamics of post-abortion women and men is extremely helpful in dealing with this fear. Many priests are silent out of the best of intentions toward such people in their congregation. Silence, however, does not interpret itself.

The person in the pew who is hurting from abortion may interpret our silence to mean, "He doesn't know my pain," or, "He doesn't care about it," or, "There is no hope." But in fact, we do know, we do care, and there is hope. The road to healing involves breaking out of denial regarding the distress of one's abortion. Honest and compassionate words about the reality of what the person has done help bring healing. We preach on abortion to save people who have had abortions and to protect others from making their mistake.

After one homily I gave on abortion, a woman told me, "Father, it often hurts when I hear about abortion, because I had one. But please keep preaching about it, because it is so consoling to know that by your words, someone else might be spared all the pain I have gone through."

11. Do I simply feel inadequate to the task of addressing abortion?

Your confidence will increase as you become more informed about the issue, speak with other priests who are active in the pro-life movement, pray, and practice. There is sometimes a fear that we will give the issue the wrong emphasis (coming down too hard, fostering guilt, sounding uncaring). We can counteract this by always mentioning the help available to women in need and the peace and forgiveness Christ offers through his Church.

12. Do I feel I have no right to address this issue because I am a man, and celibate at that?

The taking of a human life is a human issue, and addressing its injustice requires no qualifications other than being a decent human being. The abortion-rights community certainly has no complaints about men—married or single—speaking out in favor of abortion; nor should the pro-life community have any fear about men speaking out against abortion.

13. Do I believe abortion is too complex an issue to address in a homily?

Abortion is psychologically complex, but morally it is quite straightforward: Abortion is a direct killing of an innocent person, and therefore it is always wrong. Nothing can justify it.

It is not too complex to denounce killing in a homily, to point out injustice toward the most defenseless members of society, to proclaim that there is help available for pregnant women and better choices than abortion. This is no more complex than addressing racism, poverty, warfare, or drug abuse.

14. Does the complexity of a large and varied congregation deter me from addressing abortion?

Any good public speaker knows that a primary rule is "Know your audience." A Sunday congregation is a varied audience in terms of age, education, and spiritual maturity. The problem of addressing such a group is not limited to the topic of abortion. For any subject, we must exercise sensitivity and prudence.

Outside the Church, our parishioners are constantly hearing messages that contradict historic Christian teaching on faith and morals. Our challenge is to provide them with truth that will counteract the confusing messages they hear elsewhere. It is unrealistic to think that every person will immediately understand everything we say.

People will also differ in their estimation about what is appropriate. We will encounter criticism no matter what we preach. We must live with that.

We should make it clear that we are always open to speaking with people privately if questions or misunderstandings arise due to our preaching.

At the same time, we must ask, "If they don't hear the truth from me, exactly where and when will they hear it?" If we are silent, we allow those who are intent on covering up the truth about abortion to have the first, last, and only word with people whom we are responsible to shepherd.

15. Do I have trouble relating abortion to Scripture?

Scripture clearly teaches the immorality of abortion. A particular word—like *abortion*—does not have to appear in the text in order for Scripture to teach about it. The word *Trinity*, for example, is not anywhere in the Bible, but the teaching is.

Abortion is the killing of an innocent human child. The teaching on abortion is contained in the numerous condemnations of the shedding of innocent blood and the numerous instructions about justice and charity, especially toward the weak, the small, the helpless, and those whom society rejects. Beyond such texts are the clear themes of Scripture and the directions in which Scripture moves.

The people of the old and new covenants are called to be a holy people, a community bound to God and one another in love. This happens because God takes the initiative not only in giving life but also in intervening to save the helpless. Such are central events of both the Old and the New Testaments. Abortion belongs to a totally contradictory dynamic of thought and life: It excludes members of the community and destroys rather than defends the helpless.

Chapters 4 and 5 of this book present scriptural themes and particular passages that point to the primacy of life. In part 2 of this book, you will find homily hints related to the specific readings assigned to every Sunday of the year. In addition to this resource, you can find help drawing out the pro-life message of the Scriptures at PreachingOnAbortion.com.

16. Am I afraid that, in addressing abortion, I might allow a personal agenda to intrude into the liturgy?

If defending innocent children from death and reaching out in practical charity to help pregnant women in need is simply a personal agenda, then what is the Church's agenda? Can it possibly *not* include this? Scripture makes it clear that liturgy that ignores the demands of justice is not true worship:

> Your new moons and festivals I detest;
>> they weigh me down, I tire of the load.
>
> When you spread out your hands,
>> I will close my eyes to you;
>
> Though you pray the more,
>> I will not listen.
>
> Your hands are full of blood!
>> Wash yourselves clean!
>
> Put away your misdeeds from before my eyes;
>> cease doing evil;
>> learn to do good.
>
> Make justice your aim: redress the wronged,
>> hear the orphan's plea, defend the widow.
>
> Come now, let us set things right,
>> says the LORD. (Isaiah 1:14–18)

17. Do I need more resources?

There is an abundance of material that Priests for Life (PriestsForLife.org) can provide for you. If we don't have what you need in your situation, we will point you to those who do.

18. Am I disillusioned by the lack of support I have in addressing abortion?

You may not be encouraged by your fellow priests, your congregation, or Church authorities. With reference to brother priests, this encouragement in standing up for life is one of the benefits Priests for Life provides. A chapter in your diocese or regular contact with other members can help. Our newsletters highlight what other priests are doing in the pro-life arena. There are also other priests' movements that can strengthen you in various aspects of your ministry.

In regard to our congregations, the encouragement is certainly there. Take a strong stand on life, and that encouragement will grow. Complaints will also come, but it is not the complainers who have to answer to God for what is preached or not preached from the pulpit!

In regard to our bishops and religious superiors, we need to heed Scripture's advice to pray for them. "I ask that supplications, prayers, petitions, and thanksgivings be offered for everyone, for kings and for all in authority, that we may lead a quiet and tranquil life in all devotion and dignity" (1 Timothy 2:1–2). If some do not encourage us regarding the life issues, we should kindly but firmly request that they do.

19. Am I turned off by the eccentricity of some pro-lifers?
There are eccentrics in every movement. The pro-life movement, the largest grassroots movement in the history of the United States, is no exception. The pro-life movement, however, more fully reflects the rich diversity of American society than the pro-abortion movement does.

A key role of the priest is to foster the gifts of the laity, encouraging them to use those gifts to transform society. This involves identifying those in our congregations who have the kind of leadership skills that can effectively guide the pro-life movement. If we call forth such individuals to take their part in local leadership, they will likewise attract others who can bring experience and professionalism to the movement. This will prevent the vacuum of leadership that can attract eccentrics.

20. Am I afraid of political issues?

Is the killing of children merely a political issue? In the moral and spiritual realm, how is abortion different from the killing of two-year-olds? Do we have any fewer obligations to speak up for our brothers and sisters before they are born than we do after they are born? Does the fact that politicians talk about abortion require us to be silent?

It is amazing to me how the Church receives praise for speaking up for peace or for economic justice, which are also political issues, but is subject to different rules when it comes to abortion. Clergy will be silent about abortion because it is a political issue; politicians will be silent because it is a religious issue. If abortion is immoral, where do we go to say so?

Actually, abortion is many things. It is an issue of public policy, which we have every right to shape. It is a moral issue, "the fundamental human rights issue for all men and women of good will."[37] It is a spiritual issue, confronting us with a challenge: Will we peacefully coexist with child killing, or will we acknowledge God as the Lord of life and worship him by defending life?

It is critical to point out, especially at election time, that no matter what position any particular party or candidate takes in any race, the message of the Church about abortion is always the same. Speaking for life can just as well help a pro-life Democrat and hurt a pro-abortion Republican as it can help a pro-life Republican and hurt a pro-abortion Democrat. Our motive is simply the defense of life.

If fear of political issues is a problem, how much more should we fear spiritual ones, in which the powers at war are much more awesome and the stakes much higher!

> For our struggle is not with flesh and blood but with the prin-
> cipalities, with the powers, with the world rulers of this present
> darkness, with the evil spirits in the heavens.... So stand fast with

your loins girded in truth, clothed with righteousness as a breast-plate. (Ephesians 6:12, 14)

We are priests. We do not undertake our tasks on human strength but in the power and authority of Christ. Hence we do not let fear deter us.

21. Will I endanger our tax exemption by speaking on abortion?

No. The law does not forbid us to speak on public policy issues. The classic legal distinction is between issue advocacy, which is permitted, and candidate advocacy, which is not.

In March of 2015, the Office of the General Counsel for the U.S. Bishops issued revised political activity guidelines for Catholic organizations. "During election campaigns," the guidelines state, "Catholic organizations may educate voters about the issues."[38]

22. Do I see no connection between abortion and the salvation of the people I serve?

The First Letter of John asks, "If someone who has worldly means sees a brother in need and refuses him compassion, how can the love of God remain in him?" (1 John 3:17). To possess the greatest of the world's goods—life itself—and to fail to defend that gift for others diminishes our relationship with the Lord and giver of life. The question behind abortion is not simply "Would I do it?" but rather "What am I doing to stop it?"

23. Do I think that abortions are rare in my congregation?

Most counties in America do not have an abortion provider, and the numbers of abortions are certainly higher in the big cities than anywhere else. But, there can be far more abortions occurring than a priest is aware of. But as Dr. Martin Luther King stressed during the civil rights movement, injustice anywhere is a threat to justice everywhere. We do not fail to preach about famines, wars, or oppression that happen in far-off places. Love does not know geographical boundaries. Preaching on abortion in our community is part of teaching people how to love one another, wherever the other may be, and whether "the other" means multitudes or just one.

24. Do I feel that my people just don't care about the issue?

How much people care about an issue depends in part on how clearly they see its connection with the things they do care about. Our teaching can help them make those connections regarding abortion.

Why, for example, do we see children killing children in our society? Might it have a connection with the fact that the law allows parents to kill children by abortion, thereby teaching children that their lives are disposable? Significant studies likewise show links between abortion and child abuse, poverty, substance abuse, suicide, breast cancer, and numerous other problems. A "consistent ethic of life" means that all these life issues are interrelated; therefore, abortion cannot be ignored.

25. Do I feel that people already hear and know enough about abortion?

It is not enough to hear and know about abortion, any more than it is enough to "hear and know" about poverty and other forms of social injustice. The point is that something must be done about these problems, and we are called to help people get involved.

People may be opposed to poverty attitudinally, but what do they do to help the poor? How do they express their opposition behaviorally?

Certainly, most of our congregations would lament abortion. But the challenge remains to bring to their attention continually both the obligations and the opportunities to actually prevent abortion in their community.

26. Do I consider my congregation too elderly to be concerned about abortion?

While many people in our pews are too old to have a child, none are too old to love one or too old to save one. They are therefore never too old to be concerned about abortion. By our active concern, any one of us can save the life of a baby scheduled to die. To try to save our youngest brothers and sisters is an expression of the love we are bound to for all our lives.

Parents and grandparents, furthermore, have a crucial, sometimes decisive role in shaping the attitudes of their children and grandchildren toward abortion. Do they pass on a concern for life? Do they convey compassion if a daughter or granddaughter becomes pregnant outside of marriage? Does that daughter or granddaughter know that she can turn to them for understanding rather than turn to the abortionist?

No matter what their age, people can make their voices heard in arenas of public opinion and the political process. Let nobody say that a person is too old to be concerned about abortion. As long as we possess life, we have the duty to defend life.

27. Am I afraid of being confrontational?

Being confrontational is not the same as being uncharitable. Our Lord, who ate with sinners, also confronted them. Love demands confrontation, because love cannot rest if the beloved is entangled in evil. Love seeks the good of the beloved, and this means love has to get tough at times in order to extricate the beloved from evil.

Many of us think of the price of confrontation, but we forget that there is also a price to be paid for *not* confronting. That price is that evil continues to flourish, relationships become shallow and superficial, and true leadership vanishes, because the leader who is no longer able to point out the right path loses the respect of those who look to him for guidance.

Successful social reform movements always confronted an unwilling culture when exposing injustices. The civil rights movement provides just one example.

28. Do I think my preaching on this issue won't do any good?

The American people are conflicted about abortion, and they are by no means as entrenched in their positions as we might imagine. People can change their views completely based on a single article they read, commercial they see, or homily they hear.

I recall one woman telling me after Mass, "Father, I came in here today 100 percent pro-abortion, and now my views are completely changed." What convinced her was the example I used: that federal law protects sea turtles from destruction but does not protect unborn babies from abortion! It can be that easy. And people sitting in the pews who are wrestling with the option to abort can be persuaded to save that life.

29. Do I think the fight against abortion is a lost cause and a waste of time?

Every day brings us new opportunities to play our part with God in the unfolding of his plan. Every day brings new opportunities to convert hearts that have not heard the truth or to save even one life that faces destruction—and to that life, it means everything. Every day brings new opportunities to speak up for the defenseless, knowing that justice is on their side and that no lie can live forever.

We must maintain our historical perspective. Evils such as slavery and segregation took a long time to overcome. Progress is in fact being made in the pro-life cause, and our goal of victory needs to be fresh before our eyes. The battle is not a matter of the pro-life movement winning or the pro-choice movement winning. If the pro-life movement does not win, nobody wins.

Yet the one who calls us already holds the victory of life.

> Now have salvation and power come,
> and the kingdom of our God
> and the authority of his Anointed.
> For the accuser of our brothers is cast out. (Revelation 12:10)

30. Am I afraid that, in addressing abortion, I may be forced to address contraception too?

As priests, we are publicly committed to teach all that the Church teaches.

Not only is there a link between abortion and contraception, but there is a marvelous link and unity among all the truths that the Church proclaims. They form one organic whole, because ultimately the message is a person, Jesus Christ.

"Be not afraid; I go before you always." These words are sung often today in our churches.[39] They are words for us priests. Never in history has there been so much assistance offered to us, particularly in papal teachings and faithful commentary, to teach the truth about contraception. Let us use the help that is available.

31. Am I uncertain about the credibility of the teaching against abortion?
All the teachings of the Church hold together in an indivisible, living unity. We have teachings about grace, about the power of God, about dying to ourselves, about union with Christ, about practical charity, and about much more. We will not see the full credibility of any of these teachings if we isolate them from the whole.

It is difficult at times to present teaching on abortion. But the teaching is very credible. We will be credible to people if we present the teaching as part of a clear, vigorous exposition of the entire Catholic faith, with no distortions or omissions, and if we place it in the context of a life of charity, compassion, and deep holiness.

32. Do I simply not know why I don't address abortion?
If you can admit to yourself that you don't know why you are not doing something you should be doing, then a privileged moment of growth has arrived. I encourage you to respond in two ways.

First, become more familiar with the issue of abortion and its connections with priestly ministry and with the lives of your congregation. Second, bring the matter before the Lord in prayer, asking him to break through any barriers, to renew your entire priesthood, and through you to renew the face of the earth.

PART TWO

Homily Hints for Every Sunday of the Year

. . . .
ADVENT

Pro-Life Themes in the Advent Liturgy
. . . .

The introduction to the lectionary, when speaking of the Sundays of Advent, says, "Each Gospel reading has a distinctive theme: the Lord's coming at the end of time (First Sunday of Advent), John the Baptist (Second and Third Sundays), and the events that prepared immediately for the Lord's birth (Fourth Sunday)."[40] We focus, in other words, on the first and second comings of the same Christ and on the one who teaches us how to prepare for his arrival: "Reform your lives! The reign of God is at hand."

The New Testament readings complement and expand on John the Baptist's exhortations of repentance. In Year A, St. Paul urges us to "throw off the works of darkness" (First Sunday) and "think in harmony with one another" (Second Sunday). He speaks of faith as an obedience (Fourth Sunday). St. James encourages, "Be patient.... Make your hearts firm" (Third Sunday).

The Old Testament prophets, furthermore, describe the results of the Messiah's coming: "One nation shall not raise the sword against another" (First Sunday); "There shall be no harm or ruin on all my holy mountain" (Second Sunday); "Then will the eyes of the blind be opened.... Sorrow and mourning will flee" (Third Sunday); "The Lord himself will give you this sign:... Immanuel" (Fourth Sunday).

The preparation for Christ's coming is reform, and the promise is reconciliation. The two are linked. If the Messiah comes to restore harmony between nations, people, and even animals ("Then the wolf shall be a guest of the lamb.... The baby shall play by the cobra's den"), then the people of the Messiah are to repent of whatever destroys that harmony. If the

Messiah comes to bring justice ("He shall judge the poor with justice and decide aright for the land's afflicted"), then the people of the Messiah are to work for justice (Second Sunday).

The "justice" referred to here in Isaiah 11 is intervention to save the helpless. The "spirit of the Lord," which rests on the Messiah and likewise on his people, leads them to and prepares them for the work of justice, as the structure of this passage indicates. This same Spirit will later be called the Advocate.

Abortion is an injustice against the most helpless. It also attacks the harmony of human relationships at their most fundamental and sensitive point, the relationship of mother and child. Preparing for the Lord's coming therefore requires a total rejection of abortion. The focus on the virgin and child at the end of Advent highlights the proper harmony of this relationship.

The Second Vatican Council reflects upon the relationship between the coming of Christ and our activity to prepare for it. In the *Constitution on the Church in the Modern World*, we read:

> Far from diminishing our concern to develop this earth, the expectancy of a new earth should spur us on, for it is here that the body of a new human family grows, foreshadowing in some way the age which is to come….
>
> When we have spread on earth the fruits of our nature and our enterprise—human dignity, brotherly communion, and freedom—according to the command of the Lord and in his Spirit, we will find them once again, cleansed this time from the stain of sin, illuminated and transfigured, when Christ presents to his Father an eternal and universal kingdom.[41]

In other words, the spirit of Advent should naturally bolster our pro-life efforts. Any progress we make in promoting human dignity is a building block for the eternal kingdom.

· · · · · · · · · · · · · · ·

ADVENT, YEAR A

· · · · · · · · · · ·

First Sunday of Advent, Year A
· ·

Readings: Isaiah 2:1–5 • Romans 13:11–14 • Matthew 24:37–44

The First Sunday of Advent is an ideal time to remind the faithful of the nature of the entire season. Advent focuses on the Lord's coming in two ways: The first part of the season focuses on his second coming, and the second part focuses on the historical fact of the Incarnation (including the Nativity).

The readings today indicate that the Lord's coming will be unexpected (Gospel), that it will separate good from evil (Gospel), that it has the nature of an invitation (first reading), that it transforms society (first reading), and that we have to change our lives now in order to prepare for it (second reading).

In particular, Christ's coming both demands and enables a change from a culture of death to a culture of life. No more "[raising] the sword" (first reading) refers to cessation not only of war but to any attack on human life and dignity. To "conduct ourselves properly as in the day" (second reading) and to "walk in the light of the Lord" (first reading) mean that we treat every human life with the respect and protection the human person deserves.

The Lord's coming transforms both individual conduct (emphasized in the second reading) and the conduct and policies of entire societies and nations (emphasized in the first reading). Building a culture of life therefore involves both as well.

A rededication during Advent to efforts on behalf of the unborn is especially appropriate also because we are preparing to commemorate the birth of God as a baby. Jesus was an unborn baby as well.

. . . .
Second Sunday of Advent, Year A
. . . .

Readings: Isaiah 11:1–10 • Romans 15:4–9 • Matthew 3:1–12

Preaching on today's readings can focus on two themes about life: justice and welcome.

The promised Messiah brings justice. The first reading indicates that this involves "[deciding] aright for the land's afflicted," and the psalm response echoes this:

> Those who go forth weeping,
>> carrying sacks of seed,
> Will return with cries of joy,
>> carrying their bundled sheaves. (Psalm 126:6)

Some people impose a negative judgment on the afflicted, including the "unwanted" child in the womb, the elderly, and the terminally ill. The culture of death deems these unworthy of protection or of other human goods. Right judgment, the judgment of God, recognizes their dignity and treats them accordingly.

This justice is accompanied by peace. "There shall be no harm or ruin." The obvious application in our day is that preparing the way of the Lord, making straight his paths, and repentance will restore the rights of all who are marginalized, including the unborn and the disabled.

Closely connected to this theme of justice is the theme of welcome, stressed by St. Paul in the second reading: "Welcome one another…as Christ welcomed you." To welcome is to recognize the dignity of the other and make room for that person—whether he or she is anticipated or not, planned or not, convenient or not.

This stands in contrast to the concept of wantedness. When someone is wanted, he or she meets some need or expectation of somebody else. The temptation is to think that a person's value rises or falls with his or her degree of wantedness. Not so in the culture of life. While Planned Parenthood may say, "Every child is a wanted child," we say, "Every child (and every person) a welcome child."

. . . .

Third Sunday of Advent, Year A

. . . .

Readings: Isaiah 35:1–6, 10 • James 5:7–10 • Matthew 11:2–11

The themes of joy, hope, and a steady heart flow from today's readings. The coming of the Lord is close at hand! The Church wants our natural joy at the approach of Christmas to be illumined by spiritual joy at the approach of Christ.

This spiritual joy is rooted in hope. We see hope's resulting steadiness of heart expressed in all three of today's readings. Isaiah declares,

> Strengthen the hands that are feeble,
> make firm the knees that are weak,
> say to those whose hearts are frightened:
> Be strong, fear not!
> Here is your God,
> he comes.

James says, "Make your hearts firm, because the coming of the Lord is at hand." In the Gospel, Jesus contrasts John the Baptist's steady heart to "a reed swayed by the wind." Steadiness of heart is what we need as we adhere to the hope of the Gospel amid a culture of death. The psalm response today declares the reason for our hope and steadiness:

> The Lord…
> secures justice for the oppressed.…
> The Lord sets captives free. (Psalm 146:2, 7)

Jesus identified these themes as the core of his mission when he quoted Isaiah in his first sermon (see Luke 4). He comes to save us and to accomplish, through us, the flowering of justice in the world. All human beings await this justice, especially those whose rights—starting with the most fundamental right, life itself—are denied.

When we have a steady heart, we are able to face evil without minimizing it. We see that God is stronger than the evil and will work through us to conquer it. We need not and must not resort to immoral means, even to achieve good ends. A steady heart keeps everything in perspective, maintains patience, and works hard each day to bring into the world the fruit of the Spirit and to help others do the same.

. . . .

Fourth Sunday of Advent, Year A

Readings: Isaiah 7:10–14 • Romans 1:1–7 • Matthew 1:18–24

On the verge of Christmas, on the verge of welcoming Christ into the world, the readings focus on the virginity of Mary. Today's homily can draw out what this says about us. Mary, after all, symbolizes the whole Church. She received Christ into her virginal body. The Church too, as the bride of Christ—and each of us individually—is called to a total fidelity that reflects the virginity of Mary.

Whatever the vocation of each of us, this spiritual (if not physical) virginity means that we have no Lord besides Jesus. We do not worship false gods or become intimate with other deities.

As Mary welcomed Christ in her virginity, so does the Church. "It is through the Holy Spirit that this child has been conceived in her," the Gospel passage tells us. So can we say, "It is through the Holy Spirit that Christ has been conceived in us." No human effort brings about Christmas. But by our virginal fidelity, the Spirit brings him forth into the world. This is the "obedience of faith" of which Paul speaks in the second reading.

And part of this virginal fidelity, part of this obedience of faith, is our commitment to be pro-life. "God is with us" means that he is on the side of every human life, against all that would destroy it. So must we be.

· · · · · · · · · · · · · · ·
ADVENT, YEAR B

· · · · · · · · · · ·
First Sunday of Advent, Year B
· ·

Readings: Isaiah 63:16b–17, 19b; 64:2–7 • 1 Corinthians 1:3–9

Mark 13:33–37

The beginning of the Advent season focuses our attention on the future coming of Christ in glory. Its theme of repentance is a preparation for that coming. Christ's coming ushers in the final triumph of life over death. The preparation for that coming, therefore, includes repentance from the works of death, including abortion. Not only individuals but also nations need to repent.

When we battle against the culture of death in its various forms, we might pray, as in today's first reading, "Lord, rend the heavens and come down!" Why does the Lord not appear from the sky to stop abortions? The fact is that God did come down, in the Incarnation.

Through the clear teachings of Our Lord Jesus Christ, God continues to put the truth in our minds and the grace in our hearts to bear witness to life amid the culture of death. His Spirit enables us to work tirelessly to transform that culture and intervene to save the helpless.

· · · · · · · · · · ·
Second Sunday of Advent, Year B
· ·

Readings: Isaiah 40:1–5, 9–11 • 2 Peter 3:8–14 • Mark 1:1–8

The theme of repentance is stressed again in today's readings. As John the Baptizer prepared the people for the coming of Christ by proclaiming repentance, so the Church prepares the world for his second coming by proclaiming and opening the way for repentance.

The Church gives not only the message of repentance but also the grace we need to live it out. Preparing a straight path in the wasteland—lowering the mountains and filling the valleys—represents the arduous task of making our hearts right in the sight of God. They extend to the task of making the terrain of society and culture right with God.

Here the building of a culture of life is central. It is, in essence, a preparation for Christ's coming. We make straight the way for him by welcoming all who are created in his image, particularly the poor, the marginalized, and the unborn. We strive "to be found without spot or blemish before him, at peace" (second reading). This peace includes peace with all our brothers and sisters, including the unborn. Let us not be stained with the sin of rejecting them.

. . . .

Third Sunday of Advent, Year B

Reading: Isaiah 61:1–2a, 10–11 • 1 Thessalonians 5:16–24
John 1:6–8, 19–28

The command to "rejoice always" (second reading) may seem demanding, given the fact that things do not always go our way. Some circumstances are beyond our control. Yet this rejoicing is always possible, because it is based on the salvation that Christ has come to bring.

Isaiah writes,

> I rejoice heartily in the LORD,...
> For he has clothed me with a robe of salvation
>   and wrapped me in a mantle of justice.

This "justice," manifested when God rescues his people (for example, from slavery in Egypt), has come to us in the divine child whose birth we are preparing to celebrate. He wrapped us in a mantle of justice when, by his death and resurrection, he rescued us from the power of death. "To proclaim liberty to the captives" is his mission, as he will state (see Luke 4:18). The Christmas song "O Holy Night" reflects this theme:

> Chains shall he break,
> for the slave is our brother,
> and in his name all oppression shall cease.[42]

We who are rescued must rescue the poor and weak among us, including the poorest and weakest, the unborn children. To celebrate the God who comes to free the oppressed, and has freed us, means to commit ourselves to ending the pro-death oppression in our culture.

· · · · · · · · · · ·

Fourth Sunday of Advent, Year B

Readings: 2 Samuel 7:1–5, 8b–12, 14a, 16 • Romans 16:25–27
Luke 1:26–38

The readings of today thrust us into reflections on the Incarnation. Christmas is not only the feast of Christ's birth but the celebration of the entire mystery of God's taking on a human nature—beginning with the event narrated in today's Gospel, whereby Christ was conceived within Mary's body.

Vatican II stated, "By his incarnation the Son of God has united himself in some fashion with every human being."[43] God redeems us by joining every aspect of our lives to his. God even becomes an unborn child. Human life was already sacred because it always was and is God's creation, made freely from his love. But in the Incarnation, it takes on an even deeper meaning and sanctity because human nature is forever united with divine life. This affects all who share human nature, even the children still in the womb. That is why Pope St. John Paul II, in *Evangelium Vitae*, could make the following two assertions:

Life, especially human life, belongs only to God: for this reason *whoever attacks human life, in some way attacks God himself.*[44]

By his Incarnation the Son of God has united himself in some fashion with every person. It is precisely in the "flesh" of every person that Christ continues to reveal himself and to enter into fellowship with us, so that *rejection of human life*, in whatever form that rejection takes, is *really a rejection of Christ.*[45]

The fact that Mary was not expecting to carry a child and was troubled at the greeting also leads us to reflect on the providence of God. No unexpected pregnancy has ever affected history so profoundly, and no woman is a better example to those who feel they cannot handle a pregnancy.

. . . .
ADVENT, YEAR C

. . . .
First Sunday of Advent, Year C
. . . .

Readings: Jeremiah 33:14–16 • 1 Thessalonians 3:12–4:2
Luke 21:25–28, 34–36

Anticipation of the Second Coming of the Lord is a theme particularly strong in the first part of Advent. To prepare for this coming of the Lord, the readings call us as individuals and as a society to repentance. The psalm response encourages us to look to the Lord with confidence:

> Good and upright is the LORD;
>> thus he shows sinners the way.
> He guides the humble to justice,
>> and teaches the humble his way. (Psalm 25:8–9)

The repentance to which God calls us goes beyond forsaking sin to cultivating active respect for every human life and building a society of justice and welcome for the most vulnerable. "May the Lord make you increase and abound in love for one another and for all" (second reading).

Jesus encourages us to persevere in our Christian life, in spite of the disarray of nations as well as the "anxieties of daily life" (Gospel). We are to "be vigilant at all times and pray" for "the strength to escape the tribulations that are imminent" (Gospel). These are strong words for Catholics today facing the culture of death. No matter how powerful our adversaries appear, we know that victory is ours because Jesus is ours.

. . . .

Second Sunday of Advent, Year C

. . . .

Readings: Baruch 5:1–9 • Philippians 1:4–6, 8–11 • Luke 3:1–6

God began "a good work" in each of us when he called us, through faith and baptism, to live in Christ and to be "filled with the fruit of righteousness" (second reading). Advent is a time to stimulate growth in this fruit in our lives. By that growth, we can then work together to "prepare the way of the Lord" (Gospel).

This Lord, the first reading makes clear, is a God of justice. Every valley shall be filled. This includes every place in which people languish because their rights are trampled, their dignity forgotten, and their lives thrown to the outskirts of society. Every mountain and hill shall be made low—the mountains of pride, whereby we think our own choices determine what is right and wrong rather than submit our choices to the truth.

This is a time of year when prayers and thoughts of peace on earth come naturally. The first reading speaks of "the peace of justice." Peace does not simply indicate that wars stop. Peace demands that nobody be so victimized that a war is the only means of defense. Peace comes only when justice is restored.

The Advent journey of God's people includes fighting for the God-given rights of every human being—from the unborn child to the prisoner on death row. Getting engaged in the work of justice, in the light of Christ, is the way to celebrate Advent and prepare the world for Christmas.

. . . .

Third Sunday of Advent, Year C

. . . .

Readings: Zephaniah 3:14–18a • Philippians 4:4–7 • Luke 3:10–18

As Christmas draws nearer, the Church's liturgy emphasizes the theme of joy. Joy is not simply a happiness based on good circumstances but a profound exultation of spirit based on the salvation that comes from God. Every human spirit longs for joy, but many do not know how to find it. We are all too aware of the things that rob human souls of joy and peace. Many are the evils, both in our own lives and in the world, from which we need to be saved.

Advent is about the expectation of complete salvation. We do not pretend that Christ has not come and imagine welcoming him for the first time. Rather, acknowledging that Christ has already come, we await the full unfolding of the effects of the salvation he brings.

That's what the first and second readings today refer to: "He has turned away your enemies…. You have no further misfortune to fear" (first reading). "Have no anxiety at all" (second reading). People may find these assurances unrealistic, but they are not, because God is real!

For one thing, the coming of Christ has destroyed the power of sin and death at its roots. No matter what misfortunes may come our way, or what anxieties may still torment us, the fact is that we always have access to God. That is why we dismiss anxiety from our minds. God has baptized us in the Holy Spirit, as John the Baptizer promised. That Holy Spirit gives us total access to God, to an understanding of his word, and to the grace of salvation. Hence, no matter what is happening in our lives, we can say, "Merry Christmas!"

The total salvation Christ brings, which is unfolding each day, is physical as well as spiritual. The whole universe will be transformed. All physical violence, such as abortion, will be overcome. Therefore we rejoice now, as we embrace the Christ who has already come and as we wait in joyful hope for him to come again.

. . . .

Fourth Sunday of Advent, Year C

Readings: Micah 5:1–4a • Hebrews 10:5–10 • Luke 1:39–45

In today's readings, we see a link between Christmas and Easter. Christmas is the Feast of the Incarnation, not simply the celebration of Christ's birth. Christ takes on a human body so as to offer the sacrifice of that body to save the world. In fact, his sacrifice is not limited to Calvary; it begins even in the womb.

"A body you prepared for me.... I come to do your will" (second reading, quoting Psalm 40). Even as an embryo, Jesus offered himself to the Father in obedience to his will and for our salvation. He is our Savior because he bears our human nature. He has a human body as we do—a body offered on the cross and in the Eucharist.

As we see in the first reading and the Gospel, the details of Christ's birth are carefully planned by God and foretold by his prophets. His birth is all about hope fulfilled and hope inspired. That hope extends beyond his birth. We experience it today as we work to build a world in harmony with the vision of peace, life, and love that Christmas inspires.

· · · · · · · · · · ·

CHRISTMAS

Pro-Life Themes in the Christmas Season

· ·

Advent leads the Church to the Silent Night when God reveals himself as one of us. This season celebrates the joy of his birth. And the joy of Jesus's birth, St. John Paul II wrote in *Evangelium Vitae*, is reflected in joy at the birth of every child.[46]

If God has joined his nature to ours, how can we ever allow our nature to be despised? If he has come to bring us divine life and will return to take us to the skies, how can it be all right to throw people in the garbage?

As we consider the circumstances of Christ's birth, this is a perfect time to commend to the prayers of people all women who are carrying children and the fathers of those children, particularly those who may be fearful and tempted to abort. May Christ's birth shed protection on all. And as we work to end abortion, may we bear in mind "the blessed hope and the coming of our Savior, Jesus Christ."[47]

. . . .
Christmas Day
. . . .

Readings:

Vigil: *Isaiah 62:1–5 • Acts 13:16–17, 22–25 • Matthew 1:1–25 or 1:18–25*

Midnight: *Isaiah 9:1–6 • Titus 2:11–14 • Luke 2:1–14*

Dawn: *Isaiah 62:11–12 • Titus 3:4–7 • Luke 2:15–20*

Day: *Isaiah 52:7–10 • Hebrews 1:1–6 • John 1:1–18 or 1:1–5, 9–14*

In the wonder of Christmas, the promised Messiah of the Lord comes in a surprising way, surpassing the hopes and dreams of all the people of old. On the first Christmas night, angels announced Christ's birth to the shepherds. But instead of saying that Jesus was the Messiah of the Lord, they said that he was Messiah *and* Lord (Gospel at midnight and dawn). God, in other words, did not simply send someone to represent him. He came himself!

Christmas means more than welcoming the child. It means welcoming the one who will preach the Sermon on the Mount, instruct us by parables, give us the sacraments, and establish his Church. All of these Christmas presents we must open and use!

Christmas is about a God who created the human family and then decided to become a member of that family. Christmas is not when Jesus began; it is when Jesus was revealed as one of us. He joined to his divinity all who share human nature: the weak and strong, the small and big, the born and unborn.

A fascinating aspect of the Christmas Gospel is the lack of room for the Holy Family in the inn. This should make us wonder, because the birth of Christ was foreseen and planned by God from all eternity. Hundreds of years before it happened, the prophet Micah announced that Bethlehem would be his birthplace (see Micah 5:2). Did God forget to make room for his only Son? The child born at Christmas owned the inn and Bethlehem and the world and the whole universe!

Obviously, God allowed this lack of room on purpose. It demonstrates that the child comes as a Savior, to reconcile a world that is at enmity with God and has rejected him. The lack of room in the inn symbolizes the lack of room we make for him in our hearts. He comes not seeking a room in an inn but room in our lives.

Welcoming the child demands that we welcome all he welcomes. We must make room for all he loves, including the unwanted, the marginalized, the burdensome, and the inconvenient. We must welcome the poor and the destitute, the stranger and the alienated, the disabled and the unborn.

If we welcome the baby Jesus, we welcome every baby. We welcome Jesus's teaching that every life is sacred, and we live accordingly. Christmas is universally about the exaltation of the human person.

· · · · · · · · · · ·
Feast of the Holy Family

Readings:
Sirach 3:2–6, 12–14 (or, for Year B, Genesis 15:1–6; 21:1–3)
Colossians 3:12–21 or 3:12–17 (or, for Year B, Hebrews 11:8, 11-12, 17-19)
Year A: Matthew 2:13–15, 19–23
Year B: Luke 2:22–40 or 2:22, 39–40
Year C: Luke 2:41–52 (or, for Year C, 1 Samuel 1:20–22, 24–28; 1 John
3:1–2, 21–24; Luke 2:41–52)

The family is the sanctuary of life and the basic cell of society. The Holy Family, of course, is unique. One member is God, another is sinless, and the third is a saint. But the great lesson of today is that, although God could have come into the world in any way he pleased, he chose to become a member of a family. He was obedient to his earthly parents and yet totally devoted to the heavenly Father's will, as we all must be.

God also shared the vulnerability that comes with being a member of a human family. "Herod is going to search for the child to destroy him" (Gospel, Year A). St. Joseph here plays the amazing role of protecting God. His readiness to do so speaks to every father about the role of protector— and to our whole society about the need we have for good fathers. The culture of life depends just as much on fathers to make the right choices as on mothers to do so.

Today's preaching can focus on the fact that strong families are an integral aspect of the culture of life. The breakdown of families increases the temptation to abort, to resort to euthanasia, and to neglect the elderly. On the other hand, the communion of persons that comes from giving oneself away to the other in selfless love creates the proper context for saying a generous yes to life. A helpful lesson to point out from the word *family* is that it stands for "Forget About Me; I Love You."

. . . .
Solemnity of Mary, Mother of God
. . . .

Readings: Numbers 6:22–27 • Galatians 4:4–7 • Luke 2:16–21

The calendar year starts with reflections on Mary's greatest title, Mother of God. Her motherhood gives us courage and hope to start anew. Life and hope are intimately related. The more we hope, the more willing we are to welcome life. Abortion is not only a sin against life but a sin against hope.

Some wonder, "How can I bring a child into this evil and dangerous world?" as though it would be better to not be born. Christ and Mary lead the way for every mother and child, for every family.

The Gospel tells us that on the first Christmas, the shepherds arrived in Bethlehem, saw the baby in the manger, and then proclaimed to others what the angels had told them. Why was that the moment when they obeyed the message? After all, the angels had announced that the Savior was born for all people. Perhaps it was because the baby was so approachable. How can God be more approachable than as a little baby?

God continues to reveal himself in the tiny babies yet in the womb. He invites us to see and love him in them.

. . . .

Solemnity of the Epiphany

Readings: Isaiah 60:1–6 • Ephesians 3:2–3a, 5–6 • Matthew 2:1–12

The opening and closing prayers, the Preface, and the readings of today's feast all work together to communicate the message of the sanctity of life. Epiphany is about revealing and manifesting, and that is what Christ does. Not only does he reveal the Father to us, but he reveals us to ourselves. He shows us that this human nature of ours, which can be so troublesome and burdened, has in fact been renewed.

The Preface proclaims, "You made us new by the glory of his immortal nature." That, indeed, is "the promise in Christ Jesus through the gospel" that Paul proclaims to the Ephesians in the second reading. It is like the alternative opening prayer, which asks that God "draw us beyond the limits which this world imposes to the life where your Spirit makes all life complete." Death is no longer the final word for the human family.

This gift is not for one nation or one people but for all humanity, extending to those still in the womb. There are no boundaries between born and unborn, wanted and unwanted, convenient and inconvenient.

The epiphany most needed in our time is the ability to see beyond appearances, to honor the value of the smallest and weakest among us. God's light pierces the illusion that declares living human beings nonpersons under the law. Breaking through this darkness is the clear light of Christ, which shines on every human life without exception, bringing God's love and giving us the sacred obligation to love as well.

. . . .
Feast of the Baptism of the Lord
. . . .

Readings:

Isaiah 42:1–4, 6–7 • Acts 10:34–38

Year A: Matthew 3:13–17

Year B: Mark 1:7–11

Year C: Luke 3:15–16, 21–22

Today we view the mystery of Christ's baptism and our own. Jesus goes to John to be baptized in order to reveal himself as God's only son and to reveal his mission of sharing that sonship with us sinners. Our status as baptized Christians leads naturally to a commitment to the culture of life.

To be a Christian is much more than to be a good person. It's about becoming a new person, sharing a new kind of life—the life of God himself. Christmas is not just about the birth of a child; it's about the birth of a whole new humanity. In Adam, all die; in Christ, all come to life again. We become sharers, by faith and baptism, in the divine nature.

At every Mass, as the priest pours a few drops of water into the wine, he prays, "By the mystery of this water and wine, may we come to share in the divinity of Christ, who humbled himself to share in our humanity." That's what the Christmas season is all about. St. Athanasius put it this way: "God became man that man might become God."[48]

Baptism gives us our identity as "the people of life."[49] Baptized into Christ's victory over death, we are also sent to proclaim, celebrate, and serve that victory.[50] At baptism, at every renewal of the vows of our baptism, we "reject Satan and all his works." Chief among those works is death. The Son of God has destroyed death, and that means that we who follow him stand against it.

Consider what the Church does in the celebration of baptism. A child is brought into the congregation and is welcomed by all as a brother, a sister. Perhaps only a few of the gathered Christians know this child, yet they declare before God that they accept the child as one of them. Baptism expresses God's unconditional welcome of his people, his call to them to share his life. Baptism expresses the hospitality of God's Church and the responsibility we accept for the care of one another.

Abortion is a contradiction to baptism. It is not a welcoming act but a rejection.

· · · · ·

LENT

Pro-Life Themes in Lent

· ·

By your gracious gift each year your faithful await the sacred paschal feasts with the joy of minds made pure.

—Preface 1 of Lent

The themes of Lent provide powerful opportunities to preach on the sanctity of life and the tragedy of abortion. The quote above from Preface 1 succinctly expresses Lent's purpose. Catechumens prepare for baptism into the paschal mystery. The faithful are reminded of their baptism, and they will renew their baptismal vows at the Easter liturgy.

This baptismal focus is a life focus. The Lenten readings illumine it, as does Pope St. John Paul II's encyclical *The Gospel of Life*. Baptism initiates us into the eternal life Christ gives us. *Eternal* does not only mean "never ending." It also refers to the fact that such life is a share in the life of the eternal God.

The baptized are sons and daughters of God and are members of the Church, "the people of life."[51] The baptized have taken hold of the eternal life promised them (see Romans 6:4) and are already living it (Galatians 2:19–20; John 6:47).

The baptized are called to realize their new identity (see Romans 6:6; Ephesians 4:17–24). We see Christ call the Samaritan woman to repent as she accepts the waters of new life (Third Sunday, Year A). Lenten repentance leads God's people to more deeply become who they are. They are called to see their sins more clearly.

Hence baptism is known as "illumination." The passage about the man born blind (John 9) is a key Lenten passage (Fourth Sunday of Lent, Year A).

Anyone who makes the Lenten journey is called to be more alert to attacks on human life and dignity. The people of life are called to reject sin and all the devil's "works" and "empty promises."[52] The pro-choice and right-to-die mentalities are parts of those empty promises that the baptized firmly reject.

Lent is the perfect time for us to call our congregations to a clearer understanding of our identity as Christ's own. Let us lead them to a deeper affirmation of life, both natural and eternal, in the celebration of the paschal mystery.

. . . .
LENT, YEAR A

. . . .
First Sunday of Lent, Year A

Readings: Genesis 2:7–9; 3:1–7 • Romans 5:12–19 or 5:12, 17–19
Matthew 4:1–11

Each of today's readings reinforces the fact that God is Lord of our choices and that freedom is found in obedience. This strikes at the heart of the culture of death, which puts choice above life. Indeed, the culture of death validates choice simply because it is choice, not because of what is chosen.

The original temptation, outlined in the first reading, was a promise that what was right and what was wrong would be up to us, that we could write our own moral law. That's what the "tree of the knowledge of good and evil" meant, and that's why Adam and Eve were not allowed to eat from it. We are all called to know good from evil but not to *decide* it. To think we decide what is good and what is evil is the error of the pro-choice mind-set. "It's all up to me and my choice, even if it means killing a baby."

The obedience of Jesus Christ, exemplified in the Gospel passage and identified in the second reading as the source of our redemption, is the foundation for the culture of life and the pattern for each believer. Obedience does not mean a slavish following of rules. It means a free embrace of what is true and good.

In that sense, the Church and the pro-life movement are the true promoters and defenders of freedom of choice. They provide the grace and the tools to do what is right. The major efforts of the pro-life movement are directed toward providing alternatives to abortion, concrete help to enable people to choose life.

Second Sunday of Lent, Year A

Readings: Genesis 12:1–4a • 2 Timothy 1:8b–10 • Matthew 17:1–9

As Paul writes to Timothy in today's second reading, Jesus Christ "destroyed death and brought life." That is the core of the Gospel, and it is the subject of the conversation that Jesus has with Moses and Elijah during the Transfiguration, as Luke's account reveals (see Luke 9:31). The word used there for the passion, death, and resurrection of Jesus is "exodus," reminding us of the great act of liberation in the Old Testament that prefigured the paschal mystery.

The Exodus was not easy for God's people, nor was the passion easy for Christ. Yet these were the paths to the destruction of death and the revelation of life. So it is for us who—as individuals and as a society—are called to make the transition from a culture of death to a culture of life.

It is like what Abram is asked to do in the first reading—to leave all that is familiar, comfortable, and predictable and to set out for "a land that I will show you." This requires absolute trust. Abram, after all, has been where he is for a long time. Is this any time to change?

When we talk about ending abortion in our society, we encounter the same kind of question. The resistance to abolishing this practice arises not so much from the conviction that abortion is acceptable as from the conviction that it's too late to change things. The Supreme Court said as much when it came close to reversing *Roe v. Wade* in 1992. Instead the court concluded, in *Planned Parenthood v. Casey*, that women have come to rely on the availability of abortion.

On a popular level, people wonder what changes would occur in society if the many children now being aborted were born instead. "Will society be able to handle the change?" is the question they ask. Incidentally, the same kind of question was asked when society faced the question of abolishing slavery. "How will society handle the slaves who will now roam free?"

Of course, the question of how to handle a change is also asked on a very personal level by the mother who is not sure she can continue her pregnancy. How will I care for this child? What does this child's existence mean for my life?

Abram is asked to leave the comfortable and familiar and set out for a whole new land, a new way of life, and a new fruitfulness. The people of God, at the edge of the Red Sea, will wonder how it can open. The apostles on the Mount of the Transfiguration ask what this vision means and what it means "to rise from the dead."

The message for God's people today is that we are to move forward into the frightening and unfamiliar changes that are required for those committed to doing what is right. "Bear your share of hardship for the gospel with the strength that comes from God" (second reading).

. . . .
Third Sunday of Lent, Year A

Readings: Exodus 17:3–7 • Romans 5:1–2, 5–8
John 4:5–42 or 4:5–15, 19b–26, 39a, 40–42

The Gospel of the Third Sunday of Lent, Year A, along with those of the Fourth and Fifth Sundays, form a triduum emphasizing the baptismal themes of water (the woman at the well), light (the healing of the man born blind), and life (the raising of Lazarus). These powerful readings remind those preparing for baptism, as well as all the baptized, what this baptismal life is all about.

The Gospel passage for today, Jesus's offer of the waters of new life to the Samaritan woman, along with the other readings point out three things:

Jesus offers his gift of life with no regard to the false barriers that society sets up between people. As noted in the Gospel, Jews have nothing to do with Samaritans, and the disciples were surprised to find him talking with a woman.

The gift of life comes through the death and resurrection of Christ. The rock in the first reading represents Christ. As Paul relates to the Corinthians (see 1 Corinthians10:4), tradition said that the rock continued to follow the Israelites on the journey through the desert. Paul identifies that rock as Christ. The rock was struck, just as Christ was struck and crucified, and water flowed from his side. The second reading also emphasizes Jesus's passion, death, and resurrection as the source of new life "poured out into our hearts," as the water poured out of the rock.

To accept the gift, repentance is required. The woman had to go find her husband, which indicates repentance for her multiple unions.

All of this illumines our pro-life commitment. The offer of eternal life necessarily presupposes the offer of natural life—without the kind of false boundaries society sets up between born and unborn.

Moreover, since Christ gives life, to stand with Christ means to stand with life and therefore to stand against whatever destroys it. One simply cannot be a pro-choice Christian.

Finally, accepting Christ necessarily means repentance, which is concrete and historical in our lives. It includes a specific rejection of abortion. Any form of participation in abortion or of support for abortion is incompatible with the acceptance of Christ and the life of the baptized.

· · · · · · · · · ·

Fourth Sunday of Lent, Year A

Readings: 1 Samuel 16:1b, 6–7, 10–13a • Ephesians 5:8–14
John 9:1–41 or 9:1, 6–9, 13–17, 34–38

The Lenten season is marked by the urgent call to repent. It is a call to make a conscious and free choice to turn away from sin, which leads to death, and embrace the Gospel, which leads to life. It is, in fact, the full flowering of the call Moses issued in Deuteronomy 30:19: "I have set before you life and death.... Choose life."

Today's Gospel passage is that of the man born blind. This passage forms a triduum along with those of the third and fifth Sundays of Lent, Year A. Together they emphasize the baptismal themes of water (the woman at the well), light (the healing of the man born blind), and life (the raising of Lazarus). These powerful readings remind those preparing for baptism, as well as all the baptized, what this baptismal life is all about.

We see here the drama of the decision to accept or reject the call of Christ. The man born blind receives his physical sight early in the story; the rest of the passage traces the birth of his spiritual sight. At first he calls Jesus a man (v. 11), then a prophet (v. 17), then one who is "from God" (v. 33), and finally, "Lord" (v. 38). He comes to see who Jesus is because he is willing to believe: "Who is he, sir, that I may believe in him?" (v. 36).

This attitude of willingness stands in stark contrast to the stubbornness and bad will of the Pharisees. Though confronted with the same physical healing, they try to explain away the evidence through their interrogations of the man and his parents. They portray Jesus as a sinner, and finally they literally throw the evidence out the door, ejecting the healed man from their midst (see v. 34).

This drama is repeated every day as our society struggles with the culture of death. The evidence is the same for all to see, made clearer than ever by genetics and fetology. That evidence points to the fact that abortion kills a human being. Some receive that evidence and, with willing hearts, choose life. Others show the stubbornness of the Pharisees and cling to their own ideology.

For me, the starkest example of this was the day a group of pro-life people conducted a wake for an aborted baby in front of an abortion facility. The baby, the size of a hand, was visible in a small white casket. Some pro-abortion demonstrators looked at the child, and a pro-lifer challenged them,

"Look at the evidence right before your eyes. This is a baby!" Believe it or not, one person's response was, "That's your opinion!"

Not to know the child in the womb is not a sin. But the refusal to know is. Jesus declares to the Pharisees at the end of the drama of John 9, "If you were blind, you would have no sin, but now you are saying, 'We see,' and your sin remains."

"Repent and believe the Good News!" What good news? The good news, in the words of *The Gospel of Life*, that "life is always a good…manifestation of God in the world, a sign of His presence, a trace of His glory."[53]

This Lent, let us choose life again!

· · · · · · · · · · ·
Fifth Sunday of Lent, Year A
· ·

Readings: Ezekiel 37:12–14 • Romans 8:8–11
John 11:1–45 or 11:3–7, 17, 20–27, 33b–45

This weekend's readings come together in an overwhelming proclamation that God is master of life and death. Lent is meant to deepen our awareness and conviction of this truth, which is in turn the basis of the pro-life movement. We are not simply counteracting an evil in society through our human strength; rather, we are on a mission, sent by the one who has authority over death, to free the human family from its oppressive regime.

Imagine going to a wake service and having someone say to you, "If you had been here sooner, my loved one would never have died." That is what both Martha and Mary said to Jesus. They knew he had power over life and death. And yet they were subject to the all-too-human fears and calculations of our own battle against the culture of death. Martha said, "By now there will be a stench."

We say the same thing. We know what is right; we know what has to be said and done to defend life. Yet we fear the stench. We fear who will object, who will get angry. Politicians fear who will vote against them; businesses fear who will stop supporting them. "Surely, there will be a stench." And that becomes the excuse not to act—even when we know that Jesus has authority over death.

As we approach the climax of Lent and proclaim these powerful readings of God's victory over death, let's call people to a confident and persistent activism for the cause of life, without fears or excuses.

· · · · · · · · · · ·
Palm Sunday of the Passion of the Lord, Year A

Readings: Matthew 21:1–11 • Isaiah 50:4–7 • Philippians 2:6–11
Matthew 26:14–27:66 or 27:11–54

We come to the week that will bring us to the center and climax of the entire liturgical year. This week we celebrate the very heart of the Gospel in which we believe Christ has died, Christ is risen, Christ will come again.

We have been preparing to celebrate the events of these days. Indeed, these events are so crucial to human history and to our own lives that they require a whole season of repentance and preparation, that we might celebrate them worthily. We are blessed and privileged to believe that in the passion narrative, God has revealed his love for us. He has opened the way for the forgiveness of all our sins, and he has placed in our hands the gift of eternal life.

St. Paul tells us that Christ, in willing obedience to the Father, came to our world and "humbled himself, becoming obedient to death, even death on a cross." By his decision to go to Jerusalem, Jesus decided to give his life for us. He knew exactly what was going to happen to him and consented to it fully.

Jesus's entry into the city was triumphant. The acclaim that greeted him is in stark contrast to the shouts of the crowd that would come on Friday to crucify him. At the same time, the triumph of Palm Sunday represents the fact that Jesus brings the triumph of grace over sin and of life over death. His being lifted up on the cross was in fact a lifting up in glory. What we see there is not weakness but strength—the strength to give one's life for others who need to be saved. What we see there is the triumphant victory of obedience over rebellion. Christ was obedient to the Father, even to death, to undo our disobedience, which led to death.

Those who acclaimed Christ as he entered Jerusalem didn't realize how right they were. There was more to celebrate than met the eye or that could meet their minds. Love was about to be revealed in a way than would change human history and usher in the kingdom of salvation.

This love, and the way it is revealed in the passion, is at the heart of the culture of life. It is a love that, through obedience, welcomes life.

· · · · · · · · · · · ·
LENT, YEAR B

· · · · · · · · · · ·
First Sunday of Lent, Year B
· ·

Readings: Genesis 9:8–15 • 1 Peter 3:18–22 • Mark 1:12–15

"This is the time of fulfillment" (Gospel). The call to repentance, issued at the start of Lent, is a call to respond to something that has already happened. The promise of the covenant after the Flood, in the days of Noah, is fulfilled in the new and everlasting covenant of Christ. God has cleansed us by the waters of baptism and given us new, eternal life.

This fulfillment brings an obligation: Reform your life, so that it will correspond to the new life that has been poured into you! "Baptism…is not a removal of dirt from the body but an appeal to God for a clear conscience" (second reading). Repentance is consistent with the gift already given.

This gift, essentially, is life. By the new and eternal covenant, renewed in each Mass, we become ever more deeply a people of life. The repentance we undertake is expressed in the self-giving that Christ shows us on the altar. We give ourselves away in order to foster life in our families, our communities, and the world.

Putting ourselves aside to welcome the gift of life in the person of the unborn child is a particularly urgent aspect of the repentance needed in our nation today. Lent gives us the opportunity to echo that call:

Reform your lives, and put aside the doubt, fear, and selfishness that would destroy another human being in the name of "choice."

Reform your lives, and repent of the silence that keeps you from defending the helpless in your midst.

Reform your lives, and work for the reformation of the laws and policies of the nation, that they may protect the rights that God has already given to all, born and unborn.

Reform your lives, reject the covenant of death, and live the covenant of life!

· · · · · · · · · · ·
Second Sunday of Lent, Year B
· ·

Readings: Genesis 22:1–2, 9a, 10–13, 15–18
Romans 8:31b–34 • Mark 9:2–10

It was a miracle that Abraham and Sarah had a son. The name Isaac means "laughter." When God promised that he would be born, Abraham was ninety-nine years old and Sarah was ninety, and they both laughed (see Genesis 17:17; 18:12). Yet the promise came to pass.

God changed the name of Abram ("exalted father") to Abraham ("father of many"). Isaac was the beginning of the fulfillment of the marvelous promise that Abraham would have "descendants as countless as the stars of the sky."

What a test, then, when God said he was going to take the only son to himself. Why would God do this? How would his promise be fulfilled? Despite these unanswerable questions, Abraham trusted and obeyed. He is truly our father in faith (see Romans 4:11–12).

God gave Abraham this test that Isaac might foreshadow Christ. The eternal Father would give his own Son for the life of the world. How could he do this? The question of Isaac echoes centuries later at Calvary. If the Father loves the Son, how could he sacrifice him on the wood of the cross?

The answer, as St. Thomas Aquinas expressed it, lies in the fact that God filled his Son with such love that he was able to sacrifice himself for us. There is no enmity between the Father and the Son. There is only love, impelling the Son to give himself away. Christ said of his own life, "I have power to lay it down, and power to take it up again" (John 10:18). He was speaking about the power of love.

That's the power at the heart of the culture of life. It is a love by which we sacrifice ourselves for others. It is a love that, like the love God showed Abraham, brings life out of death. It is a love that sees and understands that, in every circumstance, "God is for us" (second reading) and nobody can be against us. That is, nobody can prevail in doing us ultimate harm. We always have the power to do what is right, to avoid injustice, and to welcome life.

Lent is an opportunity to exercise the faith, the trust, and the love we need to do precisely that. This is no mere exercise of the will. It is the response to the gift of God in Christ Jesus, the only beloved Son, to whom we listen and whom alone we obey.

· · · · · · · · · · ·

Third Sunday of Lent, Year B

Readings: Exodus 20:1–17 or 20:1–3, 7–8, 12–17
1 Corinthians 1:22–25 • John 2:13–25

The reading from Exodus, of the giving of the commandments, puts into context the absolute prohibition of killing human beings. For before he says, "You shall not kill," God says, "I, the Lord, am your God, who brought you out of the land of Egypt."

In other words, he gives his commands in the context of his relationship with us. He rescues us, he frees us, he makes a covenant with us, and he shares his life with us. From these realities flow the commandments. God does not simply impose something on us from the outside; rather, he shows us what his new way of life entails.

We obey the commandments because we're God's children. We respect life not just because God said so but because God is life. We are to be truthful because God is truth. We are to be just because God is justice. If we share in God's life, we will act as he does.

This is the context in which people can understand the absolute command to respect, promote, and defend life. It is not a burdensome command; rather, it shows the soul the way to happiness and fulfillment. As today's psalm tells us,

> The law of the LORD is perfect,
> refreshing the soul. (Psalm 19:8)

Our Lord's promise to raise up the temple of his body (today's Gospel passage) completes this picture. It is only through his resurrection that the life of God can be given to us. That risen life is what the catechumens are preparing all during Lent to receive. Moreover, each of us is preparing, through Lenten penance, to renew the promises of our baptism at Easter—the promises to follow the new way of life that the commandments reflect.

. . . .
Fourth Sunday of Lent, Year B
. . . .

Readings: 2 Chronicles 36:14–16, 19–23 • Ephesians 2:4–10 • John 3:14–21

The Gospel for today brings us to the most well-known verse of the Bible, John 3:16, "God so loved the world that he gave his only Son, so that everyone who believes in him might not perish but might have eternal life."

As Lent draws closer to its culmination in the Easter Triduum, it becomes clearer in the readings and prayers of the liturgy that this season is a great preparation for receiving the gift of eternal life obtained for us through the Lord's passion and resurrection. The catechumens of the Church prepare to receive this gift in baptism; the rest of us prepare for the renewal of our baptismal vows at Easter Mass. All of us live the fulfillment of John 3:16.

The homilist might reflect that the purpose of Christ's coming is that we "might not perish…but have life." As The Gospel of Life makes clear, this promise of eternal life implies the sacrosanct character of natural life, which provides the foundation and context in which we accept this gift of everlasting life. "God's eternal life is in fact the end to which our living in this world is directed and called."[54]

God's will is that human beings not perish—neither by losing their salvation nor by being deprived of the opportunity to grasp it. All have the right to be born and eventually hear God's word so that they might live the faith. God shows himself to be on the side of human life.

Yet the acceptance of life, natural and supernatural, and the defense of that life create division. "The light came into the world, but people preferred darkness to light." We have to fight against the forces in our world that would destroy human life. He who would destroy it "does not come toward the light, so that his works might not be exposed." Injustice in the world always flourishes when it is hidden. Those who support the culture of death in all its forms want to keep their actions hidden.

Sr. Helen Prejean, a renowned advocate for abolishing the death penalty, writes, "I am convinced that if executions were made public, the torture and violence would be unmasked, and we would be shamed into abolishing executions."[55] Those responsible for killing Terri Schiavo in 2005 likewise kept people out of her room—including volunteers in the facility where she was staying. Armed police officers manned the door at all times. As I revealed to the news media, because I was in the room, her death was far more horrific than the euthanasia advocates wanted the public to believe.

And of course, the reality of abortion continues to lie hidden. Few people see the procedure on video or in print. People who do are often converted on the spot. That's why we at Priests for Life present images of aborted children at the website unborn.info. Words alone cannot describe the horror of abortion.

Our Lenten journey, and our acceptance of light and life (baptismal symbols), empowers us to face both good and evil head-on. Our confidence is in the ultimate triumph of grace over sin, truth over falsehood, and life over death.

. . . .
Fifth Sunday of Lent, Year B
. . . .

Readings: Jeremiah 31:31–34 • Hebrews 5:7–9 • John 12:20–33

The Gospel of Christ is the Gospel of life, precisely because, when the "grain of wheat falls to the ground and dies,…it produces much fruit" (Gospel). The paradox is that life is poured out on the world precisely when life is given away for the good of others. In *Evangelium Vitae* we read:

> He who had come "not to be served but to serve, and to give his life as a ransom for many" (Mark 10:45) attains on the Cross the heights of love: "Greater love has no man than this, that a man lay down his life for his friends" (John 15:13). And he died for us while we were yet sinners (see Romans 5:8).
>
> In this way Jesus proclaims that life finds its centre, its meaning and its fulfillment when it is given up.
>
> At this point our meditation becomes praise and thanksgiving, and at the same time urges us to imitate Christ and follow in his footsteps (see 1 Peter 2:21).
>
> We too are called to give our lives for our brothers and sisters, and thus to realize in the fullness of truth the meaning and destiny of our existence.[56]

Christ is the grain of wheat that falls to the earth but is also "lifted up from the earth"—both on the cross and in the resurrection and ascension. And the fruit is that he "draws all people to himself."

We have here the powerful themes of life-giving fruitfulness and unity. The culture of death denies both. It embraces the loving of one's own life that Christ rejects in this Gospel teaching. It uses the words, "This is my body," to say, "I control my life." Christ and the Christian say, "I give my life."

As we approach Holy Week and meditate on the passion, it is a perfect time to call people to a renewed commitment to give themselves away in defense of the vulnerable—particularly the most oppressed, the unborn.

. . . .

Palm Sunday of the Passion of the Lord, Year B

Readings: *Mark 11:1–10 or John 12:12–16 • Isaiah 50:4–7*
Philippians 2:6–11 • Mark 14:1–15:47 or 15:1–39

The Church as the people of life is born from the cross. Jesus's passion and death are his self-giving, and he gives the power of that self-giving to us, that we might give ourselves to one another in serving, protecting, and celebrating the gift of life.

The preaching on Palm Sunday and throughout Holy Week, including Easter, can be opportunities to ground pro-life convictions in the heart of our faith. In other words, being pro-life and defending life are not things added on to our faith. Pro-life works are not optional, extracurricular activities. On the contrary, the culmination of the liturgical year leads us to the days when Jesus, by dying, destroyed our death and, by rising, restored our life. That is why the liturgy, especially in these days, is a most appropriate place to speak about life as a gift of inestimable value.

Jesus endured the rigors of the passion—described in today's liturgy in great detail—precisely because of how much he values human life. He did it for us. He did it because he wanted to raise human life to the heights of heaven. Through his passion and resurrection, he not only conquered his own death; he overturned the very kingdom of death.

We cannot believe the Gospel of the passion without marveling at how much God loves each human life. The Gospel impels us to respond when that human life is trampled underfoot. Christ gave his life for us; we are to give our lives for one another. Like Peter, we are "with the Nazorean."

Christ died once for all, but Calvary continues today, as innocent people are killed in abortion clinics nationwide. As St. John Paul II wrote, "It is precisely in the 'flesh' of every person that Christ continues to reveal himself and to enter into fellowship with us, so that rejection of human life, in whatever form that rejection takes, is really a rejection of Christ."[57] The Gospel of the passion continues in our day.

• • • • • • • • • • •

LENT, YEAR C

First Sunday of Lent, Year C

• •

Readings: Deuteronomy 26:4–10 • Romans 10:8–13 • Luke 4:1–13

The season of Lent prepares the faithful, through a special emphasis on penitence, to celebrate the paschal mystery and to renew the vows of their baptism. It is also a time of final preparation of catechumens to receive the new life in water and the Holy Spirit. This double meaning of Lent incorporates and illumines the Church's pro-life stance and provides a liturgically consistent way of preaching about it.

The dynamics of baptism are those of life, welcome, and mutual responsibility. Baptism immerses us into the death and resurrection of Christ, by which death in all its forms is destroyed. Moreover, God's sovereign choice is the first step in the process. He has chosen us, and he has chosen our brothers and sisters in the family of the Church through baptism. Hence we learn that we have responsibility not only for those we choose but for those whom God chooses to entrust to our care.

The penitential preparation for baptism—whether for its reception or renewal—is necessary precisely because the dynamics of sin lead us to exalt our own choices over and above the moral demands of justice and charity. Sin, furthermore, obscures our judgment about the dignity and rights of others and makes us all too ready to ignore them. Hence, the sacrament by which we become brothers and sisters in one body is also the sacrament of enlightenment.

The temptations of Jesus in today's Gospel passage summarize our own. Living "on bread alone" points to our dependence on material things rather than God. The one whom we worship, other than the Lord our God, might be ourselves. Is our own will more important in the end than God's?

Attempts to control the future or surmount obstacles on our own lead to frustration and despair. Failing to trust in the Lord can lead to the violence of abortion. Many people today see the economic challenges of having a child more determinative than the value of that child.

Lenten penance consists in fighting these temptations and fostering a more pure and trusting dependence on God. Fasting helps us look to the Lord for our sustenance. Prayer is all about worshiping God alone. And almsgiving is our serving him in the least of his brethren. These also build a culture of life.

· · · · · · · · · · ·

Second Sunday of Lent, Year C

· ·

*Readings: Genesis 15:5–12, 17–18 • Philippians 3:17–4:1 or 3:20–4:1
Luke 9:28b–36*

Abram (in the first reading) was enveloped by a deep sleep and terrifying darkness. On the mountain of the Transfiguration, the theme of discussion was the deep sleep and terrifying darkness that would envelop the Lord on Calvary (Gospel). In both cases, God makes a covenant amid the darkness, which gives way to new light and promise.

The name *Abram* means "exalted father"; it will soon be changed to *Abraham*, meaning "father of many." The stars in the sky don't measure up to the number of descendants he will have. God tells him when he is ninety-nine years old that he will bear a son and be the father of many nations! And it comes to pass.

Abraham's descendants include us: He is our father in faith, as St. Paul teaches us (see Romans 4:11–12). We too have seen that, despite the apparent power of death, God makes life victorious. The deep, terrifying darkness that enveloped the Lord on Calvary made the apostles flee. Yet the memory of the Transfiguration must have strengthened them, because they did not abandon their faith. On Easter it became clear that the light overcomes the darkness and life overcomes death. Furthermore, the new covenant in Christ's blood gives rise to countless children of God, among whom we are privileged to be numbered.

We renew this covenant of life at every Mass, the celebration of the victory of life. We recommit ourselves to the God of life and to standing up for life in the midst of a culture that has been enveloped in a deep sleep and terrifying darkness—a culture that mistakes death for a solution to its problems. Today we see the Lord in glory, and we are strengthened to listen to him, for he is the final Word among all the contradictory messages in our culture.

. . . .

Third Sunday of Lent, Year C

Readings: Exodus 3:1–8a, 13–15 • 1 Corinthians 10:1–6, 10–12
Luke 13:1–9

"I have witnessed the affliction of my people in Egypt and have heard their cry of complaint against their slave drivers.... Therefore I have come down to rescue them." So God speaks to Moses in today's first reading.

We enter now into a more intense period of Lent, preparing those who are to be baptized and preparing to renew the vows of our own baptism. We reflect on the central mysteries of our faith to better celebrate the passion, death, and resurrection of the Lord.

The Exodus of the Israelites from Egypt as well as the paschal mystery—that is, the central events of the Old and New Testaments—are both about God rescuing his people from oppression. Our forefathers were slaves in Egypt, and they were rescued through the waters of the Red Sea. We are oppressed by sin and death, and we are rescued through the waters of baptism.

Yet the rescued must also rescue. The saved must also save. We cannot turn to God for mercy and be deaf to the cries of others for mercy. One of the three key Lenten activities, almsgiving, symbolizes this basic truth about living our faith. We are not allowed simply to look at God and thank him for rescuing us. We are rather to let our gratitude become service, directed at rescuing others. This is the fruit of which Jesus speaks in the Gospel passage; this is the repentance he seeks of us.

God's name, as revealed to Moses, is "I AM." It does not only mean "the fullness of being." It means, "I am here *for you*, to rescue and save you." God uses the same words to announce the rescue of his people from their captivity in Babylon (see Isaiah 45). Jesus uses them to announce the liberating effects of his passion (see John 8:58). Now our obligation is to rescue vulnerable human beings in the name of our God, the great I AM.

. . . .

Fourth Sunday of Lent, Year C

Readings: Joshua 5:9a, 10–12 • 2 Corinthians 5:17–21
Luke 15:1–3, 11–32

The readings today present two equally important aspects of reconciliation, which have profound implications for the battle between the culture of death and the culture of life.

The second reading says, "God was reconciling the world to himself in Christ," and, "We implore you on behalf of Christ: be reconciled to God." The preacher can raise the question, "Who is doing the reconciling? If God is doing it, then why are we implored to 'be reconciled'?"

The Israelites, as the first reading says, were freed from Egypt and given the Promised Land—yet they still had to fight for it, and they still had to struggle to observe the way of life of the covenant. The Prodigal Son, in today's Gospel passage, was greeted by a father who was already working out reconciliation for him, eagerly anticipating his return. Yet the son too had to work out his salvation. He had to struggle. He had to make a deliberate decision to renounce his way of life, get up, and make the journey back to the father.

Reconciliation is never achieved passively. And both in the case of the Israelites and in the case of the Prodigal Son, a key reason for being reconciled was a dead end. Life in slavery was not appealing, and life for the son, far away from the father, had likewise lost its appeal. A dead end has tremendous persuasive power.

We have reached a dead end in this nation with the practice of abortion. Though abortion advocates promised decades ago that legalizing it would reduce child abuse and a host of other social ills, just the opposite has happened. The men and women of the Silent No More Awareness Campaign witness to the nation that their involvement in abortion solved nothing but rather brought many problems. That is why, as they recall their abortions, they demand that the government recall this dangerous product.[58]

It is time for the nation to be reconciled with God. The hard work of reconciliation includes being reconciled with all our brothers and sisters, including our unborn brothers and sisters. We must recognize them as persons like ourselves, speak up for their rights, and work for their protection.

. . . .
Fifth Sunday of Lent, Year C
. . . .

Readings: Isaiah 43:16–21 • Philippians 3:8–14 • John 8:1–11

"See, I am doing something new!" the Lord declares today through the prophet Isaiah.

That is what we proclaim to the world as we build the culture of life, and that is what Lent prepares us for. "By your gracious gift each year, your faithful await the sacred paschal feasts with the joy of minds made pure," says Preface 1 of Lent. The paschal mystery renews the world and ushers in the new humanity, built on Christ and reconciled with God. That is the source of the culture of life.

The error of excluding entire segments of the human family, like the unborn, from personhood and protection is an old error. It has cropped up throughout human history, leading to genocide, holocausts, and various forms of slavery, segregation, and oppression. But Christ makes all things new. As today's Gospel passage reveals, he does not condemn us but reveals to us the mercy that flows from his love for every human life. That mercy is not permission to return to our old life of sin but rather power to rise beyond the life of sin to a new way of responding to the people around us.

Some will maintain that it is not really possible to overcome the culture of death or to stop the advance of abortion, euthanasia, and other forms of violence. But we celebrate the paschal mystery with mind and heart renewed. We hear the message, "See, I am doing something new," and know that the victory of life really is possible. And we are called to use our gifts and energy to make that victory real.

In addition to these themes, the homily today may well speak about the post-abortion healing ministries of the Church. "Woman…has no one condemned you?… Neither do I condemn you. Go, and from now on do not sin any more." A good clearinghouse for such healing ministries is SilentNoMore.com.

. . . .

Palm Sunday of the Passion of the Lord, Year C

Readings: Luke 19:28–40 • Isaiah 50:4–7 • Philippians 2:6–11
Luke 22:14–23:56 or 23:1–49

The events of this day bring eternal life to the world. God is in the business of destroying death. He submits to it, "becoming obedient to the point of death, even death on a cross" (second reading), and then robs it of his power through his resurrection. God continues to destroy death through us.

Our entire faith is centered on the events of Holy Week. From them all the sacraments and all our prayers derive their effectiveness. Every teaching of the Church and all her preaching announce these events. The purpose of the Church and her ministries is to apply the fruits of these events to every human being and to society itself.

In light of the passion and death of Christ, which is the passion and death of God himself, no human being can be indifferent to violence. In the light of what Christ did to rescue us from death, we realize our call to rescue others from death.

This rescue starts with the most vulnerable human beings in our midst, the children still living within their mothers' wombs and deprived of the right to life by abortion. "Do not weep for me," Jesus told the women of Jerusalem, "weep instead for yourselves and for your children." We can apply this not just to the children in the womb but to all God's children whom the evil one assaults, particularly those who are tempted to take life rather than sacrifice themselves to protect and nurture it.

Because of what Jesus has done for us, "God greatly exalted him" (second reading). Here we find the very meaning of life: to give ourselves for the good of the other. In the light of Palm Sunday, it makes no sense to hold back our love or our sacrifice on behalf of human life.

The palm branches that we carry home today should remind us throughout the year of that simple truth. Let us run to the cross of Christ, thanking him for the eternal life he brings and resolving to be the people of life in the world.

. . . .
EASTER SEASON

Easter Is Pro-Life
. . . .

Christ is risen! "Death no longer has power over him" (Epistle of Easter Vigil). The central fact of human history and the foundational truth of our faith is celebrated in the Easter season. The Easter Proclamation tells us, "Christ broke the prison-bars of death and rose victorious from the underworld."

Jesus broke the chains of death not for himself but for us! If someone who died in your town were seen alive again, it would be an astonishing event, but it would leave your life, and the prospect of your death, unchanged. But when Jesus Christ rose from the dead, he overthrew the entire kingdom of death. He robbed death of its power! By his resurrection, he opened the door for our resurrection!

God is in the business of destroying death.

> He will destroy death forever.
> The Lord God will wipe away
>   the tears from all faces;
> The reproach of his people he will remove
>   from the whole earth; for the Lord has spoken. (Isaiah 25:8)

God says, "O death, I will be your death" (see Hosea 13:14).

Since we are God's people, we are the people of life. We bear witness to what God continues to do in our midst. We stand against death in all its forms. Its most destructive form, both in principle and statistically, is abortion.

The people of life cannot ignore the taking of life. The people of life cannot espouse death as a legitimate option to solve a problem. Nor, in fighting the power of death, can they ever doubt the outcome. Christ is risen! Life is victorious!

. . . .
Easter Sunday
. . . .

Readings: Acts 10:34a, 37–43 • Colossians 3:1–4
or 1 Corinthians 5:6b–8 • John 20:1–9
Year A: Matthew 28:1–10
Year B: Mark 16:1–8
Year C: Luke 24:1–12
Or at an Afternoon or Evening Mass, Luke 24:13–35

There is no day on which it is easier to preach on the victory of life than today, the feast of life, the feast of Christ's victory over death. Moreover, on this day, many people will be in church who do not hear our messages during the rest of the year.

Easter makes it clear that being pro-life is not something that flows primarily from any political or ideological loyalty, nor simply from a cause, plan, project, or organization. Being pro-life, with all its manifestations and activities, flows from what happened on Easter. Christ did not only conquer his death; he overturned the entire kingdom of death!

We share his risen life now, and so we are "an Easter people" or, as *Evangelium Vitae* says, "the people of life." This means that we proclaim this victory of life and stand strong against all the forces in our society that eclipse or destroy the value of life—foremost among them all is abortion. We are not intimidated, hesitant, or unsure of our ability to overcome these forces. We stand before them in strength, declaring that they no longer have any ground to stand on nor any place in our midst. Christ is risen!

On this day, let us preach with all the vigor and conviction that the Gospel inspires. Let us send people forth to apply the Easter victory of Christ to every segment of society!

Here are some specific pro-life points to incorporate in the Easter homily:

Easter is about the resurrection of Christ, which was a physical resurrection. The disciples found an empty tomb (John 20). They "embraced his feet" and heard his voice (Matthew 28). Jesus's human body and soul are free from death. The way is opened for us to share this risen life.

This puts every human being in a particular light. All "are hidden with Christ in God" and will be raised to the heights of heaven (Colossians reading). We are to "become a fresh batch of dough" (from 1 Corinthians).

We share Christ's victory by baptism. After the homily, we will renew our baptismal vows. By rejecting the "works" and "empty promises" of Satan, we overcome the power of death at work in our world today. We promise to live in Christ, which is a promise to be pro-life.

The first reading indicates that the apostles were to preach to the people about the meaning of the resurrection. So must we. We are apostles of life, spreading hope amid people who might be tempted to see death as a solution to their problems.

The Gospel tells us that the apostles "ran." So must we. This feast fills us with spiritual energy that makes us run to the Lord and then run from the empty tomb, to tell the world that life, not death, is what God wants for us and from us! We are the people of life! Let's celebrate that with confidence and joy!

• • • • • • • • • • •
Second Sunday of Easter (Divine Mercy Sunday), Year A
• •

Readings: Acts 2:42–47 • 1 Peter 1:3–9 • John 20:19–31

It is one thing to doubt the fact that Jesus is risen, as Thomas did. We, however, are more likely to doubt the power flowing from that resurrection—a power that can keep us from sin.

Today is Divine Mercy Sunday. Mercy is not to be confused with presumption or with permission to sin. In fact, it is precisely in giving us his commandments that God shows his mercy. He understands our need of him and the fact that we flourish only by living a life in union with his will. His mercy provides us with every ounce of strength we need to actually fulfill the commandments, the demands of love. He gives us "a new birth to a living hope through the resurrection of Jesus Christ" (second reading).

Love has concrete demands, beginning with a reverence and absolute respect for others' lives, including the lives of the weakest and most vulnerable in our midst. Here we recognize him whom we "have not seen" but "yet believe in" (second reading). He gives us the power to love as he loves, even to the point of sacrificing ourselves as he sacrificed himself.

Perhaps Thomas was missing on Easter night because he was out looking for Jesus on his own. After all, he was the kind of person who wanted to see for himself. But he found Jesus only when he returned to be with Peter and the other apostles. He found the strength to believe when he returned to the unity of the Church.

We too will find the strength to believe, to carry out the commandments, and to respect every human life when we maintain close unity with the Church, the community of believers built on the apostles. Let us rejoice with Christ's disciples in the presence of our risen Lord!

. . . .
Third Sunday of Easter, Year A
. . . .

Readings: Acts 2:14, 22–33 • 1 Peter 1:17–21 • Luke 24:13–35

"Lord, you will show us the path to life" (Psalm 16). This line from today's responsorial psalm sums up the message of this liturgy and of the Easter season. Christ Jesus, risen from the dead, fills his people with the same life he enjoys. This is a path, a way of life. Hence Peter can say in the second reading, "You were ransomed from your futile conduct."

The journey of the disciples on the road to Emmaus symbolizes this "path of life" and the new way in which we are called to walk. Along this way, and amid the challenges of life, we can be tempted, as these disciples were, to "look downcast." We can get caught up in discussing how we were hoping that things would be better. By giving death more credit than it deserves, we can fail to recognize that Jesus is walking with us through the most difficult hours.

In a culture of death, those difficult hours can tempt people to resort to abortion or euthanasia. Christ rescues us from such "futile conduct." Life, not death, is the solution to our problems. The kingdom of death has been conquered!

Embracing life-giving repentance, we are now filled with the Holy Spirit, as the first reading declares. That Spirit, whom the risen Christ sends upon us, not only purifies us but enables us to announce the gospel of life. We become advocates for all men and women, just as the Holy Spirit is an advocate for us.

. . . .
Fourth Sunday of Easter, Year A
. . . .

Readings: Acts 2:14a, 36–41 • 1 Peter 2:20b–25 • John 10:1–10

Jesus is revealed as the Good Shepherd who fulfills Psalm 23 (today's responsorial psalm) in all its promises. He does this precisely through the paschal mystery. The Shepherd leads the sheep to life, and this is how Christ defines his ministry: "I came so that they may have life, and have it more abundantly" (Gospel).

In order to have life more abundantly—that is, unto the resurrection of the dead and a seat on God's throne—we must first have life! Natural life is the necessary precondition for supernatural life. Therefore the defense of natural life is necessarily an aspect of the proclamation of the gift of supernatural life and the mission of the Church.

In a culture of death, the preaching of Peter about repentance has a particular significance. Peter assures us that repentance leads to "the forgiveness of our sins" and "the gift of the Holy Spirit," both for the Church and for "all those far off, whomever the Lord our God will call." Surely we could identify those who are guilty of the sins of abortion and euthanasia as "far off" the Lord's path. There is forgiveness and life in the Spirit for them.

The beginning of the encyclical *The Gospel of Life* can inform our preaching today:

> When he presents the heart of his redemptive mission, Jesus says: "I came that they may have life, and have it abundantly" (John 10:10). In truth, he is referring to that "new" and "eternal" life which consists in communion with the Father, to which every person is freely called in the Son by the power of the Sanctifying Spirit....
>
> Man is called to a fullness of life which far exceeds the dimensions of his earthly existence, because it consists in sharing the very life of God. The loftiness of this supernatural vocation reveals the greatness and the inestimable value of human life even in its temporal phase. Life in time, in fact, is the fundamental condition, the initial stage and an integral part of the entire unified process of human existence....

In a special way, believers in Christ must defend and promote this right, aware as they are of the wonderful truth recalled by the Second Vatican Council: "By his incarnation the Son of God has united himself in some fashion with every human being." This saving event reveals to humanity not only the boundless love of God who "so loved the world that he gave his only Son" (John 3:16), but also the incomparable value of every human person.[59]

. . . .

Fifth Sunday of Easter, Year A

Readings: Acts 6:1–7 • 1 Peter 2:4–9 • John 14:1–12

In relation to the culture of life, this weekend's readings reflect on our nature as "a chosen race…a holy…people" (second reading). This truth is expressed by the Church in our day through Pope St. John Paul II's expression "the people of life" in *Evangelium Vitae*:

> We are the people of life because God, in his unconditional love, has given us the Gospel of life and by this same Gospel we have been transformed and saved. We have been ransomed by the "Author of life" (Acts 3:15) at the price of his precious blood (see 1 Corinthians 6:20; 7:23; 1 Peter 1:19). Through the waters of Baptism we have been made a part of him (Romans 6:4–5; Colossians 2:12), as branches which draw nourishment and fruitfulness from the one tree (John 15:5). Interiorly renewed by the grace of the Spirit, "who is the Lord and giver of life," we have become a people for life and we are called to act accordingly.[60]

Jesus's declaration that he is "the way and the truth and the life," can be effectively summarized: Jesus is the way precisely because he is truth and life. Moreover, the "works" that he and his people do "destroy the works of the devil" (1 John 3:8), which John 8:44 reveals as lies and murder. Jesus, the way, overcomes those works precisely by being the truth (undoing the devil's lies) and the life (undoing the devil's works of death.)

The Church's commitment to the defense of human life takes its motivation from this truth. We are the people of life.

. . . .
Sixth Sunday of Easter, Year A
. . . .

Readings: Acts 8:5–8, 14–17 • 1 Peter 3:15–18 • John 14:15–21

When Our Lord promises in today's Gospel passage, "I will come to you," he is referring to the presence of his Holy Spirit. The Spirit does not bring a new divinity or a new Gospel but rather the presence of Jesus Christ. The Lord's constant promise of life comes to fulfillment with the outpouring of the Spirit of life; therefore Jesus can say, "I live and you will live."

The preaching of this weekend, therefore, can focus on the relationship between Easter and the approaching Feasts of Ascension and Pentecost. The victory of Christ over death is shared with all his people: He brings our humanity to the heights of heaven and pours out his life-giving Spirit.

The truth brought out in today's passage regarding the Advocate is also crucial to the Church's role in building the culture of life. Jesus Christ himself is our first Advocate (see 1 John 2:1). Now that Advocate is promising us "another Advocate" who will be with us always—the Holy Spirit. Indeed, the Spirit advocates for us in the heights of heaven, that all the power of the redemptive work of Christ might have its full effect.

But if the Advocate fills us, he makes *us* advocates! The Spirit gives speech to the tongue, as we will see powerfully at Pentecost. He makes us advocates for the helpless, for those who cannot speak for themselves— the unborn and all the vulnerable. In him we can "always be ready to give an explanation" for our hope, "with gentleness and reverence" (second reading).

. . . .
Seventh Sunday of Easter, Year A
. . . .

Readings: Acts 1:12–14 • 1 Peter 4:13–16 • John 17:1–11a

Jesus prayed on the night before he died, "Now glorify me, Father, with you, with the glory that I had with you before the world began." The glory he has in the ascension is the same glory he had "before the world began." It differs only in that now, he has that glory in a human nature. Our humanity has been taken to the heights of heaven, fulfilling the destiny God intended for human life from the beginning.

Revelation 3:21 declares, "I will give to the victor the right to sit with me on my throne." God's plan for us is not just that we will gather around the throne or fall down before the throne but that we will sit with him on the throne! The Gospel extends this hope to the human family. All human beings are destined for the heights of heaven. Such is our dignity.

The human nature that Jesus brings to glory in the ascension is the same human nature that you and I share. It is the human nature that the babies in the womb share. Celebrating the ascension means treating each human life as one destined to sit with Christ on his throne.

The faithful can be encouraged to use this Sunday as a launching point to pray to the Holy Spirit each day this week, as we approach Pentecost. The Spirit, who is the Advocate, makes us advocates when he fills our hearts. We can become advocates for the weakest and most vulnerable among us, including the unborn.

To support the people of God in this prayer, Priests for Life has prepared a special pro-life Pentecost Novena, which people can download from PrayerCampaign.org. Let us pray as Mary and the apostles did, "with one accord" (first reading).

And let us not be ashamed of our pro-life witness, as the second reading reminds us. We may suffer for it, but suffering for the name of Christ also brings joy.

. . . .
Second Sunday of Easter (Divine Mercy Sunday), Year B
. . . .

Readings: Acts 4:32–35 • 1 John 5:1–6 • John 20:19–31

Thomas doubted the victory of life over death. Where was he the first Easter night? Scripture tells us only that he was not with the other apostles, to whom the Lord appeared. Maybe Thomas was out looking for the Lord! After all, if he was the kind of person who had to see for himself and had heard that the women had seen the Lord on the road, maybe he had gone out on the same road to find him!

But that was a mistake. Thomas separated himself from the community of believers gathered around Peter. It was only when he reunited with the community that he too saw the Lord.

Today we are "the community of believers…of one heart and mind" (first reading). And the Lord whom we find in the Church is the Lord whose "mercy endures forever" (Psalm 18).

When the Lord appeared to St. Faustina, he made it clear that this mercy was particularly needed for the sin of abortion:

> On another occasion, she had a vision of an angel coming with thunderbolts to destroy one of the most beautiful cities of her country. And she felt powerless to do anything about it. What antidote did the Lord give her? The Chaplet of Divine Mercy. [She explained] that the city was to be chastised for its sins, primarily the sin of abortion.[61]

Let us invite people today to the mercy the Lord extends. It is mercy for all who repent of sin, including the sin of abortion.

. . . .
Third Sunday of Easter, Year B
. . . .

Readings: Acts 3:13–15, 17–19 • 1 John 2:1–5a • Luke 24:35–48

The readings today make it clear that the events of Good Friday, Holy Saturday, and Easter Sunday were foretold, and they occurred for the purpose of repentance. In the same way that God "foresaw" these events, he foresaw the opportunity each of us would have to receive the grace and salvation that these events bring.

The way to celebrate the Easter season, in other words, is to actually repent, to take hold of the transforming power of Christ's death and resurrection, and to have "the love of God...truly perfected" in us, as John describes in the second reading. What happens in our lives—and what can happen still—is just as much in God's sight, from all eternity, as what happened to Christ.

Peter, in the first reading, calls Christ "the author of life," and the Gospel passage clearly reveals that this author of life is not a ghost but a person who has real flesh and blood. As we are transformed by Easter and grow in God's love, we grow in our deep appreciation for the gift of life (natural and supernatural) and our appreciation of the body.

This counters one key theme of the culture of death: the false separation of the body from the person. People think they can do what they want with their bodies and look the other way when the bodies of children are aborted. They believe that the body is not important or is not as much an aspect of the person as is the soul. But the physical resurrection of Christ reveals the sacredness of the human body. The love God calls us to bear, the commandments he calls us to obey, and the repentance he calls us to practice all involve a deep reverence for physical human life.

· · · · · · · · · · ·
Fourth Sunday of Easter, Year B
· ·

Readings: Acts 4:8–12 • 1 John 3:1–2 • John 10:11–18

The Good Shepherd does not run away when the sheep are to be devoured but rather lays down his life for them. The love by which the Shepherd does that is precisely the "power" to which Jesus refers when he says of his life, "I have power to lay it down" (Gospel).

What a difference between this divine idea of power and the worldly concept, which says that power consists in being able to lay down someone else's life. In particular, the culture of death says that there is some kind of power in the right to choose abortion and in the right to determine the timing and manner of one's death by euthanasia and physician-assisted suicide. But that is not power at all.

The real power spoken about in today's readings is the power to give ourselves away in love. It is power that transforms suffering into life-giving sacrifice, that heals others and brings salvation, as the first reading indicates. It is a power that ultimately transforms us into the likeness of the God who is love (second reading).

· · · · · · · · · · ·
Fifth Sunday of Easter, Year B
· ·

Readings: Acts 9:26–31 • 1 John 3:18–24 • John 15:1–8

The Lord's words in the Gospel passage for today speak about what Easter has accomplished: a new human community that takes birth from the Spirit and is filled with the very life of the risen Christ. "I am the vine, you are the branches." We all are descended from Adam on a natural level; we all are built into Christ on the supernatural level. He is the new Adam, and Easter begins the new humanity, victorious over the grave and sharing the life that lasts forever.

This supernatural community obviously builds on the natural community. To enjoy supernatural life, we must have natural life, and to appreciate the meaning of supernatural community, we must have some appreciation of natural community. In our day, however, the very notion of community, even on a natural level, has been obscured by false notions of freedom that separate everyone into his or her own sphere of choices and purely personal evaluations of what is true and right. The fruit of this freedom disconnected from truth is the culture of death, in which people think that they have responsibility only to those for whom they choose to take responsibility.

In the natural and supernatural community established by God, however, we have responsibility before we choose. The other branches on the vine, the other members of the community, have been chosen by God, not by us. We must welcome them all.

What is this fruit that the Lord says we must "bear"? It is the fruit of love, concretely visible in the life of self-giving that the commandments specify (second reading). The fruit is to be visible in the community through our welcome and service of all—born and unborn, healthy and sick, convenient and inconvenient. This can be challenging, as the first reading demonstrates. We must overcome our prejudices and be open to all whom the Lord calls.

We can't bear fruit on our own power. We have to stay united to the vine. Christ's love in us makes it possible for us to love as he has commanded. It is the very same love that led Christ to the cross and to the glory of the resurrection.

. . . .
Sixth Sunday of Easter, Year B
. . . .

Readings: Acts 10:25–26, 34–35, 44–48 • 1 John 4:7–10 • John 15:9–17

The readings today teach us that God's love for us takes precedence over our love for him and that his choice of us takes precedence over our choice for him. "In this is love: not that we have loved God, but that he loved us" (second reading); "It was not you who chose me, but I who chose you" (Gospel).

In a society that values freedom of choice, this truth is especially important. It is God's choice of a human life that gives it value, not our choice. It is God's decision to entrust us to the care of each other that creates the responsibilities we have toward human life, not the choice we make to be responsible for others. If our responsibility to love and care for human life, starting with our own children (born and unborn), is rooted in God's eternal choice and his decision to love us (and those children), then we do not have the moral right to reject that responsibility, love, and life.

Giving life, moreover, is the very revelation of God's love. "In this way the love of God was revealed to us: God sent his only Son into the world so that we might have life through him" (second reading). The command given to us to love, therefore, is a command both to receive and give the kind of love God shows. "Love one another as I love you" (Gospel). We are to lay down our lives for one another. "God shows no partiality" (first reading); neither should we.

. . . .

Seventh Sunday of Easter, Year B

Readings: Acts 1:15–17, 20a, 20c–26 • 1 John 4:11–16 • John 17:11b–19

The readings today point to our role as witnesses. In the first reading, we see the apostles choosing Matthias to join the eleven "in this apostolic ministry." The second reading encourages us to "testify that the Father sent his Son as savior of the world." We learn from the Gospel passage that we are "consecrated in truth."

What is this truth in which we are consecrated and to which we bear witness? It is the truth about the meaning of love. God's love, and God himself, is revealed first of all in the love Christ showed on the cross and furthermore in the concrete love we have toward one another. Love has a truth to it, a logic, that flows from the action of God in saving the world. As he gave himself for us, so we give ourselves for one another.

Taking innocent human life is a contradiction of love; it is also a contradiction of truth. To treat the human person as disposable is to say something that is contrary to the truth of that person's dignity and inviolable rights. It is to say something false about God, who alone owns that person. Thus it is not only the fifth commandment, "You shall not kill," that is broken outside the culture of life. It is also the eighth commandment, "You shall not bear false witness against your neighbor."

We, the people of life, are witnesses to the love of God and to the dignity of every human life. Jesus prays for us that we may be guarded from the evils of the world and "share [his] joy completely."

Second Sunday of Easter (Divine Mercy Sunday), Year C
• •

Readings: Acts 5:12–16 • Revelation 1:9–11a, 12–13, 17–19 • John 20:19–31

"I hold the keys to death." Only the Lord Jesus Christ, risen from the dead, can say these words from today's second reading.

Yet a fundamental temptation of the human family is to think that someday—by our ingenuity, technology, and power—we can hold the keys of death. The desire for control drives the culture of death. Advocates of assisted suicide call for the right of people to control the timing and manner of their own deaths. We want to tame death so we can use it as a tool to escape suffering.

Some people impose this tool on the unborn, especially the unborn who are deemed inconvenient or who have disabilities like Down syndrome. A high percentage of unborn children who are diagnosed with Down syndrome are killed by abortion.[62]

But we want victory over death, so it is to the Lord Jesus Christ that we turn. With him we proclaim a kingdom of life—but not without sacrifice. When John "heard…a voice as loud as a trumpet," he was exiled on the island of Patmos precisely because he had proclaimed the message of Christ.

The first reading shows us that the apostles' preaching of the resurrection was accompanied by tremendous signs. The resurrection gives rise to a community who believes in, proclaims, and employs Christ's power. So must we. We believe in the pro-life message. Now we must trumpet it and do all we can to support the culture of life.

· · · · · · · · · · ·
Third Sunday of Easter, Year C
· ·

Readings: Acts 5:27–32, 40b–41 • Revelation 5:11–14
John 21:1–19 or 21:1–14

Today's readings make it clear that Jesus's resurrection does not only bring life to him. Rather, it begins a process whereby, through our obedience, life comes to us and extends through us to all the world.

The theme of obedience to the risen Christ comes in the Gospel passage, in which the fruitless, all-night efforts of the fishermen-apostles are contrasted to a simple act of obedience to one command of the risen Lord. The 153 fish, as some commentators have pointed out, represent the number of known kinds of fish in that day and therefore symbolize the people of every race, nation, and language called to acknowledge the Lord and be brought into the kingdom by the preaching of the Church. As the second reading tells us, "every creature in heaven and on earth" will worship before the throne. Obedience to God and to the Lamb is the call of everyone.

In the first reading, the apostles obey the Risen Lord rather than the misguided commands of human authority. More fundamentally, they point out that obedience to the Lord yields the fruit of the Holy Spirit, who gives life to all through repentance and faith. This theme of obedience leading to life contrasts powerfully with the attitude of the culture of death. Real freedom does not consist in forging our own way through life, insisting on our own choices, and arranging both our private lives and public policies to protect personal autonomy. The only way to earthly happiness and eternal salvation is a resounding yes to life, in obedience to the one who conquers death and gives life abundantly.

. . . .
Fourth Sunday of Easter, Year C
. . . .

Readings: Acts 13:14, 43–52 • Revelation 7:9, 14b–17 • John 10:27–30

The proclamation in today's readings is the very foundation of the culture of life and the pro-life movement. The first and second readings illumine the meaning of Jesus's title "Good Shepherd." In particular, they shed light on his assertion in the Gospel that he knows his sheep and they follow him. This does not simply mean that his sheep know his teachings in this life. The Good Shepherd, who died for the sheep, shepherds them through death and beyond to the life that conquers all death.

"I know them," Jesus says of his "sheep." He knows our life and the pain of our death. "They follow me," he says. We follow him to the exalted glory of a life, in our human body and soul, that will be freed from the corruption of sin and death. We follow him to our own resurrection from the dead.

The first reading speaks about the proclamation of this gift and the ways in which people either accept or reject it. "The Gentiles were delighted.… The Jews, however…stirred up a persecution." The second reading shows the end result of accepting the gift—a multitude from every nation, risen from the dead, gathered around the throne and the Lamb, sharing his life forever.

God is not indifferent to the power of death over his people. "No one can take them out of my hand," Jesus says in the Gospel. He vigorously defends us against the power of death. As the people who have accepted his life and who follow him, we too defend our brothers and sisters from the grip of death.

· · · · · · · · · · ·
Fifth Sunday of Easter, Year C
· ·

Readings: Acts 14:21–27 • Revelation 21:1–5a • John 13:31–33a, 34–35

Tying this Sunday's readings to the theme of life brings us right to the powerful promise in the second reading, from Revelation 21, "There shall be no more death." The Easter season celebrates the basis of this promise: Christ has conquered the kingdom of death by his own death and resurrection, and he has given us a share in this victory through our baptism.

Moreover, the victory embraces the entire universe, spiritual and physical: "I...saw a new heaven and a new earth." Any power that death exercises now, through evils like abortion, is a temporary and fleeting power; it has lost both its foundation and finality. The Church proclaims the gospel of life with utter confidence, and we are to engage in pro-life activities with the same confidence. We do not just work *for* victory; we work *from* victory.

Christ's victory over death, which we now share, is a victory to which we give expression by changing the shape of society and its policies. We are called to bring this world into line with the truths of a culture of life. A new heaven and new earth have already begun in Christ and the Church. "Behold, I make all things new." These are words God speaks daily. He speaks them to us and through us.

This new order of reality, in which death no longer has the final word, is the context in which the Lord says that his commandment "love one another" is "new." The law and the prophets had already instructed love; but only in Jesus Christ's victory over sin and death can love and life have the final word. Only in him can we love with a divine as well as human love. Only in him can we love the vulnerable and the unborn and all people, with the very love that he has. Only in him can we "undergo many hardships to enter the kingdom of God" (first reading).

. . . .
Sixth Sunday of Easter, Year C
. . . .

Readings: Acts 15:1–2, 22–29 • Revelation 21:10–14, 22–23 • John 14:23–29

The readings today teach us that, as a fruit of the resurrection, we enjoy the presence of Christ forever, through his Holy Spirit. That Spirit enlightens us both interiorly and as a society, bringing about peace and right relationships.

The truth that the Spirit brings, first of all, is one with the word of Jesus and the Father, as the Gospel passage explains. No new gospel can come along under the purported inspiration of the Spirit. No new inspiration will contradict the settled teachings of the Church. Jesus says that the Spirit will remind us of what he said.

Such reminders are necessary as we journey through history—particularly through periods when trends obscure fundamental truths, such as that of the sanctity of life. When the decisions of government and the messages of mass media line up against the sanctity of life, the Spirit reminds the faithful and the Church of the truth about life and how it is to be respected. The Spirit guides individuals in whom God makes his dwelling.

We see in the first reading that the Spirit also guides the community. Moreover, the second reading indicates, the guidance of God will be the center of the community in the world to come. In the New Jerusalem, there will be "no need of sun or moon," because "the glory of God [gives] it light and its lamp [is] the Lamb." The truth of God holds his people together and brings the peace of which Jesus speaks in the Gospel. This truth is the foundation of right relationships between us, including our relationships with the youngest and most vulnerable members of the human family.

. . . .
Seventh Sunday of Easter, Year C
. . . .

Readings: Acts 7:55–60 • Revelation 22:12–14, 16–17, 20 • John 17:20–26

Today's second reading brings us to the conclusion of the Bible, its culmination. The bride of Christ, the Church, yearns for him to come again so that the marriage may be brought to the fullness of its joy and promise: total union, forever.

Through Old Testament prophets, God promised a marriage between himself and his people. Isaiah 62:4–5 reads,

> For the Lord delights in you,
>   and your land shall be espoused.
> For as a young man marries a virgin,
>   your Builder shall marry you;
>   And as a bridegroom rejoices in his bride,
>   so shall your God rejoice in you.

In his public ministry, Jesus referred to himself as the Bridegroom (see Matthew 9:15). And St. Paul, reflecting on Christ's perfect sacrifice, says that the sacrament of Christian marriage symbolizes this marriage of Christ and the Church (see Ephesians 5:25–32).

This union between God and his people, more intimate than we can dare to imagine, is the subject of Jesus's prayer in the Gospel passage. The unity of Jesus with the Father is ours through his Spirit. What is equally clear is that this union with God unites human beings with one another. "That they may all be one" is his prayer for all "who will believe." We are one with each other because we are one with him.

This teaches us a twofold lesson:

The unity of the human family is not something we build and achieve through our own strength and ingenuity. It is the fruit of union with God.

The work we do for peace, justice, and respect for life must flow from our intimate union with God.

Spirituality cannot grow or be considered authentic if it does not lead to committed action for peace, justice, and respect for human life. Union with God makes us more aware of and responsive to the sufferings and needs of all our brothers and sisters in the human family. We can exclude nobody.

· · · · · · · · · · ·

Solemnity of the Ascension

In some places, this feast is celebrated on the seventh Sunday of Easter.

Readings:
Acts 1:1–11 • Ephesians 1:17–23 or Hebrews 9:24–28; 10:19–23
Year A: Matthew 28:16–20
Year B: Mark 16:15–20
Year C: Luke 24:46–53

The ascension is a powerful feast on which to preach the sanctity of human life, because at its core, this feast is about our human nature being exalted to the heights of heaven. Our humanity has been lifted up to the heights of heaven, fulfilling the destiny God intended for human life from the beginning. This is "the hope that belongs to his call" (second reading). God's plan is that the Church be "his body, the fullness of the one who fills all things in every way."

Human beings are destined for the heights of heaven, not the garbage heap. The human nature Jesus brings to glory in the ascension is the same human nature that the babies in the womb share. Celebrating the ascension means treating each human life as one destined to sit with Christ on his throne.

. . . .

Pentecost

. . . .

Readings:

Vigil Mass:

Genesis 11:1–9 or Exodus 19:3–8a, 16–20b or Ezekiel 37:1–14
or Joel 3:1–5 • Romans 8:22–27 • John 7:37–39

Mass during the Day:

Acts 2:1–11 • 1 Corinthians 12:3b–7, 12–13 or Romans 8:8–17
John 20:19–23 or John 14:15–16, 23b–26

Fifty days after the Passover, the people of Israel observe the giving of the law on Mount Sinai, when God wrote the law with his own finger on the tablets of stone. This Feast of Pentecost was originally rooted in the celebration of the harvest. It was on this feast that the apostles reaped the harvest of the Lord's Passover of suffering, crucifixion, and resurrection. They received the Holy Spirit, who writes the law on our hearts (see Jeremiah 31:33).

This same Holy Spirit who came mightily on Pentecost comes to us. The same Spirit is in us, by our baptism and confirmation—the same Spirit who transforms the apostles, who raises the dead, and who changes bread and wine into Christ's Body and Blood. That same Spirit gives us confidence in following Christ. "For those who are led by the Spirit of God are children of God" (alternate second reading, from Romans).

The Spirit brings many gifts, and one of them is the ability to see creation in its proper relationship to God. This includes the crown of his creation, the gift of human life. The Lord and giver of life brings us to our truest selves as he illumines us regarding the sanctity of life.

When we do not have this light of the Holy Spirit, the law of God seems like an imposition from the outside that limits our freedom. People in the world sometimes think that we seek to restrict rights when we speak out against abortion and euthanasia. But the Holy Spirit within us attracts us to all that is right and good. We do not feel pushed where we would rather not go but rather pulled by what is good and true and beautiful.

The Holy Spirit is also the Advocate who pleads our cause. When he fills us, he makes us advocates for all our brothers and sisters in need, including the most vulnerable, the unborn.

. . . .
Solemnity of the Most Holy Trinity
. . . .

Readings:
Year A: Exodus 34:4b–6, 8–9 • 2 Corinthians 13:11–13 • John 3:16–18
Year B: Deuteronomy 4:32–34, 39–40 • Romans 8:14–17
Matthew 28:16–20
Year C: Proverbs 8:22–31 • Romans 5:1–5 • John 16:12–15

Our preaching on the Feast of the Holy Trinity leads us to the reality of *communio*. Seen in a unique way in the Trinity, this is lived on a human level as well. *Communio* is first of all a gift and secondly a task, consisting of a total self-giving to one another. The unity of families, nations, and the world depends on it.

We find a particular application of *communio* in the matter of the unborn and their mothers. There are no two human beings closer than a mother and her unborn child. Abortion disrupts, denies, and distorts the union of these two persons. In doing so, it further destroys family and societal unity. Many marriages endure significant stress after an abortion, sometimes leading to separation and divorce. Further, the woman can experience difficulty in bonding with her other children. Abortion impairs the ability to trust and to make life decisions.

Standing for life and protecting the unborn means fostering the *communio* that we see, in its ultimate form, in the Trinity. Life is preserved precisely when it is given away in self-sacrificing love.

· · · · · · · · · · ·

The Most Holy Body and Blood of Christ (Corpus Christi), Year A

· ·

Readings: Deuteronomy 8:2–3, 14b–16a • 1 Corinthians 10:16–17
John 6:51–58

As I stated in chapter 6, our commitment to defend our preborn brothers and sisters is shaped by our faith in the Eucharist as a sacrament of faith, unity, life, worship, and love. I suggest that you review that section of the chapter to help you connect the pro-life message to this great feast of the Eucharist, "the source and summit of the Christian life."[63]

The first reading today tells of God's freeing his people from bondage in Egypt, leading them through the desert, and providing sustenance for them along the way. Moses commands the people, "Do not forget the Lord, your God…who guided you through the vast and terrible desert with its saraph serpents and scorpions, its parched and waterless ground." The same God guides us today to proclaim the gospel of life to a dry and dreary world. God will care for us—and for the young pregnant woman who feels abandoned and destitute.

St. Paul comments on the unity we experience in the Eucharist: "We, though many, are one body, for we all partake of the one loaf" (second reading). We should be as concerned for each other as we are for our own selves. This concern extends to all of Christ's members, including those in the womb, wanted or unwanted.

The Eucharist is the sacrament of life. Jesus says in the Gospel today, "I am the living bread that came down from heaven; whoever eats this bread will live forever; and the bread that I will give is my flesh for the life of the world." Whenever we gather for the Eucharistic sacrifice, we celebrate the victory of life over death. This victory extends to our fight against abortion. "He has blessed your children within you," the psalm response says. "Praise the Lord, Jerusalem" (Psalm 147).

· · · · · · · · · · ·

The Most Holy Body and Blood of Christ (Corpus Christi), Year B

· ·

Readings: Exodus 24:3–8 • Hebrews 9:11–15 • Mark 14:12–16, 22–26

Today we celebrate the Body and Blood of Christ, the great gift Jesus has given for our "eternal redemption" (second reading). Chapter 6 of this book has extensive thoughts on how the doctrine of the Eucharist inspires our pro-life efforts. I suggest that you review that section to help you connect the pro-life message to this feast.

We have some bloody readings today. According to the ancients, blood is the seat of life. There is much blood being shed in our country today, unseen by the masses, draining the life of the human family.

In the first reading, we might cringe at Moses's sprinkling of "the blood of the covenant" on the Israelites. The Israelites received it as a sign of their commitment to God: "We will do everything that the Lord has told us." Thus the Israelites, freed from their slavery in Egypt, embraced the real freedom that is found only in submission to the will of God.

Paul tells us that "if the blood of goats and bulls" was able to sanctify the defiled, "how much more will the blood of Christ, who through the eternal Spirit offered himself unblemished to God, cleanse our consciences from dead works to worship the living God." Yes, we are made to worship the living God, the God of life, not one of "dead works."

Jesus offers us this "blood of the covenant...shed for many" (Gospel). These are his words of sacrifice, his words of love. They extend to the mom in distress. Let us give her the power to say, "This is my body, my blood, my life, given up for you, my child."

· · · · · · · · · · ·

The Most Holy Body and Blood of Christ (Corpus Christi), Year C

· ·

Readings: Genesis 14:18–20 • 1 Corinthians 11:23–26 • Luke 9:11b–17

Here the new law's new oblation,

By the new king's revelation,

   Ends the form of ancient rite:

Now the new the old effaces,

Truth away the shadow chases,

   Light dispels the gloom of night.

    —from the sequence for Corpus Christi, "Laud, O Zion"

As you prepare to celebrate this Feast of the Body and Blood of Our Lord, I suggest that you review the section of chapter 6 that shows how the doctrine of the Eucharist illumines the pro-life effort.

The first reading and the psalm response today bring us the ancient figure Melchizedek, who "brought out bread and wine, and…blessed Abram." We priests today are privileged to offer people the Bread of Life and the Blood of the new covenant. As the sequence for today concludes:

Jesus still the same abides,

   still unbroken does remain.

Melchizedek extolled "God Most High, who delivered your foes into your hand." Our God is the deliverer of all who trust in him. Everyone who wants to fight abortion needs to be aware of this.

In the Gospel of today, Jesus multiplies five loaves and two fish to feed a crowd of five thousand men and who knows how many women and children. All are told to sit down, and "all ate and were satisfied." In God's kingdom, there is room and provision for all. This is our message today to the world. None of our little ones, none of our elderly, need be abandoned out of fear of limited resources. God has grace and life for all, and we the Church are his distributors.

· · · · · · · · · · · · · ·
ORDINARY TIME

Ordinary Time, Year A
· ·

Ordinary time begins after the Feast of the Baptism of the Lord, at the end of the Christmas season.

. . . .
Second Sunday of Ordinary Time, Year A
. . . .

Readings: Isaiah 49:3, 5–6 • 1 Corinthians 1:1–3 • John 1:29–34

"Called to be holy" and "a light to the nations" are two themes from today's readings that speak powerfully of our call as individuals and as a Church. Paul includes among those "called to be holy" all "who call upon the name of our Lord Jesus Christ" (second reading). The name of the Second Vatican Council's key document on the Church, *Lumen Gentium*, is from today's first reading. It reminds us that we are a light, a beacon, to every people. We are this primarily by the way we live, both in our private lives and in the activities and policies of the Church.

In American society these days, we have three observances whose themes converge powerfully to show us in what direction our nation must go and how the Church's "light to the nations" is to be shed. We honor the dream of equal human rights articulated by Dr. Martin Luther King, Jr. His advocacy for the equality of African Americans was a corollary of his advocacy for the equality of every human being. His niece, Dr. Alveda King, is a full-time pro-life activist with Priests for Life. She declares that the civil rights movement of today is the pro-life movement.

On January 22, we also mark the anniversary of the egregious violation of human rights through the Supreme Court decision *Roe v. Wade*. This decision permitted the killing of children in the womb. Observances, rallies, and marches take place throughout the nation this month to call for the protection of these children.

Christians observe the Week of Prayer for Christian Unity from January 18 to 25. Pope St. John Paul II, in his encyclical *Ut Unum Sint*, called for ecumenical collaboration in the works of justice and human rights.

Each of these events can inform our preaching today. We pray that Christians will unite in effective service to all who are deprived of their rights. May we together bring about a culture of life, justice, and love.

· · · · · · · · · · ·
Third Sunday of Ordinary Time, Year A
· ·

Readings: Isaiah 8:23–9:3 • 1 Corinthians 1:10–13, 17
Matthew 4:12–23 or 4:12–17

When Jesus begins to preach, he starts by saying, "Repent" (today's Gospel). When John the Baptist began to preach, he said, "Repent" (see Matthew 3:1–2). When Peter begins to preach on the Day of Pentecost, he says, "Repent" (Acts 2:38).

Repentance, whose Greek word means "a change of mind," is enlightenment. It is the realization that what one may have thought was right is actually wrong. What one thought led to happiness and fulfillment actually does not. The readings today talk about enlightenment—light breaking into darkness.

Jesus says in the Gospel passage that the reason, motive, and basis for repentance is that "the kingdom of heaven is at hand." We see this kingdom's light, are attracted by it, and begin to move in its direction. This entails breaking from sin and from all that leads us away from the light.

The great darkness of our day is the myth that some human lives, particularly those in the womb, just don't count. To many, these lives are not worthy of constitutional protection, of our public witness, or even of discussion. In the second reading, Paul describes a spirit of division, which ignores the common truths we are all called to embrace. There is legitimate cultural, religious, and political diversity in our world. But that diversity cannot divide the human family between those who are recognized as persons and those who are not. Yet that is precisely what support for abortion does.

Christ breaks through false divisions. He unites all human life in himself and gives us all an equal call to salvation and eternal life. He has raised men and women, born and unborn, to the heights of heaven. There is only one human nature, and by the Incarnation and the paschal mystery, everyone who shares that human nature now also shares access to the very life of God.

Christ's light breaks into the darkness of our world, even the darkness of our hearts. Let us repent and allow God's light to shine.

. . . .

Fourth Sunday of Ordinary Time, Year A

. . . .

Readings: Zephaniah 2:3; 3:12–13 • 1 Corinthians 1:26–31
Matthew 5:1–12a

It would be hard to find a set of readings more appropriate for pro-life comment than those of this weekend. The Beatitudes (in the Gospel) are all about turning upside down the ways the world evaluates who is important and worthy of attention. The Lord and the Church point us to consider "those who count for nothing" in the eyes of the world as those specially favored by God (second reading).

When the Beatitudes speak of "the poor," they do not only mean those who are materially deprived. Scripture refers to "the poor" as those who are completely dependent upon God. These have no worldly help. They have been marginalized.

The unborn are the poorest of the poor. In the eyes of many in the world, and in the eyes of the law, they "count for nothing." They have little or no defense. Let us apply to them the words of today's responsorial psalm:

> The LORD...
> secures justice for the oppressed....
> The LORD sets captives free....
> The LORD raises up those who were bowed down. (Psalm 146:2, 7, 9)

The Lord does this through his people. We in the pro-life movement are among those "who mourn," for we weep over the world's injustices, such as abortion. We "hunger and thirst for righteousness," longing to see the rights of all respected. We "are merciful," particularly toward those in danger of death. We are "peacemakers," for as Mother Teresa said, the greatest destroyer of peace is abortion. And we are insulted and persecuted for Jesus's sake.

The Lord "secures justice," as the psalm says. Zephaniah urges the Lord's people to "seek justice," and the Beatitudes declare that those who do so are blessed. To be like God, we must do the works of God. Today let us call God's people to active involvement in the pro-life cause.

· · · · · · · · · · ·
Fifth Sunday of Ordinary Time, Year A
· ·

Readings: Isaiah 58:7–10 • 1 Corinthians 2:1–5 • Matthew 5:13–16

The readings today focus on how the children of the King are to show to the world who their Father is by acting like him. This, in fact, is the best way to accomplish the New Evangelization, the reannouncement of the Gospel in places where it has been eclipsed by secularism. Where that eclipse happens, Pope Benedict XVI has said, people lose a proper understanding of the meaning of the most basic human experiences, like birth and death.[64] That is why it is so hard for some to perceive that abortion is always wrong.

We can pursue many arguments, but even more powerful, as Paul declares in the second reading, is "a demonstration of Spirit and power." People see the Spirit's effects in our lives and are convinced. We become "the light of the world," as Jesus indicates in the Gospel.

We are called to let people see that we not only choose life in our own situations but also sacrifice convenience, plans, and resources that others may live. As individuals and as a community, we accept the gift of new life God gives and also work to eradicate injustice from our world.

Isaiah speaks about sheltering the oppressed and providing for the afflicted. Children in the womb are more oppressed than any other segment of the population in our day. The prophet's words call us to pro-life action.

Isaiah also points out that this action must begin with our own flesh and blood by "not turning your back on your own." These are powerful words for our culture. Parents, do not turn your backs on the children you have conceived! Grandparents, do not turn your backs on your daughter's unborn child. Speak up for that life, and intervene to help both your children and theirs!

Some people think that because the child in the womb is the mother's, she has the right to abort that child. But Isaiah's words declare the opposite: When someone is your own flesh and blood, your obligations to that person increase. You are all the more obliged to do them good.

Only when God's people are actively and generously living as the people of life can the words of today's readings be fulfilled. At the start of The Gospel of Life, Pope John Paul II wrote: "The Gospel of life is at the heart of Jesus' message. Lovingly received day after day by the Church, it is to be preached with dauntless fidelity as 'good news' to the people of every age and culture."[65]

. . . .

Sixth Sunday of Ordinary Time, Year A

Readings: Sirach 15:15–20 • 1 Corinthians 2:6–10
Matthew 5:17–37 or 5:20–22a, 27–28, 33–34a, 37

Today we hear the Lord proclaim through Sirach, "If you choose you can keep the commandments." God is not unfair. He does not give us burdens we cannot handle.

Now, one might say, upon understanding the commandments, that they *are* impossible to keep. But we do not rely on human strength. Christ lives in us, and that is the ultimate fulfillment of the truth spoken through Sirach. Jesus can say that his yoke is easy and his burden light (see Matthew 11:30) because he transforms our nature so that we can know, love, and serve God with the very same Spirit he has.

Paul will later declare, "God is faithful and will not let you be tried beyond your strength; but with the trial he will also provide a way out, so that you may be able to bear it" (1 Corinthians 10:13). Relative to pro-life, this means that no matter what circumstances may tempt someone to abort, those forces can be resisted. The power to say yes to life is always there.

Jesus reiterates the commandment not to murder (that is, not to kill the innocent) in the Gospel, but he goes further and warns us to avoid things that lead to murder. One of them is abusive language toward our brothers and sisters. Professor William Brennan authored a book called *Dehumanizing the Vulnerable: When Word Games Take Lives.*[66] He shows in this study that the same kinds of words and phrases are used throughout history to insult the dignity of groups of people who are being oppressed— black people, Jewish victims of the Holocaust, and children in the womb. They are referred to as "waste, parasites, non-persons" and in other derogatory terms. This kind of language is certainly among what Jesus prohibits in today's Gospel passage.

Professor Brennan ends his book by urging us to a language of affirmation, which uplifts rather than degrades. Jesus tells us that we cannot worship God unless we "go first to be reconciled" with our brothers and sisters. If we are using degrading language toward them, then we are not yet reconciled. We cannot bring our gift to the altar.

This, incidentally, is the fundamental reason why being pro-choice is incompatible with receiving Communion. To want to be in communion with (and hence fully reconciled with) Jesus, we have to be in communion with and fully reconciled with all our brothers and sisters, born and unborn. We must recognize them all as persons like ourselves.

Seventh Sunday of Ordinary Time, Year A

Readings: Leviticus 19:1–2, 17–18 • 1 Corinthians 3:16–23
Matthew 5:38–48

The Lord Jesus makes universal the commandment of love. The Father, he tells us in the Gospel, "makes his sun rise on the bad and the good, and causes rain to fall on the just and the unjust." So Christians are not to draw false boundaries to their love.

Christ, after all, now has full authority in heaven and on earth. He has embraced and redeemed the entire universe and has given us a share in his dominion and in his power to love. "All belong to you, and you to Christ and Christ to God," Paul tells us in the second reading. Loving everybody comes with the territory.

There can be no difference between our love for the born and our love for the unborn. The size or age or level of dependency of a child do not determine our love and care for the life of that child. Nor can any of these exempt us from recognizing the personhood of that child.

"You shall love your neighbor" does not simply mean that we love our neighbor in the way or to the extent that we love ourselves. It means that we love our neighbor as a person like ourselves. We recognize that, whatever differences there may be between ourselves and our neighbors, they have the same human dignity that we have. We must see through all the differences, recognize that common dignity, and love each as a person like ourselves.

Ultimately, this command of universal love is not simply an external command. God is not saying, "Do this because I told you." It is not just an item on a list of dos and don'ts. Rather, we are to love because we are called to be like God. "Be perfect, just as your heavenly Father is perfect." We must be perfect in love, in service, in selflessness.

"Be holy, for I, the Lord, your God, am holy," the Lord declared to Moses and the Israelites (first reading). When we hold up the standard of love for born and unborn alike, we do not claim to be better than anyone else. Rather we point to the one who made us all and who wants us all to be just like him.

. . . .

Eighth Sunday of Ordinary Time, Year A

Readings: Isaiah 49:14–15 • 1 Corinthians 4:1–5 • Matthew 6:24–34

The pro-life connections in today's readings are powerful and poignant. The first reading declares that for a mother to forsake her own child is almost as unimaginable as God forsaking his own people. Almost—because God knows full well that mothers might and in fact do sometimes forsake their children, yet he will never forsake us.

Abortion is a forsaking of one's own child. God declares in this passage that such an action reflects the most dramatic form of infidelity of which human beings are capable.

The comparison of the mother-child bond to God's own care for us also reflects the fact that God, in giving us all life, has entrusted our lives to the care of one another. This is, in fact, an aspect of being made in the image and likeness of God. This "image" is not just a matter of what each of us is in him or herself; it is a matter of our communion with each other, our self-giving service and love and unity. This reflects the inner life of Father, Son, and Holy Spirit, who give themselves completely to one another and cannot possibly be unfaithful to one another.

The Gospel gives us one of the causes of our human infidelity. We worry about daily provisions for our needs. Is this not at the core of many temptations to abort? "How will I provide for the child?" "How will I afford what this child deserves?"

The Lord tells us to stop worrying about such things. This does not mean that we are to be imprudent and to avoid planning for what we need. It means, however, that we are called to trust in God's care. "Seek first the kingdom of God."

God alone has dominion over human life. Nobody is authorized to choose that another will live or die. Nobody can predict the future or weigh the value of a person's life. No person owns another, and no nation can negate the personhood of anyone, born or unborn.

Seeking God's kingship means that we both acknowledge his dominion and trust his providence. That fills us with hope, which gives us the courage to say yes to life.

Ninth Sunday of Ordinary Time, Year A

Readings: Deuteronomy 11:18, 26–28, 32 • Romans 3:21–25, 28
Matthew 7:21–27

The theme today is the grace that freely justifies us (second reading) and leads us to a life of obedience. That obedience is linked to life. The first reading finds an echo in the well-known "choose life" passage of Deuteronomy 30. In the Gospel, Jesus exhorts us to "listen to these words of mine and [act] on them." Then we will flourish, withstand the trials of life, and ultimately inherit the life that never ends.

The scene of the judgment in the Gospel passage raises a distinction that at first is surprising. One might think that those who exercised gifts of prophecy and exorcism knew the Lord and were close to him. But it is not the gifts one is given or the skills one has that make one holy. It is obedience, union with the will of God.

We see striking examples in the culture of death of the external symbols of Christianity coexisting with actions that take human lives. I have seen more than one set of rosaries hanging from the rearview mirrors of cars heading into abortion facilities. The challenge of today's readings is to allow the externals of our faith to shape our interior lives. We must let God be the source of our decisions.

· · · · · · · · · · ·

Tenth Sunday of Ordinary Time, Year A

Readings: Hosea 6:3–6 • Romans 4:18–25 • Matthew 9:9–13

The readings today lead us to reflect on the fact that God's call—a call of his initiative—is not based either on merit or on human judgment. By either of those standards, the Lord would have called neither Abraham, nor Matthew, nor the people of whom Hosea speaks. God's people doubted him time and time again: Abraham and Sarah wondered how God's promise of descendants stood to reason, Matthew served the Roman government as a tax collector and was labeled a sinner by the Pharisees, and the devotion of Israel in Hosea's time was "like a morning cloud, like the dew that early passes away."

But the readings make it clear that God did call these people. God's call just doesn't meet our earthly standards. Moreover, it is a call that transforms. God calls sinners not to reward them for their sinful lives but to make them saints.

Today he calls us in the midst of a culture of death. He calls us to transform our culture, its practices, and its policies. He calls us to follow him, as he instructed Matthew. This following involves advancing his ways, proclaiming his truth, and defending life.

· · · · · · · · · · ·

Eleventh Sunday of Ordinary Time, Year A

Readings: Exodus 19:2–6a • Romans 5:6–11 • Matthew 9:36–10:8

Jesus as Shepherd and his need for "laborers for his harvest" are familiar themes. One thing we can point out from the Gospel today is that the sheep are "troubled and abandoned." The laborers have to gather the people in because, as God says in today's first reading, they are to be his "special possession." The psalm says, "He made us; his we are" (Psalm 100).

This is the basis for Jesus's giving his disciples the authority to cure diseases and expel demons. Diseases and demons ravage people who belong to God. In a sense, they steal God's possession away from him.

And that's exactly what abortion does, thousands of times a day in the United States alone. At the heart of the debate is not the question "When does life begin?" Rather, it is the question "To whom do we belong?" Intervening for the child—proclaiming that he or she belongs to God—is an aspect of gathering in the flock who are abandoned.

Our goal is to inspire hope and strength in the mother and father to say yes to life. This is a place where we can follow the Lord's example of helping the "troubled and abandoned," those who are "like sheep without a shepherd." Catholic fathers have a particular role in this work.

We may wrestle with the command in today's Gospel to "raise the dead." In what sense do we fulfill this command of Jesus? Was it only for the apostles? Does it only refer to those dead in spirit, whom we can rouse to life-giving repentance? Or can it also refer to those who are tottering at the brink of death, including children in the womb who are scheduled to be aborted? Can our pro-life efforts save them from death? Can we rescue their parents from the clutches of the culture of death, offering alternatives and assistance? Indeed, we can!

Twelfth Sunday of Ordinary Time, Year A

Readings: Jeremiah 20:10–13 • Romans 5:12–15 • Matthew 10:26–33

"Even the hairs of your head are counted.... You are worth more than many sparrows." This assertion in today's Gospel forms the basis for preaching on how much God values human life.

God values all that he has created. But it is human beings—worth more than other living beings—who are privileged to have a particular relationship with God. This capacity for God marks what we mean by the sanctity of human life. A relationship with the Creator is possible for us—a relationship of which lower forms of life are not capable. We can know God, praise him, receive a share in his divine nature, and one day see him face-to-face. We were made for him, as St. Augustine said, and our hearts are restless until we rest in him.[67]

If a sparrow does not fall to the ground without the Father's knowledge, what about a tiny unborn child killed in secret by chemical abortion, sometimes masquerading as birth control? What about the new human embryo destroyed in secret in a laboratory, in the name of research? Part of acknowledging Jesus before others is bearing witness to the care that he and the Father give to the smallest human lives.

. . . .

Thirteenth Sunday of Ordinary Time, Year A

Readings: 2 Kings 4:8–11, 14–16a • Romans 6:3–4, 8–11
Matthew 10:37–42

The readings of today are all about life and welcome and the relationship between the two. As a result of welcoming Elisha, the holy man of God, the woman of Shunem receives the gift of a child. As a result of welcoming Christ, the Holy One of God, we all receive the new life of which the second reading speaks. These readings have immediate application to the theme of welcoming the representatives of God who come preaching his word. This welcome extends to every human being.

Christ is the one who welcomes us into the life he shares with the Father. The only appropriate response for us—as individuals and as a community—is to extend welcome to all whom Christ welcomes, that is, to every human life. It would be a contradiction to accept the welcome of Christ but to reject another human life.

In welcoming other human lives, furthermore, it is necessary to apply the first part of the Gospel reading, namely, the embrace of the cross and the bringing of ourselves to naught. This is the opposite of the self-centered assertion of pro-choice and "my rights, my life." In contradiction to the idea that we are fulfilled by asserting ourselves, even at the cost of the life of an unborn child, the Lord teaches here that it is precisely in self-giving that we find ourselves. Parents give themselves to their children, whether born or in the womb, and in so doing, they experience the very love of Christ and the life to which that love leads.

. . . .
Fourteenth Sunday of Ordinary Time, Year A
. . . .

Readings: Zechariah 9:9–10 • Romans 8:9, 11–13 • Matthew 11:25–30

"His dominion" (first reading) is brought about through "the Spirit of the one who raised Jesus from the dead" (second reading). It is the dominion of life over death, not only in our bodies but in our culture, institutions, laws, and policies.

That Spirit dwells in us, the second reading says. We, therefore, are life givers! In fact, human beings can spread either life or death; there is no neutrality. The yoke that Jesus calls us to take in the Gospel is one that embraces and spreads life. This is an easy yoke because we were made to be life givers.

The Son wishes to reveal the Father to us (the Gospel) precisely through that Spirit. What do we learn when he does so reveal the Father? We find the revelation of ourselves—people of life, people of self-giving, people who can love as the Father loves!

Fifteenth Sunday of Ordinary Time, Year A

Readings: Isaiah 55:10–11 • Romans 8:18–23 • Matthew 13:1–23 or 13:1–9

The Word of God created the whole world. Genesis shows God creating by speaking, and John's Gospel points out, in its first chapter, that this Word that God spoke in the beginning was in fact Christ. Paul expounds this truth in the first chapter of Colossians, which in fact contains a commentary on the first verse of the Bible. Christ is that "beginning" of which Genesis speaks, and "all things were created through him and for him" (Colossians 1:16).

When, therefore, today's readings speak about the fruitfulness of the Word of God—Isaiah declaring that the word accomplishes the end for which it is sent, and Jesus explaining how the seed will bear fruit—they are not to be understood only in a spiritual sense. The fruitfulness of the Word is also physical, starting with human life itself. Mary said, "May it be done to me according to your word" (Luke 1:38), and by that word, the physical conception of Christ took place.

Likewise, the conception and birth of each human being is a fulfillment of the promises in today's readings. When did God decide that you or the people around you should start to exist? The answer is, "From all eternity." There was never a time when God did not intend each living person to exist, nor a time when he did not have definitive plans for each person's life.

"My word shall not return to me void" (first reading). The plan, the eternal word, that God has for each person is not to return void because of a veto on someone else's part. Contraception, abortion, and euthanasia all constitute an offensive *no* to this word, an attempt to veto an eternal decision of God regarding the fruitfulness of each life. Part of the reason for these vetoes is the "worldly anxiety" referred to in the Gospel. This anxiety leads to the temptation to cut off the fruitfulness of life.

Paul, in the second reading, puts those anxieties in an eschatological perspective. He invites us to hold firm through life's difficulties and continue saying yes to God's plan. Interestingly, it is the process of childbirth that he uses to describe the full unfolding of God's plan for all creation.

. . . .
Sixteenth Sunday of Ordinary Time, Year A
. . . .

Readings: Wisdom 12:13, 16–19 • Romans 8:26–27
Matthew 13:24–43 or 13:24–30

God gives time for repentance. This is a key theme of today's readings. For the people of life, a key area of repentance might be impatience. Our efforts to build a culture of life may seem painstakingly slow, though our steps are steady. Why, some might ask, does God not just stop all abortions today? He certainly does not justify a single one of them, nor does he allow us to justify them. In fact, he calls us to do what we can to restore justice today.

Yet the Gospel tells us that weeds and wheat grow together; good and evil coexist. The generous patience of the Lord, by which he allows the sinner room to find repentance, has led to many conversions. The website of the Silent No More Awareness Campaign contains numerous testimonies of women about their abortions and subsequent healings. Even many abortionists have converted and now speak publicly about it. See AbortionTestimonies.com.

As we try to elect pro-life candidates and lobby public officials, it is particularly important to emphasize the theme of patience. The United States Catholic bishops indicate in *Living the Gospel of Life* that we are called to use our votes to advance the culture of life. Yet no candidate has a magic wand to end the culture of death.[68]

Weeds and wheat grow together, but the Lord will eventually gather his own. "Then the righteous will shine like the sun in the kingdom of their Father."

· · · · · · · · · · ·

Seventeenth Sunday of Ordinary Time, Year A

Readings: 1 Kings 3:5, 7–12 • Romans 8:28–30 • Matthew 13:44–52 or 13:44–46

Solomon requests the gift of "an understanding heart." His solemn duty is to be king of the people, and he acknowledges that he is "a mere youth, not knowing at all how to act." Therefore he asks for this gift, that he might "distinguish right from wrong." The psalm picks up on this theme, praising the revelation of the Lord's word because it "sheds light, giving understanding to the simple" (Psalm 119).

Jesus, in the Gospel, asks his disciples, "Do you understand all these things?" By his words to them, he seeks to impart that gift of understanding.

We are beneficiaries of this gift as well. If the psalmist could praise God's commands for giving understanding, how much more can we, who have the added benefit of the Gospels and the Church? Human reason can distinguish right from wrong, but we are further enlightened and strengthened by revelation in Christ. We have no reason to be ignorant of moral truth.

Yet we see all around us Solomons without wisdom: public officials who have responsibility to govern but who claim that what is right or wrong for the human family cannot be known with certainty. This problem has been addressed frequently by the Magisterium. The 2002 Doctrinal Note on Some Questions Regarding the Participation of Catholics in Political Life, issued by the Congregation for the Doctrine of the Faith, describes the problem this way:

> Citizens claim complete autonomy with regard to their moral choices, and lawmakers maintain that they are respecting this freedom of choice by enacting laws which ignore the principles of natural ethics and yield to ephemeral cultural and moral trends, as if every possible outlook on life were of equal value.[69]

Today's readings make it clear that no believer can make this claim. Part of the Good News is that we can indeed know the difference between right and wrong, and we have the strength to act accordingly. Among the goods we need to preserve, the "pearl of great price" is life itself. For life is the foundation and condition of every other right and good that we possess.

. . . .

Eighteenth Sunday of Ordinary Time, Year A

Readings: Isaiah 55:1–3 • Romans 8:35, 37–39 • Matthew 14:13–21

Abortions do not happen because of freedom of choice but rather because some mothers and fathers feel they have no freedom and no choice. They have needs that they think cannot be met without aborting their child. They are captive to the coercive power of despair.

Today's readings are about the Lord providing for our needs, issuing an invitation to us to come to him confidently and to trust that he can fulfill all those needs. Fundamentally, of course, this is an invitation to salvation. But salvation is integral: It is bodily as well as spiritual, it is communitarian as well as individual, and it extends its effects to our daily needs, including those related to parenting. No trial, such as the anxieties that can accompany pregnancy, is too great for the love of Christ.

It is in the power and confidence of God that we are to come to him in our need—for the grace to do what is right, to choose life in every circumstance, and to strengthen others in their needs and trials. The Gospel passage for today does not say that the Lord fed the crowds himself. He ordered his disciples to feed them. They weren't sure how to do that, but he enabled them to do so. We too are to feed one another.

Together, as the people of life, we can meet the needs faced by those who are tempted to abort. We can meet their anguish and distress with the victorious love of Christ.

. . . .
Nineteenth Sunday of Ordinary Time, Year A
. . . .

Readings: 1 Kings 19:9a, 11–13a • Romans 9:1–5 • Matthew 14:22–33

St. Paul expresses profound anguish for his people in today's second reading. He longs that they accept Christ, who is "God blessed forever" and the only hope of the human family. For every disciple, Christ is everything. Each event and decision of life, each project and plan, finds its standard, meaning, and fulfillment in him.

Yet the events, projects, and plans of life, and the circumstances under which they unfold, are very much like the tempestuous behavior of nature that we see in both the first reading and the Gospel. Wind, waves, earthquakes, noise, danger, and the confusion of constant change mark many chapters of life. We need to remember that there is no single chapter, nor a single moment, in which we cannot cling to Christ, find him present, and embrace his hand, which will save us from drowning in the cares of this world.

This applies directly to those confused by a pregnancy that they feel they cannot handle. It also speaks to those who have had an abortion and are suffering the storms of anguish, possibly drowning in despair. And it is encouragement for all those who are in the heat of the battle, defending life against numerous attacks and seemingly hopeless odds.

In all of this, we seek and cling to Christ. He gives us the strength to stand on the side of life. He gives his forgiveness to those who seek it. And he gives strength for the battle.

. . . .
Twentieth Sunday of Ordinary Time, Year A
. . . .

Readings: Isaiah 56:1, 6–7 • Romans 11:13–15, 29–32 • Matthew 15:21–28

Catholic means "universal." Everyone is called to salvation in Christ; everyone is called to his "house of prayer," his Church, his family. The

Church, at her core, is missionary. All her efforts are geared toward an ever wider expansion and growth. She seeks to embrace every human being, as Jesus embraces the Canaanite woman in his ministry.

This universality, reflected in all of today's readings, is rooted ultimately in the meaning of the Incarnation. The Second Vatican Council teaches, "By his incarnation the Son of God has united himself in some fashion with every human being."[70] This reality raises the dignity of human life beyond what it already had as God's creation in his own image. It also lends urgency to the task of announcing the Gospel to all people, that they may know the meaning and promise of the dignity they have.

"The gifts and the call of God are irrevocable," today's second reading tells us. That is why the Church is pro-life. As Blessed Pope Paul VI declared in *Humanae Vitae* and Pope St. John Paul II firmly stated in *Evangelium Vitae*, "this tradition is unchanged and unchangeable."[71] Our stance in favor of life and in defense of life does not spring from us or from some inclination we have toward a particular philosophy, ideology, or political platform. It is based, rather, in "the gifts and the call of God," which "are irrevocable" and universal. He has chosen to create and redeem us, and he reserves a place for us on his throne! His choice is what makes human life sacred, and it is the basis for our choices.

Today's readings, therefore, provide a foundation for a strong affirmation of the essential and integral pro-life stance of the Church, of its meaning and origin, and of the need for that pro-life witness to be given to the whole world and to every culture and subculture. The fact that God calls enables us to echo that call. Each in our own way, we can urge people to participate in the work of advancing the kingdom and building the culture of life.

We are not content, as Christians, to observe those who do not follow the Lord. We do not await an invitation but rather go boldly into the territory of others and invite them to accept God's call. It will transform their lives.

. . . .

Twenty-First Sunday of Ordinary Time, Year A

Readings: Isaiah 22:19–23 • Romans 11:33–36 • Matthew 16:13–20

If some mistook Jesus for John the Baptist, Elijah, or Jeremiah, as today's Gospel passage indicates, then his preaching must have borne a resemblance to theirs. John the Baptist, Elijah, and Jeremiah were tough characters. They did not hesitate to confront power with the truth and the demands of the moral law. They did not hesitate to point out that violation of the covenant brings ruin to the people. They did not shy away from moral absolutes and from the absolute requirements of fidelity to God.

The Church takes the same stand in the world, assured, as we also see in the Gospel, of her union with Christ in her mission of teaching and transformation. "Whatever you bind on earth shall be bound in heaven; and whatever you loose on earth shall be loosed in heaven." Challenging every culture with which it communicates, the Church takes the initiative and storms "the gates of the netherworld."

Gates, after all, do not run out on the battlefield to attack the enemy. Rather, gates stand still and defend the city against the enemy attacking it. To say that the gates of hell will not prevail against the Church is to say that it is the Church who is taking the offensive. We storm the gates of hell in order to win ground for Jesus Christ. "For from him and through him and for him are all things" (second reading).

This provides a context for understanding the fight against abortion and all the manifestations of the culture of death. The Church's pro-life teachings are faithful to Christ, consistent, and unchangeable. Her mission is to transform the culture of death into the culture of life. The people of life will not be deterred from that mission.

. . . .
Twenty-Second Sunday of Ordinary Time, Year A
. . . .

Readings: Jeremiah 20:7–9 • Romans 12:1–2 • Matthew 16:21–27

The Church's efforts to proclaim, celebrate, and serve the gospel of life find support in today's readings.

First, the effort to defend life is based on the thirst for God, which today's first reading and psalm express. We long for him who is life itself, and we long for others to possess him as well. We serve the kingdom of life because it has first captured us, enthralled us, and convinced us that all our happiness and fulfillment are found in it. God's kingdom is the kingdom of truth and life, of holiness and grace, of justice, love, and peace.

Second, St. Paul says in the second reading that we must not conform ourselves to this age. We reject the worldly disconnect of freedom from truth. The pro-life movement is based on the renewal of our minds, which results in the ability to discern "what is good and pleasing and perfect." We can see, as Pope St. John Paul II wrote in *Evangelium Vitae*, that "life is always a good."[72]

Third, the Gospel passage reinforces the need for this discernment of what is good. Peter was thinking in a worldly way when he saw suffering and crucifixion ahead. These, he thought, the Lord should avoid at all costs. Such thinking today leads some to see abortion as a solution to the suffering of a crisis pregnancy or euthanasia as an escape from illness and disability. But that is not godly thinking.

As Simone Weil has said, "The false god transforms suffering into violence; the true God transforms violence into suffering."[73] Thus Jesus did by his cross; thus he calls us to do by embracing ours.

. . . .

Twenty-Third Sunday of Ordinary Time, Year A
. . . .

Readings: Ezekiel 33:7–9 • Romans 13:8–10 • Matthew 18:15–20

The readings today provide important insight into the pro-life witness of the Church and of each member of the Church. Combining the themes of the readings, we can say that the Church consists of "loving watchmen." Because we love God, we love others and therefore try to persuade others to love the same God and to keep themselves from the destructive harm of sin.

Yet when we try to fulfill the exhortations of Ezekiel and Jesus to engage in the spiritual work of mercy of "admonishing the sinner," often we are told that we should mind our own business. This is particularly the case when the sin we try to prevent is abortion. This criticism is not heard when we try to prevent politically correct sins, such as harm to the environment.

Yet it is our business to engage in fraternal correction, because God has entrusted us to each other. Pope St. John Paul II stated, "The God of the Covenant has entrusted the life of every individual to his or her fellow human beings."[74] There is a natural bond of responsibility, because we are all one human family. Within the Church there is a mystical communion in grace, and the sins of the individual harm the entire body of Christ. Hence fraternal correction makes sense.

Especially urgent is the task to speak up for the unborn and the ill. These are defenseless human beings who cannot speak for themselves.

The love that Paul describes in the second reading infuses the pro-life movement and motivates its participants. Defending the unborn is simply an application of loving your neighbor. It is love in action. This love inspires pregnancy centers, post-abortion healing ministries, legislative efforts, protests, and every other form of pro-life activity.

The Gospel passage today ends with the words, "Where two or three are gathered together in my name, there am I in the midst of them." Why did the Lord say "two or three"? He is there when just one person is present, isn't he?

Certainly, he is. But it is when the other or others show up that we are able to give ourselves in love. The bond of active love between human beings manifests Jesus's presence in the particular way that he highlights in this passage.

. . . .

Twenty-Fourth Sunday of Ordinary Time, Year A

. . . .

Readings: Sirach 27:30–28:9 • Romans 14:7–9 • Matthew 18:21–35

"None of us lives for oneself, and no one dies for oneself." This assertion and what follows it in today's second reading speak of the dominion of God over human life. This, of course, is the basis for the Church's opposition to abortion and euthanasia and any other kind of violence against human life.

The pro-choice side chants, "My body, my choice, my life!" and the pro-euthanasia side chants, "My body, my choice, my death!" But this reading declares that Christ is Lord of both the living and the dead. When the Church defends life, she defends not only the rights of the human person but also the rights of God.

God's dominion over human life is the basis for the mercy and forgiveness of which today's first reading, psalm, and Gospel speak. God is over all and therefore can have mercy on all. The first act of mercy is creation itself, and therefore, just as we are called to imitate God's mercy by forgiving our neighbor, so are we called to imitate his mercy by protecting our neighbor's life.

These powerful readings about mercy are a good opening to remind the congregation about the forgiveness the Lord and the Church offer to those who have had abortions. They remind us of our responsibility to welcome such individuals with tenderness and kindness, and never with harshness or judgment.

. . . .
Twenty-Fifth Sunday of Ordinary Time, Year A
. . . .

Readings: Isaiah 55:6–9 • Philippians 1:20c–24, 27a • Matthew 20:1–16a

The contrast God indicates between his way of thinking and ours (first reading) is exemplified in the Gospel passage, where the landowner's (the Lord's) generosity to those who started late astonishes those who worked all day. Those who come late to the kingdom of God (the gentiles, and those in our midst who seem far off) can still enjoy its full benefits.

The emphasis on right thinking that these readings convey goes to the heart of repentance. *Metanoia* is a change of mind, of thinking. Elsewhere Paul writes that "we take every thought captive in obedience to Christ" (2 Corinthians 10:5).

This is at the core of the battle between the culture of death and the culture of life. Pope St. John Paul II, in *Evangelium Vitae*, writes,

> At the root of every act of violence against one's neighbor there is a concession to the "thinking" of the evil one, the one who "was a murderer from the beginning" (John 8:44). As the apostle John reminds us: "For this is the message which you have heard from the beginning, that we should love one another, and not be like Cain who was of the evil one and murdered his brother" (1 John 3:11–12)[75]

Either life has priority over choice, or choice can be used to destroy life. These two ways of thinking cannot coexist. One who thinks according to the culture of death needs a true metanoia. As the Lord says in today's first reading, we must think his way about the relationship between life and choice.

The readings also put a strong emphasis on mercy and forgiveness, themes that always accompany our teaching about abortion. They impel us to invite to reconciliation those who have been far from the Church because of past involvement with abortion. We also invite people to think in God's way about those who have had abortions—not with condemnation but with eagerness to welcome and console.

· · · · · · · · · · ·

Twenty-Sixth Sunday of Ordinary Time, Year A

· ·

Readings: Ezekiel 18:25–28 • Philippians 2:1–11 or 2:1–5
Matthew 21:28–32

People indeed can convert. God asks us to believe that in today's readings. The son who first said no can later say yes (Gospel); the wicked one can turn from his wickedness and find life (first reading).

This proves true in the pro-life effort. In fact, the flow of conversions is in the direction of life, not death. I was privileged to receive into the Catholic Church Norma McCorvey, the former "Jane Roe" plaintiff (and winner) of the Supreme Court's 1973 *Roe v. Wade* decision legalizing abortion. She now devotes her time to ending abortion. The late Dr. Bernard Nathanson, one of the chief engineers of the abortion rights movement, also became a strong pro-life advocate. There are so many others that an international society of ex-abortionists has been formed, called the Society of Centurions.

But even more common is the testimony, "I regret my abortion," from the women of the Silent No More Awareness Campaign. This is the largest mobilization in history of those who have had abortions and now speak out against it. "I regret lost fatherhood" is the message that the men of the campaign offer, as they grieve the children they lost to abortion. Today's readings call us to welcome these individuals and to learn from their experience.

The longer form of the second reading can lead us to reflect on the cross as the denial of self. Pro-choice is the assertion of oneself; the cross is the emptying of oneself. Pro-choice says we can lift ourselves up; the cross says that we are obedient and that God lifts us up.

The notion that we can exalt ourselves goes right back to the original sin and, in fact, to the sin of the devil himself. "You will be like gods" (Genesis 3:5), he said to our first parents. Scholars apply these words from Isaiah to Satan:

In your heart you said:
  "I will scale the heavens;
Above the stars of God
  I will set up my throne." (Isaiah 14:13)

The attitude we learn from Christ is to humble ourselves in obedience. Our exaltation, our freedom, and our fulfillment come from a humble acceptance of and obedience to a truth that we did not create. The tree of the knowledge of good and evil marks the limit of our choices. True freedom is the power to choose what is right and to love as Christ did by embracing the cross and giving ourselves away for the good of the other.

. . . .

Twenty-Seventh Sunday of Ordinary Time, Year A

Readings: Isaiah 5:1–7 • Philippians 4:6–9 • Matthew 21:33–43

The first reading and Gospel passage assigned to this Sunday talk about the vineyard of the Lord. Those to whom the vineyard was entrusted did not properly respond to the Lord or yield the fruit for which he was looking. Instead, they broke his covenant, killing his prophets and eventually his son. And so the master took the vineyard away from them.

God entered into a covenant of life with his people of old, and the prophets spoke untiringly of the demands of that covenant, both what the people owed God and what they owed one another. Those who worshipped God were to help their neighbor; those whom God had rescued were bound to care for and rescue one another. The failure to do this led to such rebukes as this from Isaiah:

> When you spread out your hands,
> I will close my eyes to you;
> Though you pray the more,
> I will not listen.
> Your hands are full of blood! (Isaiah 1:15)

The theme carries over into Isaiah 5, today's first reading.

> Why, when I looked for the crop of grapes,
> did it bring forth wild grapes?

A good summary of the history of the people's rejection of the covenant is found in Psalm 106. God's people, having inherited the Promised Land, still had to do battle with the foreign nations around them. They were told not to adopt the practices of those people, for they did not know the true God. God's people, however, mingled with these other nations and even joined in their rituals. The most grievous of the sins of God's people was when, in imitation of the pagan nations,

> They sacrificed to demons
> their own sons and daughters,
> Shedding innocent blood,
> the blood of their own sons and daughters. (Psalm 106:37–38)

Rather than bearing the fruit of life, rooted in true worship, they bore the fruit of death, rooted in false worship. True worship would have led the people to embrace the prophets' admonition:

> Make justice your aim: redress the wronged,
> hear the orphan's plea, defend the widow. (Isaiah 1:17)

As James puts it, "Religion that is pure and undefiled before God and the Father is this: to care for orphans and widows in their affliction" (James 1:27).

Today we are entrusted with a vineyard too: It is the new and everlasting covenant in the blood of Christ. That covenant is renewed at the Eucharist, where we resolve to bear good fruit for the Lord as we receive his life-giving Body and Blood. We will not betray the covenant with which we are entrusted.

As of old, so today, that covenant gives us obligations to one another. The vineyard we have here in the United States guarantees profound gifts of freedom. We can shape our culture and government. God asks us to bear fruits of life rather than abuse our freedom with perversions that take away life.

. . . .

Twenty-Eighth Sunday of Ordinary Time, Year A

Readings: Isaiah 25:6–10 • Philippians 4:12–14, 19–20
Matthew 22:1–14 or 22:1–10

The readings for today speak about the banquet to which God—in the old and new covenants—calls his people. The homilist can point out that this is a banquet of life.

Isaiah tells us that God is in the business of destroying death:

> On this mountain he will destroy
>   the veil that veils all peoples,
> the web that is woven over all nations;
>   he will destroy death forever.

This is the same mountain on which God "will provide for all peoples a feast of rich food and pure, choice wines."

God did not make death; rather he destroys it. He does so in Christ, for whom the wedding banquet (the marriage of Christ the Bridegroom with the Church, his bride) is celebrated. To stand with Christ is to stand with life, and to stand with life is to stand against whatever destroys it. And nothing destroys more life than abortion.

We are on the holy mountain now—in the Eucharist, where the Church, and each of us individually, renews our vows to the Lord and receives (not simply recalls) his victory over death. It remains for us to "proclaim, celebrate and serve the Gospel of Life," as Pope St. John Paul II put it in *Evangelium Vitae*.[76] We must apply Christ's victory to every sector of society.

· · · · · · · · · · ·
Twenty-Ninth Sunday of Ordinary Time, Year A
· ·

Readings: Isaiah 45:1, 4–6 • 1 Thessalonians 1:1–5b • Matthew 22:15–21

The first reading emphasizes the fact that the Lord alone is God; there is no other. In a culture of death, that is precisely the truth that is denied. The battle between pro-life and pro-choice is really about the dominion of God. "Life, especially human life, belongs only to God: for this reason whoever attacks human life in some way attacks God himself," Pope St. John Paul II wrote.[77]

Abortion advocates more and more openly admit that abortion kills a child, but they claim the right to do that. The late Dr. James McMahon was an abortionist in southern California who performed partial-birth abortions. He admitted that the baby was a child but then said, "Who owns the child? It's got to be the mother."[78]

In the Gospel's familiar account of Jesus's answer about taxes, Jesus says that the coin belongs to Caesar because it bears his image. What then belongs to God? That which bears his image, namely, human life itself, including the life of Caesar!

Jesus teaches here the hierarchy of divine and human authority. Christians must be good citizens, but citizens and their governing authorities alike must obey God, acknowledging his dominion over human life and protecting it.

· · · · · · · · · · ·

Thirtieth Sunday of Ordinary Time, Year A

Readings: Exodus 22:20–26 • 1 Thessalonians 1:5c–10 • Matthew 22:34–40

The readings for today make it clear that love of God and practical, concrete attention to the needs of one's neighbor are inseparable. To love one's neighbor as oneself implies loving the neighbor as a person like oneself. It means recognizing, in other words, that despite any differences the neighbor may have, he or she is a person with human dignity.

So it is with our relationship with the unborn child. Recognizing that child as a person like ourselves is the foundation of extending our love to and protecting him or her.

Moreover, the Gospel says that the second commandment "is like" the first. The love of God cannot coexist with indifference toward the slaughter of the unborn. As the First Letter of John to the Thessalonians explains in detail, we cannot love God without loving our neighbor. And on these two great commandments depend the whole law and the prophets. Failure to love our neighbor in the womb undermines all other efforts for social justice and the common good.

· · · · · · · · · · ·

Thirty-First Sunday of Ordinary Time, Year A

Readings: Malachi 1:14b–2:2b, 8–10 • 1 Thessalonians 2:7b–9, 13
Matthew 23:1–12

The first reading, from Malachi, asks,

> Have we not all the one Father?
> Has not the one God created us?

This theme is echoed in the Gospel's teaching, "Call no one on earth your father; you have but one Father in heaven."

In a culture of death, the worldview is that we are responsible only for those for whom we choose to be responsible. This choice is a purely individual, private matter. Such a culture would have us believe that someone's decision to abort a child is none of our business.

But if we all have one Father, then that makes us brothers and sisters. Our lives are entrusted to one another's care. We are responsible for each other before we choose to be. The abortions that others have are our business, because those children—as well as their parents—are entrusted to our care in the one family of God.

Ours is the business of love. We are to care as much as we can for all our brothers and sisters.

. . . .
Thirty-Second Sunday of Ordinary Time, Year A

Readings: Wisdom 6:12–16 • 1 Thessalonians 4:13–18 or 4:13–14
Matthew 25:1–13

The second reading today reminds us, "Jesus died and rose." This is the basis for the pro-life efforts of the Church. We stand with life and proclaim life precisely because we stand with and proclaim Christ, who conquered the power of death. His resurrection does not conquer only his death; it conquers ours, overthrowing the entire kingdom of death. Christ has already defeated the power of abortion.

We, the people of life, have the task of announcing that victory, celebrating it, and serving it. We must apply it to every sector of society. We must do this with confidence, because victory is our starting point. In the pro-life cause, we are not just working for victory; we are working *from* victory.

The lesson of vigilance that comes from the Gospel translates to the constant vigilance that we as individuals and as a nation must keep over the sacredness of life. Stay awake. We must not allow our attitudes, actions, laws, or public policies to degrade or deny the right to life.

. . . .
Thirty-Third Sunday of Ordinary Time, Year A
. . . .

Readings: Proverbs 31:10–13, 19–20, 30–31 • 1 Thessalonians 5:1–6
Matthew 25:14–30 or 25:14–15, 19–21

We all have talents, the use of which will be judged at the end of time. In preaching about the use of our talents in a fruitful way, we can focus on how they apply to the effort to defend and promote the sacredness of human life. People in the pro-life movement provide alternatives to abortion, legal advice, counseling, medical services, adoption services, employment searches, housing, education. Many services can be accessed through hotline numbers and websites.

There is also a wide range of healing ministries for those who have had abortions. Moreover, the pro-life effort is advanced through research, medical expertise, litigation, lobbying, media work, writing, speaking, grassroots activism, and much more.

In short, there is room for everyone in the pro-life movement. The greatest fruit of our talents is to present to the Lord the lives saved through our efforts.

· · · · · · · · · · ·

Solemnity of Christ the King (Thirty-Fourth or Last Sunday of the Year), Year A

Readings: Ezekiel 34:11–12, 15–17 • 1 Corinthians 15:20–26, 28
Matthew 25:31–46

The Solemnity of Christ the King suggests many themes related to the defense of life and the care of the vulnerable. Christ's kingdom is a kingdom of life and justice, as the Preface reminds us. It is a kingdom of life because Christ identified himself on various occasions as "the life" and said that his mission was to bring life. To stand with Christ is to stand with life, and to stand with life is to stand against whatever destroys life. "The last enemy to be destroyed is death," the second reading tells us. Our union with God means that we share in the process by which he destroys the power of death in the world.

The kingship of Christ also reminds us that we are subject to his laws—not only as individuals but also as nations. We do not want a theocracy in which, for example, civil law would require belief in the Eucharist or attendance at Sunday Mass. We do, however, want a society that acknowledges its dependence on God, is accountable to him, and adheres to the fundamental requirements of his law relating to the protection of basic human rights.

The first reading and psalm speak about God's care for the sheep, particularly the weak ones. His care for his people puts the same obligation on us, as the Gospel relates. What we do to the least, we do to him.

Defending the unborn, who are the weakest of the weak and the poorest of the poor, flows from this Gospel passage. When we defend the child in the womb, we defend Christ in the womb. It is our business to intervene.

Ordinary Time, Year B

Ordinary time begins after the Feast of the Baptism of the Lord, at the end of the Christmas season.

· · · · · · · · · · ·
Second Sunday of Ordinary Time, Year B

Readings: 1 Samuel 3:3b–10, 19 • 1 Corinthians 6:13c–15a, 17–20
John 1:35–42

A powerful way to draw the pro-life theme from today's readings is to build on Paul's declaration to the Corinthians, "You are not your own" (second reading). The battle cry of pro-choice is "My body, my life, my decision." The idea is that we are our own, each the captain of our own ship. "Nobody can tell me what to do." Christianity challenges all that.

Because of what Jesus Christ did, we are no longer our own. He owns us—not to oppress or enslave us but to incorporate us into his body. In Christ, we go beyond the natural concept of the common good to enter into a new humanity, a level of love and unity with one another (including the unborn) that could never be achieved by human effort alone.

A striking contrast to this truth comes from the late Dr. James McMahon, an abortionist from southern California who performed partial-birth abortions. In response to a question posed by the *American Medical Association News*, he said, "After 20 weeks (4½ months), where it frankly is a child to me, I really agonize over it.… On the other hand, I have another position, which I think is superior in the hierarchy of questions, and that is: 'Who owns the child?' It's got to be the mother."[79]

Paul would counter, "Do you not know that your body is a temple of the Holy Spirit within you, whom you have from God?"

· · · · · · · · · · ·
Third Sunday of Ordinary Time, Year B

Readings: Jonah 3:1–5, 10 • 1 Corinthians 7:29–31 • Mark 1:14–20

January 22, 1973, was the date of the tragic *Roe* v. *Wade* decision, and this date falls close to the time when we hear these readings that accent the theme of repentance. "Repent" is the first message of Jesus as he begins his public ministry (today's Gospel). It was also the first message of John the Baptizer as he began preparing the way for Christ (see Mark 1:4) and will be the first theme that Peter proclaims on the first Pentecost (Acts 2:38). The preaching of Jonah foreshadowed all of this, and the work of the Church today echoes it.

Many believers, as they learn more about the facts of abortion and *Roe v. Wade*, think that our first spiritual duty in the face of abortion is to pray. But it is not. Our first duty is to repent. God does not simply prohibit us from committing abortion. He prohibits us from tolerating it. He calls us to become active in fighting it.

Today provides an excellent opportunity to sound the call of repentance and to educate parishioners on some of the key facts of *Roe v. Wade*, such as can be found at PriestsForLife.org. Simply knowing what *Roe v. Wade* permitted—which is far more than most Americans realize—can spur people to start doing more for the pro-life effort.

· · · · · · · · · · ·

Fourth Sunday of Ordinary Time, Year B

Readings: Deuteronomy 18:15–20 • 1 Corinthians 7:32–35 • Mark 1:21–28

The Gospel and first reading for this Sunday raise the issue of the authority of those who speak the Word of God. Jesus taught with authority because he is the Word of God. The prophets taught with authority because God put his own words into their mouths. The Church today teaches with authority because, as the body of Christ, she continues his teaching mission—or to be more precise, Christ continues teaching through her. Each member of the Church, by virtue of baptism and confirmation, has a prophetic role, echoing the Word of God by words and example.

These themes are important in the battle between the culture of life and the culture of death. Our opponents ask why we are imposing our morality on everyone else. In reality, however, we are not imposing anything; we are speaking a truth that is not our own. It is the truth that simply reflects the reality of how we are made and what the moral law is.

If anything is imposed, it is imposed by God. We are witnesses to him. We have no authority of our own; we simply proclaim his Word. By that fact, moreover, we are bound by what we proclaim as are those to whom we proclaim it.

The pro-life message does not imply any kind of moral superiority on the part of those who proclaim it. Rather, it implies solidarity and a common acknowledgement of the God of life. He is Lord of those who preach and those who hear.

· · · · · · · · · · ·
Fifth Sunday of Ordinary Time, Year B

Readings: Job 7:1–4, 6–7 • 1 Corinthians 9:16–19, 22–23 • Mark 1:29–39

Jesus loved the poor, the weak, the sick, and the demon-possessed. These individuals and those who cared for them knew that they could come to Jesus to find what they needed. What they needed, however, was often much more than what they thought they needed.

Jesus indicates in today's Gospel passage that his mission is to preach the Word of God. "For this purpose I have come." People need to hear the truth of God. By accepting it and being formed in it, they can establish right relationships with God and one another. They can conquer sin. They can have integral salvation, in body and soul.

As Jesus was the one to whom the people brought the ill and those possessed by demons, so the Church is the place that people should go first today for healing and help. The Church preaches integral salvation, as the *Compendium of the Social Doctrine of the Catholic Church* so clearly explains.[80] The feeding of the soul and the care for temporal needs go hand in hand.

The Church, which teaches the truth that all life belongs to God, is reaching out each day to those who are tempted to take life by abortion. The thousands of pregnancy centers run by Christians across our nation bear witness to this fact. These centers provide medical help, financial assistance, legal advice, counseling, job and education opportunities, and assistance to keep and raise children or to make adoption plans. National hotlines—like the Option Line, 1-800-712-HELP (4357)—and websites, like pregnancycenters.org, bring this concrete help to countless people daily. Members of your parish can extend the ministry of Jesus by referring people to this kind of help—thus saving lives, sparing people grief, and proclaiming the Word of God about human life.

· · · · · · · · · · ·
Sixth Sunday of Ordinary Time, Year B
· ·

Readings: Leviticus 13:1–2, 44–46 • 1 Corinthians 10:31–11:1
Mark 1:40–45

I do will it. Be made clean. (Mark 1:41)

Lepers, the first reading makes clear, were outcasts from their community. Jesus's healing of the lepers in today's Gospel demonstrates two key lessons that relate to the Church's stand on life.

First, Jesus is always on the side of human life. His healing of some represents his liberation of all from the power of sin and death. The healings described in the Gospels point to the overthrow of the entire kingdom of death and the final triumph of life. Christ is life, and to stand with him is to stand with life and against whatever destroys it.

Second, the Lord broke down false barriers between different classes of human beings. He saw the humanity of all, the image of God inscribed on them from creation. This image is not obscured by the false distinctions people make according to their prejudices or customs. He touched clean and unclean.

The Lord's determination to eliminate false barriers is seen in many other ways in the Gospels. We see him reach out to children, despite the efforts of the apostles to keep them away (see Matthew 19:13–15); to tax collectors and sinners, despite the objections of the scribes (Mark 2:16); to the blind, despite the warnings of the surrounding crowd (Matthew 20:29–34); to a foreign woman, despite the utter surprise of the disciples and of the woman herself (John 4:9, 27); and to gentiles, despite the anger of the Jews (Matthew 21:41–46).

When it comes to human dignity, Christ erases distinctions. St. Paul declares, "There is neither Jew nor Greek, there is neither slave nor free person, there is not male and female; for you are all one in Christ Jesus" (Galatians 3:28).

We can likewise say, "There is neither born nor unborn." The unborn are the segment of our society that is most neglected and discriminated against. Christ surely has a special love for them.

Seventh Sunday of Ordinary Time, Year B

Readings: Isaiah 43:18–19, 21–22, 24b–25 • 2 Corinthians 1:18–22
Mark 2:1–12

The emphasis of this weekend's first reading and Gospel is on the forgiveness of sins. I suggest that as we speak about God's mercy, we mention that the Church extends that mercy to all who have been involved in abortion. These words from Pope St. John Paul II's *Evangelium Vitae* are worth reading to your congregation:

I would now like to say a special word to women who have had an abortion. The Church is aware of the many factors which may have influenced your decision, and she does not doubt that in many cases it was a painful and even shattering decision. The wound in your heart may not yet have healed. Certainly what happened was and remains terribly wrong. But do not give in to discouragement and do not lose hope. Try rather to understand what happened and face it honestly. If you have not already done so, give yourselves over with humility and trust to repentance. The Father of mercies is ready to give you his forgiveness and his peace in the Sacrament of Reconciliation. To the same Father and to his mercy you can with sure hope entrust your child. With the friendly and expert help and advice of other people, and as a result of your own painful experience, you can be among the most eloquent defenders of everyone's right to life. Through your commitment to life, whether by accepting the birth of other children or by welcoming and caring for those most in need of someone to be close to them, you will become promoters of a new way of looking at human life.[81]

A practical resource like the Silent No More Awareness Campaign (SilentNoMore.com) can also be mentioned. Parishioners can find referrals to various ministries of post-abortion healing at that website. The Silent No More gatherings, furthermore, at which women share their regrets about their abortions, show forth the mercy of God to the local community. A powerful addition to this weekend's message would be a three-to-five-minute testimony after Communion from one of these women.

The theme of Jesus Christ as the *yes* is a powerful pro-life theme of the second reading. Yes is what Jesus says to human life, and in his yes we find the strength to say yes. We affirm and receive the promises God holds out to all whom he creates, including his promise of life.

. . . .
Eighth Sunday of Ordinary Time, Year B
. . . .

Readings: Hosea 2:16b, 17b, 21–22 • 2 Corinthians 3:1–6
Mark 2:18–22

Today's readings lead us to reflect on the marriage between God and his people. This in turn illumines why we are pro-life.

In the first reading and the Gospel, God describes himself as our spouse. So great is his love for us, he is not content to watch us from a distance or simply send us his love. Rather, he comes radically close to us, fills us with his being, and gives himself entirely to us.

We, in turn, are called to give ourselves entirely to him, as to a spouse. The marriage between God and his people, between Christ and his Church, is both permanent and fruitful. This bond of love cannot be broken. Moreover, it always brings about new life in the Spirit. Thus the Church, the bride of Christ, proclaims the dignity of all human life and calls us to welcome every life with generosity.

Some criticize the Church for what they see as a failure to recognize the full rights and dignity of women. The more radical pro-choice elements of society, in fact, see our pro-life stance as oppressive toward women. In reality, however, the Church is a woman, a bride, a mother! The welcome of life springs from her very nature.

In giving himself to us, God teaches us how to give ourselves to him and to each other—including our children, born and unborn. God also gives us the very power to do this, as he lives in us and loves through us. Pro-life action, then, is a powerful way to live out our marriage vows with God.

· · · · · · · · · · ·
Ninth Sunday of Ordinary Time, Year B

Readings: Deuteronomy 5:12–15 • 2 Corinthians 4:6–11
Mark 2:23–3:6 or 2:23–28

The preserving of life is more important than the law. This simple truth is obvious in our daily lives and in our public policy. "No trespassing" signs, for example, preserve privacy and property, but one can violate such a sign in order to save a life. Life is a value that towers above all.

Even with regard to the sacred law of the Sabbath, Jesus says that the preserving of life is more important. "The sabbath was made for man, not man for the sabbath." Indeed, all the law is made for man. It all points to Christ, and in Christ, human life is taken to the throne of God. All of salvation history is for the fulfillment of this plan of the exaltation of the human person in God. That is why we are pro-life, and that is why the work of preserving and celebrating human life is more important than any other.

The principle of the primacy of the human person applies to all other institutions as well. The state is made for man, not man for the state. The courts are made for man, not man for the courts. The medical profession is made for man, not man for the medical profession. And so on. When this principle is obscured or contradicted, we end up with abortion and similar forms of slavery and exploitation.

· · · · · · · · · · ·
Tenth Sunday of Ordinary Time, Year B

Readings: Genesis 3:9–15 • 2 Corinthians 4:13–5:1 • Mark 3:20–35

Two kingdoms are at war. One has already been defeated yet still exercises a harmful though limited power. The strife between the kingdoms is described in the first reading, as is the outcome. The serpent strikes the heel of the seed of the woman.

The seed of the woman is Christ, into whom we are all incorporated by our obedience to the Word of God. As Jesus explains in the Gospel, that obedient union with his will is what makes us his brothers, sisters, and mothers. And this is precisely how he (and we in him) cast out devils and crush the head of the serpent: Obedience, leading to unity, undoes the disobedience of Adam and Eve, which led to chaos and strife.

The fight over abortion is not simply a worldly struggle between philosophies or political parties. It is the embodiment of the biblical struggle laid out in today's readings. Abortion is a great *no* to the will of God. It brings division within the most basic relationship, that of a mother and her child, and spreads more division throughout the human family.

The solution is in the promise of God: The divine offspring "will strike" at the devil's head (Genesis 3:15). The culture of life is a great *yes* to God, spoken in Christ. It comes by obedience to his will. The fruit of that obedience is the unity of all God's children and, as the second reading indicates, life eternal.

. . . .
Eleventh Sunday of Ordinary Time, Year B
. . . .

Readings: Ezekiel 17:22–24 • 2 Corinthians 5:6–10 • Mark 4:26–34

Building the culture of life is a combination of our responsibility and God's responsibility. In Christ, God has already conquered death and brought about the victory of life. This is the starting point both of the Church and of the pro-life movement. And the kingdom of life is constantly growing in the world and in the hearts of those who are open to it.

The images, in the first reading and the Gospel, of constant growth under the hand of God inspire confidence in his plan for the ultimate triumph of life and of all that is good. "The kingdom of God…is like a mustard seed that…springs up and becomes the largest of plants and puts forth large branches."

Our responsibility becomes clear in the second reading. We will be judged according to what we do. Either our actions will promote and defend life, or they will promote and defend death. God gives the growth, but we must constantly plant the seeds.

This is an opportunity to exhort people to practical action on behalf of the defense of life. When one life is saved, that brings into the world all the good that the saved individual and his or her descendants will do.

. . . .

Twelfth Sunday of Ordinary Time, Year B

Readings: Job 38:1, 8–11 • 2 Corinthians 5:14–17 • Mark 4:35–41

Job's life and sufferings raised many questions for him and those around him. What did he do wrong? If he didn't commit a great sin, why was he experiencing so much misfortune? How can one find strength in the midst of so much loss, and how can one trust God in the midst of so much adversity?

Job ponders his fate, and his wife and his friends chime in with their advice. Then, after all the human words are spoken, God breaks his silence and speaks to Job. God responds to the puzzlement of human beings by asking a series of questions that highlight the difference between God and his creatures. It would be instructive in this homily to read some of these questions, which give a tremendous sense of perspective that we so easily miss:

> Who shut within doors the sea,
> when it burst forth from the womb;
> when I made the clouds its garment
> and thick darkness its swaddling bands?

We find it so easy to question God and to take the role of God. Yet when God asks us if we are really able to take his role or claim to do any of the things he does, he shows the absurdity of human pride. How foolish, he shows us, is our lack of trust in him.

The apostles learned the lesson of trust in the midst of a dangerous sea. There Jesus showed himself to be the one who can answer God's questions in Job 38. He rules the sea, setting limits for it, because he is God.

This lesson of trust and utter humility in the face of God's infinite providence is a tremendous antidote to the temptation of individuals and families to resort to abortion and euthanasia. "How will I handle this child I did not anticipate?" "How will I handle this terminal illness?" When these questions confront us—like stormy waves on the sea, threatening to sink our boat—we need to hear the questions of Job 38. And we need to know the power of the one who, though he may seem asleep, is in control.

This set of readings not only inspires the trust and hope we need to choose life but also challenges the arrogance displayed by the culture of death. Trying to control the timing and manner of death through euthanasia and assisted suicide, trying to control the circumstances of conception and birth by contraception, genetic manipulation, and abortion—these are examples of trying to play God. Yet far beyond anything that human intelligence, in its pride, can accomplish is the "new creation" of which the second reading speaks. The true victory over the evils of this life comes in the transformation available to us in Christ.

. . . .

Thirteenth Sunday of Ordinary Time, Year B

Readings: Wisdom 1:13–15; 2:23–24 • 2 Corinthians 8:7, 9, 13–15
Mark 5:21–43 or 5:21–24, 35–43

God did not make death....
For he fashioned all things that they might have being.

This line from the first reading is not only an assertion about God; it is a mandate for his people to stand against the power of death and to defend and promote life. Likewise, the raising of the dead girl to life, recounted in the Gospel passage, is not simply a story about what Jesus did; it is a summons to his people to build a culture of life in the world.

One could ask, in the face of miracles like the raising of the dead, why Jesus did not do it more frequently. The answer is that his miracles were signs of his mission and ours. His occasional raising of the dead reveals the meaning of everything he did, at every moment. He reconciled humanity to God and hence destroyed the very source of death. In the end, all will rise—but they are called first to come to Christ, who is life itself, and embrace that gift of natural and supernatural life.

The pro-life movement is not simply a response to *Roe v. Wade*. Rather, the pro-life movement is a response to Jesus Christ. God is in the business of destroying death, and he has done so through Christ. To stand with Christ is to stand with life and therefore to stand against whatever destroys life. Nothing in our world destroys more life than abortion.

Some wonder why we would preach about abortion at Mass or why we are concerned about what, in the eyes of some, is none of our business. Yet it is our business, because we serve a God who destroys death. We are the people of God and the people of life. It is the business of love to save human lives.

In the Mass, we literally touch the victory of life over death. What can be a more appropriate time and place to speak the pro-life message?

· · · · · · · · · · ·
Fourteenth Sunday of Ordinary Time, Year B
· ·

Readings: Ezekiel 2:2–5 • 2 Corinthians 12:7–10 • Mark 6:1–6a

The readings today invite us to reflect on what it means to be a prophet—and how we can be "content with...insults" and "persecutions."

At our baptism, we were declared to be "priest, prophet, and king," like the Lord Jesus, into whose body and mission we were baptized. A prophet does not primarily tell the future; rather, a prophet tells the present, declaring to the people what the Lord says about current circumstances, culture, and lifestyle. The prophet declares the next good step for God's people to take on their constant road of repentance and growth in holiness.

As the people of life amid a culture of death, we are all prophets regarding the sanctity of life. We are prophets who declare that the only appropriate response to life at all stages, especially when most vulnerable, is a generous and loving yes. We are prophets as we teach our children about the dignity of life. We are prophets when we share the pro-life message with friends and coworkers and with the community through letters to the local papers or online. We are prophets when we enter the voting booth, as we have the obligation to do at each election, and vote for candidates who are committed to protect the unborn.

Because a prophetic stance calls people to change and to repent of sin, the prophet will often be rejected, "without honor...in his native place and among his own kin and in his own house" (Gospel). It is easy to think that this rejection means that we need to go back to the drawing board or perhaps hire a public relations firm to refine our message. But in fact, it doesn't mean that at all. We are called to be faithful, as Mother Teresa noted, whether or not we are successful. "They shall know that a prophet has been among them" (first reading).

Paul learned to be "content with weaknesses, insults, hardships, persecutions, and constraints for the sake of Christ." Some people take this passage to refer only to moral weaknesses. But Paul also means persecutions and insults—the very things that we try too hard to avoid.

. . . .
Fifteenth Sunday of Ordinary Time, Year B

Readings: Amos 7:12–15 • Ephesians 1:3–14 or 1:3–10 • Mark 6:7–13

The apostles "preached repentance," as the Church is called to do today. This is a key aspect of being a prophet. Prophecy is not so much about telling the future as it is about telling the present, pointing out to God's people how they have to change in order to be faithful to him today. Amos did that, and the first reading shows that he was not always well received.

A key aspect of repentance in our present circumstances is suggested by the second reading, which is all about God's choice. He chose us in Christ before the world began. That in itself is a subject for profound reflection. Before anything ever existed, before the first event that any history book relates, we were already chosen to exist, to believe, and to be holy. God knew us, wanted us, and loved us.

God's choice is primary; human choice is secondary. "It was not you who chose me," Jesus teaches elsewhere, "but I who chose you" (John 15:16). "In this is love: not that we have loved God, but that he loved us and sent his Son as an expiation for our sins" (1 John 4:10). Since God chose each human person to exist, no human can choose for that person to not exist.

The pro-choice mentality puts human choice above God's; it is directly contrary to the lesson of these readings. Pro-choice essentially says that we have responsibility only to those lives for which we choose to have responsibility. Scripture teaches, on the other hand, that we have responsibility for those God gives us. We have the duty to take that preexisting responsibility into account in all the decisions we make. Here lies a matter of repentance, for each of us personally and for our culture.

· · · · · · · · · · ·
Sixteenth Sunday of Ordinary Time, Year B

Readings: Jeremiah 23:1–6 • Ephesians 2:13–18 • Mark 6:30–34

The first reading and the Gospel passage echo the theme of God as our Shepherd. The second reading shows how Christ shepherds us—through the reconciliation achieved in his blood. He shepherds us not simply by teaching us but by destroying the very power of death.

The Church's pro-life efforts fit firmly within this context. They are aspects of the reconciliation of the world with God in Christ. The "enmity" of which St. Paul speaks has many dimensions. In its widest spiritual sense, it includes the enmity that all sin places between us and God and between us and one another.

The exaltation of individual choice above our responsibilities to others, especially our children, creates a destructive enmity. The peace that Christ gives is not something to be received only in an internal, spiritual way but a reality that transforms relationships, cultures, and nations. That peace demands respect for life and a rejection of the enmity that constitutes the culture of death.

· · · · · · · · · · ·
Seventeenth Sunday of Ordinary Time, Year B

Readings: 2 Kings 4:42–44 • Ephesians 4:1–6 • John 6:1–15

The signs that God offers in the Old and New Testaments of his ability to multiply food in miraculous ways are really messages to us about his dominion over life. Today's first reading and Gospel offer two examples. The second reading echoes this theme. God is the "one God and Father of all, who is over all and through all and in all."

Along with the theme of God's dominion, we see the theme of human solidarity. The crowd that had to be fed were united in their need. Moreover, even the miraculous solution to their need was fulfilled with the active collaboration of the boy who gave of the little he had.

The Church's witness to the sanctity of life is rooted in these two themes— God's dominion over life and human solidarity. The God who made us entrusted us to the care of one another. No human choice can trample his decision that another human should live. Nor can anyone deny the solemn duty we have to care for each other rather than destroy each other.

· · · · · · · · · · ·

Eighteenth Sunday of Ordinary Time, Year B

Readings: Exodus 16:2–4, 12–15 • Ephesians 4:17, 20–24 • John 6:24–35

Human hunger is deeper than physical hunger. The readings today point to Christ as the Bread of Life. The manna prefigures this (first reading), and Christ continues to provide our "daily bread" in the Eucharist.

In his encyclical *Caritas in Veritate*, Pope Benedict XVI states, "Development must include not just material growth but also spiritual growth."[82] Today's readings help us to focus on both realities and on the relationship between the two.

Moreover, these readings point out that the spiritual growth we acquire in Christ, the Bread of Life, impels us to take on a whole new way of life. It is a way that generously affirms life and firmly rejects the culture of death.

Embracing life, particularly amid economic difficulties, requires the kind of trust in God and human solidarity experienced by the Israelites on their journey in the desert. It requires the kind of trust, furthermore, that the promises of Christ in today's Gospel inspire. Drawing again from the encyclical *Caritas in Veritate*, we find this summary of these truths:

Development needs Christians with their arms raised towards God in prayer, Christians moved by the knowledge that truth-filled love, *caritas in veritate*, from which authentic development proceeds, is not produced by us, but given to us. For this reason, even in the most difficult and complex times, besides recognizing what is happening, we must above all else turn to God's love. Development requires attention to the spiritual life, a serious consideration of the experiences of trust in God, spiritual fellowship in Christ, reliance upon God's providence and mercy, love and forgiveness, self-denial, acceptance of others, justice and peace. All this is essential if "hearts of stone" are to be transformed into "hearts of flesh" (Ezekiel 36:26), rendering life on earth "divine" and thus more worthy of humanity. All this is of *man*, because man is the subject of his own existence; and at the same time it is of *God*, because God is at the beginning and end of all that is good, all that leads to salvation: "the world or life or death or the present or the future, all are yours; and you are Christ's; and Christ is God's" (1 Corinthians 3:22–23). Christians long for the entire human family to call upon God as "Our Father!" In union with the only-begotten Son, may all people learn to pray to the Father and to ask him, in the words that Jesus himself taught us, for the grace to glorify him by living according to his will, to receive the daily bread that we need, to be understanding and generous towards our debtors, not to be tempted beyond our limits, and to be delivered from evil (see Matthew 6:9–13).[83]

· · · · · · · · · ·
Nineteenth Sunday of Ordinary Time, Year B

Readings: 1 Kings 19:4–8 • Ephesians 4:30–5:2 • John 6:41–51

Elijah was fed on his journey to Horeb; the Israelites were fed on their journey to the Promised Land; we are fed on our journey to heaven. In all three cases, God does the feeding. We also see that in all three cases, God's children complain when they face the struggles of the journey. The greatest temptation is to fail to trust God—and a failure to trust is what often leads to the devastating results we see in the culture of death.

In their desert journey (see Exodus 15–17), the sin of the Israelites was to grumble in distrust. Their lack of trust, in fact, was the reason they had to wander for forty years instead of going directly on a journey that could have taken a few weeks. Even when God fed them with manna, they continued to grumble, tired of the same food every day. Some even wanted to go back to Egypt. Slavery seemed less challenging. At least in Egypt they knew what to expect.

The Gospel passage from John 6 is like a replay of that desert grumbling. "The Jews murmured about [Jesus]," John says—just as their ancestors had murmured about the manna. We grumble too about the difficulties of the journey. Paul's admonitions in today's second reading were not just for the Ephesians. They sound familiar to us today!

But Paul also gives the answer: "Be imitators of God…and live in love, as Christ loved us and handed himself over for us as a sacrificial offering." The Gospel passage shows how Christ hands himself over to us—in the flesh, on the cross, in the Eucharist—that we may have life. We are to imitate the mysteries we celebrate at the altar. The Eucharist teaches us how to live. The food we receive gives us strength for a journey in which we can give ourselves away.

Some people may grumble about having to sacrifice, but we see sacrifice as a life-giving gift. Some may grumble because things get in the way of their plans for life, but we pray for God to give us "our daily bread." God is already in our future. Yes, we must plan certain things, but we must trust even more. The more we trust, and the more we sacrifice, the more life we will give.

· · · · · · · · · · ·
Twentieth Sunday of Ordinary Time, Year B
· ·

Readings: Proverbs 9:1–6 • Ephesians 5:15–20 • John 6:51–58

The focus of this Sunday's Gospel passage provides an opportunity to preach on any of the numerous connections between our Eucharistic faith and our pro-life commitment. The flesh of Christ as our food reminds us of some of Jesus's earlier words to his disciples, that his food was to do the will of the Father (see John 4:34). Now, two chapters later, he tells us that our food is his body and blood, which give us life just as the Father gives him life. It follows that our participation in the Eucharist is geared toward our doing the will of Christ.

The Eucharist is indeed the very sacrifice and sacrament of life. For through his sacrifice, Christ destroys our death and restores our life, and in the Eucharistic banquet, he gives us the Bread of Life. This unites us all with him and with one another. Such life and unity are the exact opposite of abortion, which divides, scatters, and kills.

The Eucharist teaches us the meaning of love, of which abortion is the exact opposite. Love says, "I sacrifice myself for the good of the other person." Abortion says, "I sacrifice the other person for the good of myself."

The very same words that the Lord uses to teach us the meaning of love are also used by those who promote abortion: "This is my body." These four little words are spoken from opposite ends of the universe, with totally opposite results. Abortion supporters cling to their own bodies and allow others to die. Christ says, "This is my body given up for you; this is my blood shed for you." These are the words of sacrifice; these are the words of love.

Paul urges us in the second reading, "Try to understand what is the will of the Lord," and he gives us some concrete examples: "Be filled with the Spirit, addressing one another in psalms and hymns and spiritual songs, singing and playing to the Lord in your hearts, giving thanks always and for everything." Our defense of life is one major aspect of our union with the will of God.

. . . .

Twenty-First Sunday of Ordinary Time, Year B

. . . .

Readings: Joshua 24:1–2a, 15–17, 18b • Ephesians 5:21–32 or 5:2a, 25–32
John 6:60–69

The apostles "have come to believe and are convinced" that Jesus is the "Holy One" of God. Even if they don't understand his words about eating his flesh and drinking his blood, they know he is trustworthy (Gospel).

There is, indeed, no evidence here that Jesus's words made any more sense to Peter and the other apostles than they did to the people who turned away. But as St. Thomas Aquinas would write centuries later in the hymn *Adoro Te Devote,*

> What God's Son has told me, take for truth I do.
> Truth himself speaks truly, or there's nothing true.

Faith is not blind. It begins with motives of credibility. In other words, we have solid reasons for believing the one we believe. We don't trust everyone who comes along and says he has a message from God. But once we have solid reasons for believing, we trust that person to lead us to knowledge that reason alone could never reach.

The Church, moreover, does not reject freedom of choice, properly understood. God demands that we "decide today whom we will serve," as Joshua told the people (first reading) and as the hearers of Jesus did. Yet our choices have corollaries and consequences.

Choosing God, in fact, means choosing life. Pope Benedict told the Roman clergy on March 2, 2006:

Choosing life, taking the option for life…means first and foremost choosing the option of a relationship with God. However, the question immediately arises: with which God? Here, once again, the Gospel helps us: with the God who showed us his face in Christ, the God who overcame hatred on the Cross, that is, in love to the very end. Thus, by choosing this God, we choose life.[84]

We choose again in the Eucharist. Coming to Communion, we renew our fundamental choice to serve God, to believe Christ, to live as the Church teaches. The Church does not propose maybes to us but certainties, by which we then find the strength to do what Paul describes in the second reading: to give ourselves for each other.

Paul speaks of a mutual subordination and the self-giving love of husband and wife. The Church by no means degrades women but rather sees them as symbols of the Church herself, the bride of Christ. All members of the Church are called to the self-giving love that Christ lived.

. . . .
Twenty-Second Sunday of Ordinary Time, Year B
. . . .

Readings: Deuteronomy 4:1–2, 6–8 • James 1:17–18, 21b–22, 27
Mark 7:1–8, 14–15, 21–23

The culture of life will come about when we practice the "religion that is pure and undefiled before God and the Father" (second reading). "To care for orphans and widows in their affliction" is what the pro-life movement does (second reading). The unborn child is the most orphaned of all when he or she is scheduled for an abortion. The mothers of these children may not be widowed in the sense that their husbands have died, but very often the father of the child is absent. Or he may be the one pressuring the mother to abort.

The Gospel passage makes it clear that the building of the culture of life comes "from within," just as the death-producing ways of thinking that guide the culture of death do. The culture is shaped by external factors, including law, and such factors can powerfully shape the heart. Yet from within the depth of the heart will spring our readiness to give life, welcome life, and defend life.

· · · · · · · · · · ·
Twenty-Third Sunday of Ordinary Time, Year B
· ·

Readings: Isaiah 35:4–7a • James 2:1–5 • Mark 7:31–37

The readings of today bring us to the heart of two key principles of our faith that undergird our pro-life commitment to defend the unborn and all the marginalized.

The first is that of "integral salvation." The Church does not only seek the "salvation of souls" but the salvation of the human person, body and soul. Our Lord reveals this integral salvation through his healing of the deaf (Gospel reading), as was foretold by the prophet (first reading).

This commitment to integral salvation includes human relationships and institutions. This is made very clear in the *Compendium of the Social Doctrine of the Catholic Church*, promulgated by the Pontifical Council for Justice and Peace in 2004.[85] Defending human rights, and creating a just social order in which those rights are protected, is at the heart of the Church's mission. It is not some kind of political add-on to that mission. Stopping the dismemberment of children is part of promoting integral salvation.

The second principle is that of nondiscrimination, which the second reading brings into clear light. "Show no partiality," James tells those who "adhere to the faith in our glorious Lord Jesus Christ." Today the legal status of the unborn in America is different from that of any other group of people. This is because *Roe v. Wade* said, "[T]he word 'person' as used in the Fourteenth Amendment does not include the unborn."[86] This is essentially a policy of exclusion and marginalization. Such a stance has no room in a Christian heart or a Christian society.

. . . .
Twenty-Fourth Sunday of Ordinary Time, Year B
. . . .

Readings: Isaiah 50:5–9a • James 2:14–18 • Mark 8:27–35

You are thinking not as God does, but as human beings do.

This Gospel rebuke of Jesus to Peter applies to us all.

Perhaps we think that to be successful in our efforts to win people over to the Gospel and the pro-life message, we have to be popular. This is a human way of thinking. It does not give room to the role of the cross in the plan God has for us. The fact is that people are converted by the truth of the message and by the integrity and faithfulness with which we convey that message, even in the face of opposition. People are ultimately inspired not by crowd pleasers but by God pleasers.

Jesus, of course, gives the primary example of this. The fact that some people thought he was John the Baptist or Elijah or one of the other prophets gives us a good insight into what he was like. These men were tough preachers, proclaiming hard truths and inviting all kinds of opposition and persecution. A homily on this Gospel might well go back to some of the preaching of these men to illustrate this point.

Success does not require popularity; rather, it requires fidelity. This is a particularly valuable lesson in relation to our efforts to proclaim the sanctity of human life in the face of abortion. People who attack the messenger are nevertheless impacted by the message. That's the very reason they attack.

The second reading illustrates the goal of our efforts. It is not to simply bring people to believe in the sanctity of life but to have them practice it, "to demonstrate faith to you from my works." All are called to respond concretely to the needs of the people we proclaim as sacred. The hungry must be fed, not just spoken about with sympathy. The unborn must be saved from the violence of abortion, not just mentioned in our prayers. Whether one is a candidate for public office or a Christian in the pew, just believing in the right to life is not enough. The pertinent question is "What will you do to protect that right?"

. . . .
Twenty-Fifth Sunday of Ordinary Time, Year B
. . . .

Readings: Wisdom 2:12, 17–20 • James 3:16–4:3 • Mark 9:30–37

Receiving the child is tantamount to receiving God, the Gospel of this weekend tells us. This is why Pope St. John Paul II could write in the *Gospel of Life*, "Whoever attacks human life, in some way attacks God himself," and, "Rejection of human life, in whatever form that rejection takes, is really a rejection of Christ."[87]

Jesus places this teaching in the context of humble service to others. He gives this lesson in the wider context of his impending passion, death, and resurrection. In other words, at the heart of the Christian life is the paschal mystery. That is what brings salvation and changes us. It changes us precisely into people who have the power to love by giving ourselves away.

The dynamic of giving ourselves away in humble service is the self-emptying of which St. Paul writes to the Philippians. The Lord Jesus "emptied himself" (Philippians 2:7). The link with today's Gospel is that self-emptying is exactly what is needed in order to welcome one another— from the unborn to the elderly, from those who are like us to those who differ in a thousand ways.

Self-emptying frees us from the prejudice that fails to see the other as our neighbor. It frees us from the selfishness that welcomes only those whom we choose to welcome. The Christian faith demands that we accept responsibility for our neighbor based on God's choice, not ours.

This ties in with the first reading. What is described in this passage from Wisdom is essentially an abdication of personal responsibility for one's actions. Those who beset the just man say to themselves, "If God is on the just man's side, then it's God's responsibility to save him. We are off the hook. If we attack and God does not intervene, then it must be OK."

We see a reflection of this mind-set in the temptation to abortion. By claiming that "circumstances" leave no other choice than to abort a child, one is placing back on God the responsibility that we each have to empty ourselves in humble service. Let us rather imitate the Master and welcome the child.

. . . .

Twenty-Sixth Sunday of Ordinary Time, Year B

Readings: Numbers 11:25–29 • James 5:1–6 • Mark 9:38–43, 45, 47–48

The Word of God calls us to have a nonterritorial attitude. Today's first reading and Gospel passage both illustrate this. If the Lord has given us a mission, we should rejoice when we find others doing the same mission rather than have a turf war with them. This applies to ministries throughout the Church. In reference to the pro-life mission, Pope St. John Paul II addressed this point in The Gospel of Life:

> No single person or group has a monopoly on the defense and promotion of life. These are everyone's task and responsibility. On the eve of the Third Millennium, the challenge facing us is an arduous one: only the concerted efforts of all those who believe in the value of life can prevent a setback of unforeseeable consequences for civilization.[88]

Furthermore, the second part of today's Gospel passage presents one of the rationales for calling people to great sacrifice to protect and preserve life, whether of the unborn, the terminally ill and disabled, or anyone else. To directly take the life of an innocent person is the kind of offense that the Lord commands us to avoid at all costs. In the case of abortion, it may not be one's hand or eye that leads to sin but rather one's relationships.

What a young, scared, pregnant mother fears losing by choosing life is usually far less than she imagines. The boyfriend pressuring her to abort may not be the best partner for her in the long run. Parents who encourage a daughter to abort are not acting in her best interests. The lost job, lost educational opportunities, and lost friends do not compare with the loss of her child and the emotional, physical, and spiritual damages that she will sustain.

Whatever the cost for choosing life, the Lord clearly tells us the right road. "Better for you to enter into the kingdom of God with one eye than with two eyes to be thrown into Gehenna." Better for you to lose all your friends, college degrees, and promotions than to be ensnared by the culture of death.

· · · · · · · · · · ·

Twenty-Seventh Sunday of Ordinary Time, Year B

Readings: Genesis 2:18–24 • Hebrews 2:9–11 • Mark 10:2–16 or 10:2–12

The proclamation of the sanctity of life and the proclamation of the sanctity of marriage go hand in hand. The image of God in the human being is fully reflected in total self-giving in the vocation of love. This is seen in marriage as well as in celibacy for the sake of the kingdom. Those who embrace the single life are likewise called to give themselves away in loving service but to the wider community. God never calls anyone to a life for oneself.

Love gives life. Welcoming the spouse in marriage includes welcoming his or her fertility. Contraception is wrong because it compromises the totality of our self-giving to one another. "I will take only part of you, not all of you."

Love leads to life. The longer form of today's Gospel passage shows Jesus welcoming children right after his teaching on faithful marriage. Faithfulness and fruitfulness are key characteristics of marriage. This forms the basis of the family, which is thereby the sanctuary of life. There is no family without life; there is no life without family.

. . . .
Twenty-Eighth Sunday of Ordinary Time, Year B
. . . .

Readings: Wisdom 7:7–11 • Hebrews 4:12–13 • Mark 10:17–30 or 10:17–27

The manifold demands and activities of life can often obscure our understanding of what is most important. As the second reading indicates, the Word of God cuts through the fog and enables us to discern clearly what matters most.

The gift of wisdom, to which the first reading refers, is actually Christ himself. He is the Word, the Wisdom, the perfect image of the Father, the ultimate desire of our hearts. He himself is the kingdom of God, the one possession above all our possessions. Both the first reading and the Gospel point us to him and urge us to desire him and to value our relationship with him above all things.

That relationship, that possession of the kingdom that comes by following him, depends concretely on our keeping the commandments. It is no accident that the first commandment Jesus mentions in this Gospel passage is "You shall not kill." The man asks how to possess God. Perhaps he imagined that Jesus was going to give some spiritual answer upon which he could then go home and meditate. But Jesus anchored the demands of spirituality to earth, asking him what he was doing and what he intended to do in relationship to people and things around him.

Our relationship with God, Jesus teaches, rises and falls with our relationship to others—people we can see, hear, and touch. And the first demand of those right relationships is that we not kill the other!

As the passage progresses, it becomes clear that "You shall not kill" is the prerequisite, not the fulfillment, of perfect love. Love demands that we seek the least, the poorest. "Give to the poor" and "Follow me" come in the same breath, because discipleship demands not that we own nothing but that we give of ourselves for the other.

Here then is revealed the wisdom of being pro-life. We can never cling to what we possess—material goods, career, reputation, and friendship—at the expense of ruining our relationship with God. If we fail to serve the least, the most vulnerable human beings—if we instead kill them or tolerate their killing—then everything else we have is false security and false joy.

. . . .
Twenty-Ninth Sunday of Ordinary Time, Year B

Readings: Isaiah 53:10–11 • Hebrews 4:14–16 • Mark 10:35–45 or 10:42–45

"Whoever wishes to be great among you will be your servant" (Gospel). In the kingdom of God, and therefore in the culture of life, even those in authority recognize that their subjects are their brothers and sisters. Distinction in role does not imply an inequality in dignity. The smallest, the weakest, the most insignificant in the eyes of the world are nonetheless persons worthy of honor, respect, protection, and service. That is because in the kingdom of God, the smallest human person still belongs to the King.

In a culture of life, therefore, government officials and candidates would never imagine that they have the authority to declare some human beings to be nonpersons. They would never contend that some people are outside the protections of the law, as *Roe v. Wade* did in regard to children in the womb.

The second reading today provides a clear basis for this respect for the very least of our brothers and sisters. Our human nature has been taken to the heights of heaven. Jesus, the "great high priest who has passed through the heavens," while remaining divine also shares our human nature—the nature common to every person, born and unborn. He has taken this human nature to the heights of heaven, where he continues to intercede for us.

Human life, sacred at its creation, becomes all the more sacred as Christ the High Priest takes it to the very throne of the Father. We who acknowledge this cannot sit idly by while human life is thrown in the garbage.

· · · · · · · · · · ·

Thirtieth Sunday of Ordinary Time, Year B

Readings: Jeremiah 31:7–9 • Hebrews 5:1–6 • Mark 10:46–52

The Gospel passage today epitomizes a key aspect of the Church's teachings on social justice, namely, our preferential option for the poor. A "sizable crowd" was passing by, and the center of attention was Jesus. People paid no attention to the blind man by the side of the road, till his cries proved a nuisance. Then they tried to silence him.

Bartimaeus symbolizes the marginalized of our society, the inconvenient and burdensome—in short, the unwanted. Crowds pass them by every day and don't even want to think about them.

Jesus, however, did not heed the crowd. He paid attention to the man at the margins. He called Bartimaeus and healed him.

As we promote a culture of life, there are some who want to silence even further the already silent screams of the unborn, who constitute the most marginalized and oppressed segment of humanity today. Yet as a Church, we are called to give "urgent attention and priority" to these children.[89] We are called to embody the response of Christ, ignoring the rebukes of the politically correct segments of our society and identifying ourselves with the man at the margins.

Not only is this an imitation of Christ, but it is a fulfillment in our day of the prophecy of Jeremiah that we hear in the first reading. God's promise regarding his scattered and oppressed people is "I will gather them." That's what the pro-life effort of the Church does: It gathers together those who were scattered by the legal fiction that their lives were not equal to those of others. It restores protection to those who would otherwise be scattered by the physical violence of abortion.

. . . .

Thirty-First Sunday of Ordinary Time, Year B

Readings: Deuteronomy 6:2–6 • Hebrews 7:23–28 • Mark 12:28–34

In the Gospel reading today, Christ puts the second commandment together with the first: "There is no other commandment greater than these." The close relationship between these two commandments is discussed at length in the First Letter of John. He makes it clear that the failure to love the neighbor we see, to attend to his needs, makes it impossible to love the God we do not see (1 John 4:20).

These two closely related commandments provide the impetus of the Church's efforts to defend the unborn and the vulnerable. Because we love God with all our mind, heart, soul, and strength, we cannot place our own plans and choices above his choice. And he has chosen to create human life and entrust it to our care.

Moreover, piety is never meant to turn us in on ourselves but rather to make us more attentive and responsive to the needs of the vulnerable. We love our neighbor—including our unborn neighbor—like ourselves, which means that we recognize the unborn as people like ourselves. Some say the unborn are too small or too unlike us in their characteristics to be considered a neighbor, a person. But the second commandment requires that we see every human being as a neighbor like ourselves and therefore love him or her. This demand of love is greater than any other commandment.

We may be tempted to excuse ourselves from the duty to intervene for the unborn because of other duties we have. We have legal concerns, often exaggerated. We shrink back because of concern for our human respect. We are afraid to part with certain possessions, relationships, guarantees of security. And sometimes those to whom we must answer tell us to tone it down regarding our outspoken defense of the unborn.

But "there is no greater commandment than these." We are to love our unborn neighbor just as we love our born neighbor, without reserve.

. . . .

Thirty-Second Sunday of Ordinary Time, Year B

Readings: 1 Kings 17:10–16 • Hebrews 9:24–28
Mark 12:38–44 or 12:41–44

Today's readings bring us a tale of two widows, both of whom gave when they had every human reason not to. The widow in the first reading prepared something for Elijah although she didn't have enough for herself and her son. The widow in the Gospel passage gave all her savings to God's temple. The Lord's prophet reassured the first widow; the Lord himself praised the second.

We, the Church, are not widowed. The Bridegroom is with us, and it is from him that we draw the courage to be generous—not just with food and money but with our witness to the Gospel and our efforts to build a world of justice and a culture of life.

Some Catholics may feel that they have enough business to mind with their own lives. They don't want to get involved in the lives of others. "I have enough problems of my own," expresses the common temptation. They barely have enough energy and attention for those problems, let alone the problems of others.

This is precisely where the lesson of the widow's might comes in. The human heart expands when it touches God. It expands to take in the needs, the business, of every vulnerable human being. We no longer measure our giving by how much *we have*; we measure it by how much *the other needs*. Then, like the miracle that surprised the widow whom Elijah visited, we find our capacity for love and concern greater than we imagined.

The demands of justice require that we measure our risk not by potential personal loss but against what the victim of injustice stands to lose. In fighting for the unborn, we defend those who risk losing their very lives— and therefore all the goods and rights they might possess in life. What we risk for defending them is little to nothing in comparison.

The tales of these two widows reflect Jesus's fundamental teaching: "No one has greater love than this, to lay down one's life for one's friends" (John 15:13).

. . . .

Thirty-Third Sunday of Ordinary Time, Year B

Readings: Daniel 12:1–3 • Hebrews 10:11–14, 18 • Mark 13:24–32

We have arrived at a time of the Church year when the readings speak of the Second Coming of Christ. This is a theme, of course, that is echoed in every Mass: "We proclaim your death…until you come again."[90] "We await the blessed hope and the coming of our Savior, Jesus Christ."[91] "As we look forward to his second coming, we offer you in thanksgiving this holy and living sacrifice."[92]

In some Gospel passages, the teaching about the effects of Christ's passion, death, and resurrection is interspersed with teaching about his second coming. These are two critical moments of salvation history: In the one, the power of sin and death are overthrown at their roots; in the other, the victory is brought to its culmination and full manifestation. Both of these moments are described with apocalyptic language and imagery from Old Testament passages, such as those of today's first reading from Daniel.

What is being conveyed here is the destruction of one kingdom and the inauguration of another. This, of course, is what Christ came to accomplish. His kingdom is among us, thanks to his death and resurrection, made present again to us in every Mass. That kingdom, the liturgy tells us, is "a kingdom of truth and life, a kingdom of holiness and grace, a kingdom of justice, love, and peace."[93]

We live now in the in-between time, when the kingdom of Christ has been inaugurated on earth but not yet brought to its full manifestation. The power of sin and death—revealed in evils such as abortion—has been destroyed at its roots. Yet we still struggle, in and through Christ, to bring about a culture of life. We must bear witness to the truth, life, holiness, grace, justice, love, and peace that characterize the kingdom.

The apocalyptic language of the readings should inspire in us both the awareness of how awesome a struggle this is and confidence in the final victory—a victory marked by the triumph of life. "Many of those who sleep in the dust of the earth shall awake" (first reading). Life has the last word. "Now he waits until his enemies are made his footstool" (second reading)—and the last enemy to be destroyed will be death itself.

Mercy also has the last word, as the second reading conveys. It is a mercy that reaches even to those who have taken life by abortion.

$\cdots\cdots\cdots$

Solemnity of Christ the King
(Thirty-Fourth or Last Sunday of the Year), Year B

Readings: Daniel 7:13–14 • Revelation 1:5–8 • John 18:33b–37

I see two ways to approach the theme of the sanctity of life on the Feast of Christ the King: in the light of Christ's dominion over human life and in the light of his victory over sin and death.

Christ's kingship is his dominion. All of today's readings reflect that. The ultimate question in the debate over abortion and euthanasia is a debate about dominion. It's not so much a question of when human life begins or ends but a question of to whom it belongs.

The only answer in the light of the Word of God and the kingship of Christ is that human life belongs to God—not only because he made it, but because he redeemed it in Christ. Human life in the womb does not belong to the mother, as the late Dr. James McMahon contended.[94] This idea that some people own others was rejected long ago in the slavery debate, yet it resurfaces in the abortion debate. It flatly contradicts the kingship of Christ and the dominion he exercises over human life.

Christ is King also because he has conquered the power of evil. The Alpha and the Omega lives and reigns—before all other life came to be and after all death will be destroyed (second reading). He holds the keys of death and has robbed it of its power. In the light of that victory, we who work to build the culture of life proclaim a kingdom that has already been established in place of the kingdom of death.

The vanquished kingdom of death still sends its echoes throughout the land—through evils like abortion. But it does not have the final word. Christ has already accomplished delivery from its power. We simply have to announce that victory and apply it through the many facets of the ministry of the Church and the pro-life movement.

This kingship over evil manifests itself in us when, despite powerful temptations (such as those that afflict a person tempted to abort a child), we choose what is right and good. We always have the power to choose life, no matter what the circumstances.

Ordinary Time, Year C

Ordinary time begins after the Feast of the Baptism of the Lord, at the end of the Christmas season.

. . . .
Second Sunday of Ordinary Time, Year C

Readings: Isaiah 62:1–5 • 1 Corinthians 12:4–11 • John 2:1–11

The wedding at Cana is not just about Jesus helping a couple in need. It is about his wedding to us, fulfilling the prophecy of Isaiah in the first reading: "Your builder shall marry you." Jesus, by revealing his glory publicly and having his disciples begin to believe in him, inaugurates the marriage that will be consummated on the cross.

The fierce love that God has for human life cannot be overstated. The sanctity of human life, and the absolute obligation to defend that sanctity, likewise cannot be exaggerated. To trample human life is to trample upon God's bride.

The water becoming wine symbolizes the fact that Jesus Christ elevates human life and human love to a new kind of life and love: that which is shared within the life of the Trinity. We have human life; now in Christ we are called to partake of divine life. We experience human love; now in Christ we are called to experience divine love.

As we do so, we help one another find, manifest, and grow in that life and love. That's where the many ministries of the Church, as summarized in the second reading, come in. All of them serve human life—life that is called to divine marriage.

. . . .
Third Sunday of Ordinary Time, Year C

Readings: Nehemiah 8:2–4a, 5–6, 8–10
1 Corinthians 12:12–30 or 12:12–14, 27 • Luke 1:1–4; 4:14–21

The Gospel reading today fits perfectly with the call for protection of children living in the womb. Such advocacy is at the heart of Jesus's mission:

He has anointed me

   to bring glad tidings to the poor,

   He has sent me to proclaim liberty to captives,…

   to let the oppressed go free.

Nobody is more oppressed in our world today than the unborn child. The Spirit of the Lord, who is our Advocate in heaven, fills us and makes us advocates for these lives.

That advocacy takes numerous forms in the pro-life movement. Just as the second reading reminds us of the diversity of the one body of Christ, so is that diversity manifested in the wide variety of activities in the pro-life movement. Driven by the Spirit, who is "Father of the poor," all seek the same ultimate goal.

We are called to remind people of the extent of this tragedy of abortion. They need to know that it is our business to intervene for the victims of abortion—no less than it is our business to help the victims of crime, war, drugs, poverty, AIDS, and any other type of violence. Ours is the business of love, the business of letting the oppressed go free, for that is what God has done for us.

· · · · · · · · · · ·

Fourth Sunday of Ordinary Time, Year C

Readings: Jeremiah 1:4–5, 17–19 • 1 Corinthians 12:31–13:13 or 13:4–13
Luke 4:21–30

The lessons of today's first reading and Gospel, regarding what a prophet faces, speak to the people of life today as we confront the culture of death. We are all prophets by our baptism, and therefore we share in both the blessings and the burdens of that vocation. We are blessed in that we have and know with certainty the Word and will of God regarding the sanctity of life. The burden we have is that we must speak that Word—in fact, proclaim it—to people who may not want to hear it.

The lessons of these readings are that (1) we should expect opposition, not be surprised at it, and (2) we should not measure the success of our mission by how we are received but rather by how faithful and loving we are in carrying it out.

The prophetic stance we take on behalf of life is a stance not only of example but also of word. The good example we set must at times be explained. Blessed Pope Paul VI, in his landmark document *Evangelii Nuntiandi* (On Evangelization in the Modern World), explained that "the Good News proclaimed by the witness of life sooner or later has to be proclaimed by the word of life."[95] People need our encouragement—as well as concrete tools—to be able to explain their pro-life position.

The second reading provides the well-known lesson about the meaning of love: "Love is patient, love is kind." The pro-life movement is a movement of love. It can be summed up as a movement that objects to the fact that the unborn are excluded from the most basic requirement of love— that is, the protection of life. It is a movement that loves these children intensely in order to make up for the lack of love they receive from others. While abortion says, "I sacrifice the other for the good of myself," love says, "I sacrifice myself for the good of the other."

. . . .
Fifth Sunday of Ordinary Time, Year C

Readings: Isaiah 6:1–2a, 3–8 • 1 Corinthians 15:1–11 or 15:3–8, 11
Luke 5:1–11

The first reading and the Gospel for this weekend both show the reaction of sinful humanity in the presence of the manifestation of holiness: "Woe is me," Isaiah says. "Depart from me, Lord," Peter says, "for I am a sinful man." In the presence of God, we see with new clarity the depths of our sin, just as we can see stains on an apparently clear window when the bright rays of the sun hit it.

If we read the letters of St. Paul in the order in which they were written (which is not the order in which they appear in Scripture), we can see that Paul displays an increasing awareness of his sinfulness as life goes on. "Paul…apostle of Christ Jesus," he begins his First Letter to the Corinthians. Later he refers to himself as "apostle and servant." In today's reading, he declares himself "the least of the apostles." And later, he calls himself "the foremost" of sinners (1 Timothy 1:15).

Yet faced with the holiness of God (in Isaiah's case, God's glory in the temple, and in Peter's case, God's glory in Christ), humanity is not crushed. Rather it receives the invitation to be purged, renewed, and sent. Isaiah was cleansed of sin and then responded to the call to be a prophet. Peter was told to put his fears aside, and he "left everything and followed" the Lord.

This provides a perfect spiritual context for the call to be pro-life and to build the culture of life. Contrary to what some of our critics say, we in the Church are not self-righteous people who think we are better than everyone else and want to tell others how to live. Rather, we begin with repentance, realizing that we can recognize the sins in the world only after we've recognized our own. When we call others to a standard of morality, we acknowledge that same standard for ourselves. When we call others to repent of sins that destroy life, we answer to a God who made us all, whose choices have priority over ours.

Throughout the country are pro-life people who counsel women against abortion. They approach these women not as strangers. Rather, these pro-life counselors know what it is to struggle with evil and to be drawn by temptation. They minister as repentant sinners, quite familiar with the struggle against evil.

Likewise, many Catholics pray the rosary in front of abortion clinics, not to harass or intimidate women but as an act of repentance. As they stand on the public sidewalk, they do not say "pray for those sinners" but rather, over and over, "pray for *us* sinners." From that stance of repentance, they can reach out to those who are on their way to a terrible mistake. By speaking up and reaching out in love to prevent abortion, these faithful people try to make up in some way for the silence and fear that keep others from doing their part to save lives.

Pro-life activity flows from humble repentance. When we help people realize that, we lay a foundation for calling them to be prophets of life, like Isaiah, and apostles of life, like Peter.

· · · · · · · · · · ·
Sixth Sunday of Ordinary Time, Year C

Readings: Jeremiah 17:5–8 • 1 Corinthians 15:12, 16–20 • Luke 6:17, 20–26

Abortion is not only a sin against life; it is a sin against hope. According to the abortion mind-set, we should trust our own (or other people's) evaluations of the problems that surround us and decide whether the world is hospitable enough for a child to be welcomed into it. The pro-life movement focuses instead on inspiring the hope that brings the courage to say yes to life. The first reading, with its exhortation to hope in the Lord, speaks right to the heart of the culture of life.

This hope is based on what the second reading identifies as the foundation of our faith: Christ is indeed raised from the dead. The evils we fight, like abortion, are ultimately defeated at their root, because the kingdom of death has already been overturned.

These truths of the first and second readings provide the basis for the Beatitudes that Jesus gives us in today's Gospel. Each bears witness to the pro-life task of the Church:

"Blessed are you who are poor." Biblically, the poor are those who have no help but God. They are not simply the materially disadvantaged but rather those who are marginalized by society. The children living in the womb are truly the poorest of the poor. They are the only group of people in our society whose very right to live is formally and explicitly denied by public policy. The Church's preferential option for the poor requires that we give them priority.

"Blessed are you who are now hungry." We are hungry for justice to be established. The unborn are hungry for recognition of their most basic rights.

"Blessed are you who are now weeping." If we are to be builders of the culture of life, we must first learn to weep over the culture of death. The evil of abortion must break our hearts. Only then will our hearts be open to receive the grace and strength to witness and battle against this evil.

"Blessed are you when people hate you." Few movements can give as direct an experience of this particular beatitude as the pro-life movement. Many people in the world today see defenders of the unborn as threats to human rights! They deem us enemies of women's rights and health and opponents of freedom. Let us remember that Jesus calls us blessed when we suffer such insult "on account of the Son of Man." Let us "rejoice and leap for joy" as we serve him through our pro-life efforts.

. . . .

Seventh Sunday of Ordinary Time, Year C

Readings: 1 Samuel 26:2, 7–9, 12–13,22–23 • 1 Corinthians 15:45–49
Luke 6:27–38

> If you love those who love you, what credit is that to you?… If you
> do good to those who do good to you, what credit is that to you?…
> Lend expecting nothing back.… Be merciful, just as your Father
> is merciful.

This Gospel passage calls us to a high standard of love, set by the example of God himself. It is particularly appropriate to draw out the application of this standard for the pro-life efforts of God's people. In striving to restore protection to the most vulnerable members of our society—the unborn and those whose illnesses have rendered them incapable of response—we in fact love those who cannot love us back. We do good to those who cannot do good in return. This is a love free of the ulterior motive of getting something in return.

Nor is that love judgmental. "Stop judging and you will not be judged." Here is an opportunity to clarify this much abused quote of Jesus. Some try to use it to defend relativism. They want it to mean, "Don't judge anyone for what they do, because you really don't know if it's right or wrong. You have your standards, and they have theirs. Who are you to say what pleases God?"

Of course, we would not be able to say what pleases God were it not for the fact that he has told us. Speaking both through reason and his revealed word, God has given us the ability to know right from wrong. In that sense, we can and must judge the difference. If we were not able to judge between right and wrong, then neither could we say, "Do not judge," for that is itself a judgment.

We can and must judge abortion to be always wrong. Killing a baby is as wrong as killing a person who is walking down the street. We can never claim ignorance here. The violence committed is never morally tolerable for the children of God.

What we cannot judge is the state of a person's soul or the motives of the heart. We do not condemn the person who kills; rather we call the person to conversion. And we are merciful, as our Father is merciful.

· · · · · · · · · · ·
Eighth Sunday of Ordinary Time, Year C
· ·

Readings: Sirach 27:4–7 • 1 Corinthians 15:54–58 • Luke 6:39–45

Building the culture of life, which is the irrevocable and fundamental commitment of the Church, is a matter of proclaiming, in word and deed, the victory that Christ has already won and applying that victory to every sector of society. "Death is swallowed up in victory," the second reading declares. That is the starting point for the Church and the pro-life movement. If death is swallowed up in victory, then so is abortion. We proclaim the victory of life, and we work to defend life from the destructive effects of the kingdom of death.

We do so not only in action but also in speech. The first reading and the Gospel shows the power of words. Words reveal the heart of a person, and they have a profound impact on others. In the culture of life, we respect and exalt life in the way that we speak about it. Our words reflect the union of our hearts with the children and with the weak and defenseless. Ours is a language of affirmation.

When people are oppressed, the oppressor uses language of degradation, of dehumanization. Thus abortion providers refer to the unborn as "tissue," "parasites," "waste," and other degrading things. But the unborn are truly our brothers and sisters, creatures of God, equal in human rights and dignity. They are blessings entrusted to us. Our language, revealing our hearts, must reflect this day by day and thereby help to change the world.

· · · · · · · · · · ·
Ninth Sunday of Ordinary Time, Year C
· ·

Readings: 1 Kings 8:41–43 • Galatians 1:1–2, 6–10 • Luke 7:1–10

Paul passionately declares in the second reading that there is and can be no other Gospel than the one that has been handed on to us. The God of all the universe gives this Gospel to us, and it is the last, best offer he has to all of humanity, without exception.

Universality marks the Church's mission of evangelization, as the first reading and the Gospel indicate. Solomon prayed "that all the peoples of the earth may know your name." And Jesus healed the slave of the Roman centurion, whose faith "amazed" him. Nobody is to be excluded from the offer of salvation in Christ.

This universality on the supernatural level is rooted in a universality in the order of nature. Even before being incorporated into Christ by faith and baptism, we share a common human nature. We are already brothers and sisters on the natural level.

It is on that basis that the Church reaches out to all humanity with the urgent plea to protect life. The pro-life mission of the Church reaches to this natural level, this common basis, which the further announcement of the Gospel presupposes. The urgent task of protecting life can never be separated from the Church's mission of evangelization and catechesis.

. . . .
Tenth Sunday of Ordinary Time, Year C
. . . .

Readings: 1 Kings 17:17–24 • Galatians 1:11–19 • Luke 7:11–17

Both the first reading and the Gospel speak to us today about a mother with no husband who loses her son. Then a man of God—in the Gospel it is Jesus, the Son of God—gives the child back to his mother, alive. In both cases, this victory of life over death for a woman's child is a sign of God's favor. God is in the business of destroying death and restoring life. In the end, he will do this for us all.

A key aspect of the mission of the Church—and of each member of the people of God—is that we be a sign of God's preference for life over death, a sign of the power of life over death. We cannot raise the dead as Elijah and

Jesus did, but we can save children from death through our involvement in the pro-life movement. The witness, the words, and the compassionate intervention of the Church bring to pass each day the words of today's psalm, "You preserved me from among those going down into the pit" (Psalm 30), and the words of the Gospel, "Jesus gave him to his mother."

A further application of this theme is in the arena of healing after abortion. Each day, through ministries like Rachel's Vineyard, parents who have lost children to abortion experience Jesus's return of those sons and daughters to them. They are led, by the Word of God and the sacraments, to life-giving repentance, to reclaimed responsibility for their children, and to the hope that they and their children are in the hands of God and will be reunited one day. Today's readings give us the opportunity to call people to healing and to a witness of life, mercy, and hope.

. . . .

Eleventh Sunday of Ordinary Time, Year C

Readings: 2 Samuel 12:7-10, 13 • Galatians 2:16, 19-21
Luke 7:36-8:3 or 7:36-50

"I live, no longer I, but Christ lives in me." This bold declaration in the second reading today indicates the foundation of the pro-life convictions of the Church: We belong to God. This statement from Galatians 2 parallels that in 1 Corinthians 6:19: "You are not your own." At issue in the pro-life struggle is not simply the question "When does life begin?" It is rather the question "To whom does life belong?"

The fact that each human life belongs to God is what we mean when we say that life is sacred. No other human being may own or kill another life, including his own, because life belongs to God. David's killing of Uriah, referenced in the first reading, brought Nathan's condemnation, leading to the king's admission, "I have sinned against the Lord."

The awesome calling of parents is also revealed here. They are entrusted with the gift of life. This gift does not belong to them, but they cooperate with the Creator to bring it about.

"Insofar as I live in the flesh, I live by faith in the Son of God." This assertion of Paul shows us another reason why the defense of life is so fundamental to the Church. As Pope St. John Paul II wrote in *Evangelium Vitae*:

> Man is called to a fullness of life which far exceeds the dimensions of his earthly existence, because it consists in sharing the very life of God. The loftiness of this supernatural vocation reveals the greatness and the inestimable value of human life even in its temporal phase. Life in time, in fact, is the fundamental condition, the initial stage and an integral part of the entire unified process of human existence.[96]

In other words, we must defend the natural gift of human life in order that people may, with that foundation secure, take hold of life eternal.

As we proclaim the absolute demands of respect for life, we proclaim the infinite mercy of God, even toward those who have taken life. This Sunday's readings give us an opportunity to renew the Church's invitation to mothers and fathers who have participated in abortion to come to him for forgiveness and peace.

· · · · · · · · · · ·
Twelfth Sunday of Ordinary Time, Year C
· ·

Readings: Zechariah 12:10–11; 13:1 • Galatians 3:26–29 • Luke 9:18–24

"Whoever wishes to save his life will lose it." The paradox of Christianity is that life finds its most profound meaning precisely when it is given away in love for God and others.

This is at the core of the pro-life effort. We confront a culture in which many seek to find their own life by taking someone else's. The pregnant mother feels she has to choose between her life—not necessarily in a physical sense but in a psychological sense—and the life of her baby. But the Lord says that those who seek to save their life will lose it, and we find our life precisely by putting the other person's life first. To deny ourselves and take up our cross brings us to the essence of life, which is to give and receive love.

The pro-life movement, in urging this dynamic, breaks down false barriers, just as Paul indicates in the second reading: "Neither slave nor free person...all one in Christ." Jesus did the same, showing his love for the outcast, those whom society rejected. All are equal. No person can enslave, own, or devalue another. No one can declare another to be a nonperson or beyond the protection of law. We come to set the slave free, to set the unborn free, to proclaim all human beings as equals.

· · · · · · · · · · ·
Thirteenth Sunday of Ordinary Time, Year C

Readings: 1 Kings 19:16b, 19–21 • Galatians 5:1, 13–18 • Luke 9:51–62

The second reading gives us the opportunity to preach today on the relationship between freedom and the right to life.

Supporters of abortion, unwilling to describe the details of dismemberment that the abortion procedure entails, have taken refuge in more positive words like *freedom* and *choice*. Ironically, abortions do not happen because of freedom of choice but rather because some pregnant women think they have no freedom and no choice. The only solution to their predicament, they think, is to have an abortion.

To invoke freedom to justify abortion twists the very notion of freedom, in a way that today's second reading warns against. The corrective truth that Paul gives is that we are to love our neighbors as ourselves. The unborn children are our neighbors, and loving them starts with protecting them from violence.

The command to "love your neighbor as yourself" means that we are to love the other as a person like ourselves. In other words, we must recognize in the other a person the same worth, value, dignity, and rights as we have. This is precisely where the pro-choice mentality has gone wrong: It fails to see the unborn child as our neighbor. The justifications for abortion would not hold as reasons to kill a born child. "Love your neighbor as a person like yourself."

Our Declaration of Independence states that life is an "unalienable right" granted to all "by their Creator," not their government. What God gives, government cannot take away. This is the foundation of the freedom we enjoy in America. God himself grants our human rights, and "to secure these rights, governments are instituted." Preserving that freedom requires preserving the fundamental rights that are its foundation, starting with life itself.

· · · · · · · · · · ·
Fourteenth Sunday of Ordinary Time, Year C
· ·

Readings: Isaiah 66:10–14c • Galatians 6:14–18
Luke 10:1–12, 17–20 or 10:1–9

"The kingdom of God is at hand." This cry from today's Gospel is what our preaching is all about. A kingdom has already arrived, created by God and having characteristics established by God. The fact that it is among us, that it is "at hand," forces a crisis. We must decide today whether or not to join it—more accurately, whether or not to let it take hold of us. If that is our decision, then we must live accordingly.

This kingdom is described in the Church's liturgy as "a kingdom of truth and life, a kingdom of holiness and grace, a kingdom of justice, love, and peace."[97] These characteristics hold together inseparably and integrally, because they are all aspects of the one God, who is King. Today's first reading and Gospel passage summarize them with the word *peace.*

The apostles are sent to proclaim peace, just as Isaiah proclaimed it to Jerusalem. This is not a peace to construct with diplomatic, political, military, or creative skills. It is a peace from on high. The appropriate response from us is to prepare the way to receive this peace by repenting of what blocks it. And then we are to live in accordance with the demands of that peace.

Respect for everyone's right to life, beginning with the unborn from fertilization and including all the disabled and terminally ill, is absolutely essential to peace. Peace is not lost when guns are fired or bombs dropped. Rather, peace is lost as soon as the human rights of even a single individual are violated. Our neighborhoods may seem peaceful, but if an abortion clinic is operating in our midst, there is no peace because the human rights of unborn children are being violated. Moreover, anywhere in a nation where an unborn child is not protected is a place where there is not yet peace.

To pursue and preserve peace means not only that we do not participate in abortion; it means that we do not tolerate it. It means we work vigorously to restore respect and protection for every human life.

The sixth chapter of Jeremiah offers a contrast with today's first reading. During the siege of Jerusalem, some prophets spoke falsely:

> They have treated lightly
> the injury to my people.
> "Peace, peace," they say,
> though there is no peace. (Jeremiah 6:14)

So it is today. If God's people seek justice, mercy, and peace while failing to see how serious the wound of abortion is, God is not pleased. There cannot be peace in the world if there is no peace in the womb. There cannot be peace between nations if there is no peace between a mother and her own child. As Mother Teresa asked in her 1994 National Prayer Breakfast speech, "If we say that a mother can kill her own child, how can we tell people not to kill each other?"[98]

The reign of God is at hand, and it is a culture of life.

. . . .
Fifteenth Sunday of Ordinary Time, Year C
. . . .

Readings: Deuteronomy 30:10–14 • Colossians 1:15–20 • Luke 10:25–37

Today's readings provide a powerful foundation for preaching on the call of God's people to be the people of life. It is a call to take concrete action to defend the lives of the unborn.

Often people complicate the Church's pro-life teaching unnecessarily. In reality, it is simple. As Moses says in the first reading, the law of God "is not too mysterious and remote." It seems that the scholar in the Gospel was not aware of this. "What must I do to inherit eternal life?" he asked Jesus. "Love…your neighbor as yourself" was the Lord's response, but the scholar required further explanation, as perhaps many do today.

"Love your neighbor" does not have distinctions, limitations, or exclusions. It includes our unborn neighbors. And to love them "as yourself" means first to recognize them as persons like ourselves. There is no room for the pro-choice mind-set, which is ultimately just another form of prejudice, in this case directed at people still in the womb.

Both the first reading, with the exhortation, "You have only to carry it out," and the Gospel passage, with its concluding command, "Go and do likewise," call us beyond being pro-life in attitude to becoming pro-life in behavior. It is not enough for us to believe abortion is wrong; we have to intervene for those in danger of being aborted.

Jesus illustrates who our neighbors are with the story of the Good Samaritan. The priest and Levite who passed by the wounded man knew the words of Moses in today's first reading. They failed, however, to carry out those words. On the night before he was killed, Dr. Martin Luther King Jr. preached about this priest and Levite.[99] Maybe they were afraid that this was a trap, King suggested. Maybe robbers were around the next curve of this road from Jerusalem to Jericho, lying ready to attack anyone who would stop to help the victim.

The mistake that the priest and Levite made was asking, "If I stop to help this man, what will happen to me?" The Samaritan reversed the question. He asked, "If I do not stop to help this man, what will happen to him?" And so we must ask this in regard to the unborn. These are today's victims of robbers, in danger of losing their lives while many people pass along the way and do nothing. We must not calculate the risk to ourselves but think about the risk to them.

All of our pro-life activity flows from our union with Christ. The second reading today is actually a commentary on the first few words of the Bible, "In the beginning, God created…" Paul shows us that this "beginning" is Christ. He is the source and purpose of all life, of all creation. To stand with him, then, is to stand with life and against all that destroys it.

. . . .

Sixteenth Sunday of Ordinary Time, Year C

Readings: Genesis 18:1–10a • Colossians 1:24–28 • Luke 10:38–42

The first reading and the Gospel of this weekend speak to us about welcome and hospitality. In the exercise of welcoming the other, we welcome God himself. The New Testament urges us in various passages not to fail to exercise hospitality. The Letter to the Hebrews, for example, says, "Do not neglect hospitality, for through it some people have unknowingly entertained angels" (Hebrews 13:2).

Today's homily can point out that hospitality is more than just a natural virtue or an integral part of good manners. There is a hospitality that goes to the very depths of our relationship with God and our neighbor. The examples of Abraham, Sarah, Martha, and Mary point us to several key truths.

First, the only proper response to the human person is welcome, acceptance, and love. This starts with the welcome we give to our own children, born and unborn, and continues in the fabric of the family, the Church, and society, to create a communion of love and service. The attitude of welcome, the virtue of hospitality, means that we make room for the other because of the value of the other, not because of some pleasure or convenience of our own.

"Every child a wanted child" is a Planned Parenthood slogan. But as psychiatrist Dr. Philip Ney explains, it is not being "wanted" that leads to psychological health but rather being "welcomed."[100] Being wanted means meeting someone else's need or desire; being welcomed means finding room for oneself because of the dignity one possesses, independent of what is going on with anyone else.

A second truth: The opportunity to welcome the other comes at times we do not expect. We are always living in the community of the human family, and we have to be ready to respond to the needs of the other person. We are not only responsible for the people we choose and plan for. We are responsible to all human beings, simply because they are our brothers and sisters. As Pope St. John Paul II stressed in *Evangelium Vitae*, we have been entrusted to the care of one another by the Creator.

Third, the welcome and hospitality we extend to others is, by that very fact, extended to God himself. This is brought out in today's readings and in many other passages of Scripture, such as the judgment scene in Matthew 25. "Amen, I say to you, whatever you did for one of these least brothers of mine, you did for me" (Matthew 25:40).

Fourth, extending welcome can bring suffering and inconvenience. We see in the Gospel that Martha was "burdened with much serving." Such burdens are opportunities to live out what St. Paul describes in the second reading, uniting our sufferings with those of Christ.

Pro-life is the attitude of welcome; pro-choice is the attitude of rejection. The following two poems display this contrast dramatically. The first was used as a prayer at a conference of the National Abortion Federation. The second was written by a pro-life activist. Both address a child in danger of abortion.

"Prayer" at National Abortion Federation Workshop

Greetings, little one. Little sister, little brother,

Great wise ancestor.

You want to come to our house,

Maybe you think we would make good parents for you—

Well, the food is short now—

The winter was too long, and the summer too hot.

We have too many mouths to feed.

My husband works too hard already.

We cannot open our home to you now.

Try again later, little one, or find a better place.

Go in peace now, go in peace.[101]

Contrast the above with this beautiful poem, sent to me by a woman named Rose Marie.

Come Forth

Come, pass this way, unseen one.

Come, walk through the shadows of life.

I invite you, want you, need you.

Do not drop back into the unknown void.

Come forward into the bright

Sunshine, feel the softness of the snow,

See the vivid brightness of the stars.

Run over the warm hot sands

Of time, with pink chubby toes,

Reach out cherub arms, innocent

Hands to catch butterflies, fish,

Worms, puppies, whatever pleases your heart.

Grow in happiness, love, agony, despair.

Let life be kind or cruel, it matters not.

Just come forth, there is love,

Delight waiting, watching, wanting

You. Come forth, dear little heart.

Come forth.[102]

—Rose Marie, December 1979

· · · · · · · · · · ·

Seventeenth Sunday of Ordinary Time, Year C

Readings: Genesis 18:20–32 • Colossians 2:12–14 • Luke 11:1–13

Jesus told us that if we ask God for what we need, we will receive. Abraham knew this when he called on God for mercy (first reading). In the Gospel, Jesus says that the greatest good we can ask for is the Holy Spirit. The Spirit brings mercy and enables us to say, "Our Father." When we pray in that way, we are (like Abraham) calling down God's mercy on all our brothers and sisters. We are in fact defining ourselves as brothers and sisters because of the fact that we all have one Father.

This has implications. No longer can we exclude any person from our love. Love is indivisible. This is the basis of our pro-life convictions. In its broadest sense, the acknowledgment of God as Father extends to his role as Creator and affirms the responsibility we have to every human being (whether Christian or not) because he or she was made by and is loved by

God. The unborn and the terminally ill cannot be excluded from person-hood, from prayer, from protection, or from practical help.

When we ask, we receive. We should invite people to join the ongoing worldwide novena to end abortion, at PrayerCampaign.org. What we receive, furthermore, is not simply an answer to our prayer in the form of God's doing something. What we receive is a share in the heart of God. He makes us compassionate as he is, and he gives us the grace to live out that compassion as true brothers and sisters united in the Holy Spirit with one Father.

· · · · · · · · · · ·
Eighteenth Sunday of Ordinary Time, Year C

Readings: Ecclesiastes 1:2; 2:21–23 • Colossians 3:1–5, 9–11
Luke 12:13–21

"One who stores up treasure for himself but is not rich in what matters to God" Jesus refers to as a "fool" (Gospel). And what is it that matters to God?

Today's second reading answers the question that arises from today's Gospel. What matters to God is that we become like him, that we "put on the new self, which is being renewed…in the image of its creator." What matters is that we do what he does—that is, that we give ourselves away in love.

The opening prayer of today's Mass refers to God's creative action. Our life is his gift. What we have received as a gift, we must give as a gift. And through our godlike generosity, we become a source of life for others.

Seeking fulfillment in earthly possessions (the way disparaged in today's Gospel) and failing to see that all earthly things pass away (the lesson of the first reading) contribute powerfully to the culture of death. Many are tempted to take life through abortion and euthanasia because they fear that the things of earth will slip away if they are generous. Yet what matters to God is that we give ourselves away at every moment, to the unborn as well as to the born and to the weak as well as to the strong.

As the Gospel indicates, judgment can come at any moment, and so can our opportunity to give life to others. "The things you have prepared, to whom will they belong?" Let us be secure at every moment in giving ourselves away so that others may live.

· · · · · · · · · · ·

Nineteenth Sunday of Ordinary Time, Year C

Readings: Wisdom 18:6–9 • Hebrews 11:1–2, 8–19 or 11:1–2, 8–12
Luke 12:32–48 or 12:35–40

"He thought that the one who had made the promise was trustworthy." So the second reading today describes Abraham, our father in faith. God made an oath to him, that though elderly and without children, he would have "descendants as numerous as the stars in the sky and as countless as the sands on the seashore." Abraham trusted the oath and acted accordingly— not because it made sense to him but because he trusted the one who was making it. He didn't measure and analyze. The evidence he had was his faith, "the realization of what is hoped for and evidence of things not seen."

The people of Abraham likewise trusted God. The first reading tells us, "With sure knowledge of the oaths in which they put their faith.... your people awaited the salvation of the just and the destruction of their foes." What was the evidence that their foes would be destroyed? It was not any apparent weakness on the part of their enemies but rather their faith, the "evidence of things not seen." They trusted the one who did see.

We are commanded to have that same faith, now rooted in the oaths God has sworn to us through the blood of Christ. We too are to have "sure knowledge" that we will be delivered from all our foes, all that oppresses the human family, all our sins, and death itself. The culture of death, no matter how strong it seems, has no secure foundation.

God swore an oath to Abraham; he swore an oath to us in Christ. He sets us free from error, sin, and death through the cross and resurrection of Christ—a cross and resurrection in which we share. Every one of the sacraments, in fact, is an oath (which is what the word *sacramentum* means).

When, for example, we receive the sacrament of penance, God gives us his oath that we are forgiven and that his grace will help us resist temptation in the future. When we are confirmed, the oath of God is that the power of the Holy Spirit will enable us to bear witness to Christ and stand faithful to his truth in our every interaction with a sometimes hostile world. In the sacrament of marriage, God makes an oath that he will provide every ounce of grace and strength that the man and woman need to be faithful.

Christ makes the oath that he is coming back, the Gospel tells us, as really and truly as he came the first time. At this second coming, which will occur on a day and at a time that nobody knows, all our trust will be rewarded and all our hope fulfilled. Total freedom from darkness, sin, and death will be ours, with the resurrection of the dead and the final separation of good from evil. All the good that has been done but unacknowledged will be rewarded, and the evil that has been done will be set right.

On that day, we will be asked to give an account of our trust and of how that trust shaped our daily lives. Did we live in a way that showed we trusted in ourselves and our worldly security (possessions, reputation, worldly cunning, and so on), or did we trust in the oath of the one who set us free? Did we try to fix things ourselves, even if it meant lying, cheating, or stealing, or did we do what was right, with trust in God for what we couldn't fix?

The culture of death resorts to the taking of life by abortion and euthanasia in order to fix things in its own eyes. But we trust in the God who makes and fulfills promises.

Twentieth Sunday of Ordinary Time, Year C

Readings: Jeremiah 38:4–6, 8–10 • Hebrews 12:1–4 • Luke 12:49–53

We are destined, in this life, to be divided from at least some people, and today's readings urge us to be divided for the right reasons. Prejudice raises walls between us, a phenomenon that happens all too naturally. The conflict between the culture of life and the culture of death is largely a problem of prejudice against the unborn, the elderly, and the disabled. None of the reasons offered for abortion would be tolerated as reasons to kill the born; it is only because the victims are unborn that they become victims. Similarly, none of the reasons for killing less functional people would be tolerated as reasons to kill the functioning; again, prejudice is the real problem.

When we stand against that prejudice, however, we may get treated like Jeremiah. He was accused of demoralizing the soldiers when he said that the Babylonians could not be stopped in their attack on Jerusalem because God was using them to punish his people. The problem was not military or political, Jeremiah said, but rather moral.

In our day, when we point out the moral problems that stand at the foundation of many societal ills, we too may be rejected and mocked. Issues like abortion will divide family members, as in the Gospel for today. We may need to resist the culture of death even "to the point of shedding blood," as the second reading suggests. Yet whether the opposition launched against us is intense or not, God calls us not to worry about what will happen when we fight for what is right.

. . . .

Twenty-First Sunday of Ordinary Time, Year C

Readings: Isaiah 66:18–21 • Hebrews 12:5–7, 11–13 • Luke 13:22–30

"We ate and drank in your company and you taught in our streets." Evidently, that type of contact with the Lord is not enough to save. The Gospel today challenges us to be disciples internally, not just externally. We may go to Mass, identify ourselves as Christians to others, have our sacramental certificates, wear crosses, and have other religious symbols around us. But that is not enough.

We may indeed hear the Lord teach in our streets. He continues to teach and proclaim his Gospel every time an ordained minister of the Church gives a homily. We hear the Lord speaking through many others too and through our own individual contact with his Word. But still that is not enough.

Discipleship requires obedience to the teaching we hear the Lord give us. It requires actual union with the one with whom we sit at the table.

This has implications for our pro-life stance. It is not enough to get our viewpoint right. Attitudinal opposition to abortion has to translate into behavioral opposition. It is not enough to reject any personal participation in abortion; we must not tolerate it. We must reach out and intervene to save those who are threatened by the culture of death.

. . . .

Twenty-Second Sunday of Ordinary Time, Year C

Readings: Sirach 3:17–18, 20, 28–29 • Hebrews 12:18–19, 22–24a
Luke 14:1, 7–14

Being pro-life is really all about the humility of which today's first reading and Gospel speak. Humility allows us to see each other and ourselves honestly, as neither more nor less than what we are. Because we see the worth of our own lives and those of our neighbors, we are not led by pride to either oppress or ignore others. Rather, humility leads us to serve those lives.

Humility keeps us from being fooled by appearances. The rich, the famous, the powerful—these do not command our attention. Instead we respect and serve the small and lowly. We don't determine their value, and neither does the law.

"When you hold a banquet, invite the poor, the crippled, the lame, the blind; blessed indeed will you be because of their inability to repay you. For you will be repaid at the resurrection of the righteous." Here Jesus urges us toward eschatological realism. We are to evaluate today's choices in the light of what will happen on the last day. This applies perfectly to our service of the unborn. Of anyone we can serve, they are the least able to repay us or even to know of our efforts on their behalf. Pro-life work is the most selfless of all kinds of love, for we love those who cannot love us back.

We love those whom today's psalm calls "the forsaken." We imitate God, "the father of orphans" who "gives a home to the forsaken" and "leads forth prisoners to prosperity" (Psalm 68).

· · · · · · · · · · ·
Twenty-Third Sunday of Ordinary Time, Year C
· ·

Readings: Wisdom 9:13–18b • Philemon 9–10, 12–17 • Luke 14:25–33

"Hating…even his own life": This is a strongly worded condition of discipleship laid out in today's Gospel passage. It takes aim at the arrogance to which the original sin has left us so inclined, the idea that Satan presented to our first parents in the Garden of Eden: "You will be like gods."

This original temptation was a promise that what was right and what was wrong would be up to us, that we could write our own moral law. That's what the "tree of the knowledge of good and evil" meant. Adam and Eve were not supposed to eat from it, for human beings are called to know good from evil but not to decide it.

To think we make decisions about other human beings is the error of the pro-choice mind-set. "It's all up to me and my choice, even if that means killing a baby." This way of thinking, of course, leads to total chaos. On what basis do we tell people not to kill each other or steal from each other if there are no standards of right and wrong that apply to everyone?

The temptation to abort is often couched in reasons and language from the Bible. One might invoke today's Gospel's advice to count the cost before building a tower or marching with an army. Yet prudence does not give license to kill in order to get ourselves out of undesirable consequences of past actions. Prudence, instead, calls us to evaluate consequences before we act. In this sense, the Gospel's lesson is a call to chastity. One should not engage in sexual relations until one is ready to welcome a child in the context of marriage.

The Gospel calls us to calculate the cost of the renunciation of our own understanding, which the first reading also reflects. "For the deliberations of mortals are timid, and uncertain our plans." When a child in the womb seems to throw life's plans out of control, today's message of total trust in the God who knows more than we do is a life-saving message indeed.

· · · · · · · · · · ·

Twenty-Fourth Sunday of Ordinary Time, Year C

Readings: *Exodus 32:7–11, 13–14* • *1 Timothy 1:12–17*
Luke 15:1–32 or 15:1–10

The readings for this Sunday all proclaim the power and depth of God's mercy. The Gospel presents three analogies for the merciful behavior of God the Father; the first reading shows an example of that mercy toward an entire people; the second reading shows an example of it toward an individual, Paul.

This is an opportunity to point out that the gospel of life is a gospel of mercy. Mercy begins with God's decision to create us. We did not ask for or earn our lives, yet God chose to be merciful and give us what we didn't (and can never) deserve. He mercifully rescued us from the nothingness in which we once were and brought us into being. Mercy always welcomes life; the destruction of life is a direct contradiction of mercy.

This weekend is an excellent opportunity to proclaim the mercy of God even in the face of the ongoing abortion tragedy. The Silent No More Awareness Campaign (SilentNoMore.com), a joint project of Priests for Life and Anglicans for Life, is essentially a proclamation of mercy. Women and men who have aborted their children find the healing of Christ and then proclaim his mercy publicly in gatherings, from pulpits, in legislatures, in the media. Some of the testimonies of these men and women can be read, heard, and viewed on the website, and many of these individuals are willing to share their testimony briefly from the pulpit—after Communion, for example. Simply inquire at the website.

Preaching on this theme also gives us the important opportunity to warn against presumption and to distinguish mercy from permission. Neither God's people of old, nor Paul, nor the Prodigal Son were ever given permission to commit evil, before or after they were forgiven. The proclamation of the greatness of God's mercy is meaningful only because the evil of sin is great. Were sin trivial, then mercy would be meaningless.

Some will say, when faced with the temptation to abort (or to commit any other sin), "Well, God is merciful—he'll understand." What he understands is that sin destroys us and that grace can keep us from sin in the first place. The promise of his mercy should never be hijacked and made into an occasion of sin. Mercy follows upon repentance; it does not replace it.

. . . .
Twenty-Fifth Sunday of Ordinary Time, Year C
. . . .

Readings: Amos 8:4–7 • 1 Timothy 2:1–8 • Luke 16:1–13 or 16:10–13

The second reading today contains a verse that forms the basis for the lessons in the other readings: "There is…one mediator between God and men, Christ Jesus, himself human." The reality of the Incarnation speaks to Christian morality, and here in particular to our moral obligations regarding the use of money. The fact that Jesus is both God and man means that our relationship with God is not of a detached spiritual realm, disconnected with the things of earth. Rather, it is precisely through the proper use of the things of earth that we connect with our salvation and our God.

Hence we recognize the importance of earthly goods. We also respect the Church's teaching that the goods of the earth are meant for all people. In the first reading and in the Gospel, the lesson is that people are more important than money. When we mistreat people for the sake of monetary benefit, we harm our relationship with God.

The priority of people over things is a theme that shapes the Church's views of economics, health care, politics, and every realm of human activity. Governments exist for people, not the other way around. Economies exist for people, not the other way around.

These truths form the basis for a culture of life. When they are reversed, societies and individuals feel free to resort to violence against people in order to make things right in some other regard. But a rejection of the human person can never make things right. Only in the affirmation of the person do we find the path to God.

. . . .
Twenty-Sixth Sunday of Ordinary Time, Year C
. . . .

Readings: Amos 6:1a, 4–7 • 1 Timothy 6:11–16 • Luke 16:19–31

We learn many lessons from those who go to heaven. In the story of the rich man and Lazarus, we learn a lesson from one who went to hell.

Why was the rich man condemned? Was it because he had so much? Was there something inherently sinful about the purple and linen in which he dressed or the feasts in which he indulged?

No. The rich man went to hell because he ignored the other man. He was condemned not for what he did but for what he did not do. He did not recognize or treat Lazarus as his equal, his brother. Because Lazarus's possessions were less valuable than his, he considered Lazarus less valuable.

The story causes us to wonder what we would do if we were there. Yet the fact is that we are there now. The Lazarus of the twenty-first century is in our midst. He is with us in the poor, the troublesome, the annoying, the person who is smaller and weaker than we are, and the person who seems different and less valuable. In particular, the Lazarus of the twenty-first century is our preborn brother or sister. This is the person rejected by society, the person who begs for help to live but whose cries are rejected some 3,300 times a day in our country. This is the person torn apart and thrown away by abortion.

The rich man was condemned for not treating Lazarus as his brother. We also will be condemned if we do not treat the preborn as our brothers and sisters. Many oppose abortion and would never have one, but they then ask, "Who am I to interfere with a woman's choice to abort?" Today I will tell you who you are.

You are a brother or a sister of that child in the womb! You are a human being who has enough decency to stand up and say *no!* when you see another human being about to be killed. You are a person who has enough wisdom to realize that injustice to one human being is injustice to every human being. You are a follower of the one who said, "Whatsoever you do to the least of my brothers, you do to me" (Matthew 25:40).

Do we not believe that if we allow a person to die of starvation, we are allowing Christ to die of starvation? Do we not believe that if we leave the sick untended, we are leaving Christ untended? Must we not then also believe that whenever a child in the womb is ripped apart, burned, crushed, and then thrown away, Christ is ripped apart, burned, crushed, and thrown away?

It is Christ in the womb! When we stand up for life, we stand up for him!

· · · · · · · · · · ·

Twenty-Seventh Sunday of Ordinary Time, Year C

Readings: Habakkuk 1:2–3; 2:2–4 • 2 Timothy 1:6–8, 13–14 • Luke 17:5–10

The prophet Habakkuk expresses what many believers say in the face of the culture of death:

How long, O LORD?…

   I cry out to you, "Violence!"

   but you do not intervene.

The Lord says to us what he said to Habakkuk:

The vision still has its time,

   presses on to fulfillment, and will not disappoint.

We have even more reason than Habakkuk to have hope, because the foundational event of the fulfillment of the vision has occurred—the death and resurrection of Christ. We live now in the in-between time, when the kingdom of Christ has been inaugurated on earth but not yet brought to its full manifestation. The power of sin and death—revealed in evils such as abortion—has been destroyed at its roots. Yet we still struggle, in and through Christ, to bring about a culture of life.

The passage from Habakkuk concludes with the familiar line, "The just man, because of his faith, shall live." Our faith gives us life. As Paul declares, God "delivered us from the power of darkness and transferred us to the kingdom of his beloved Son" (Colossians 1:13). This is deliverance from the grip of death, from the kingdom of death, from the covenant with death that is brought about by sin.

The apostles, in the Gospel passage, ask the Lord to increase their faith. Our Lord's response indicates that we need not worry about the quantity of our faith but rather how we use that faith. Paul writes to Timothy, in today's second reading, "God did not give us a spirit of cowardice."

In other words, as we live in the world and fight for what is right, we do not look at the world's evils and the culture of death and wonder how we are ever going to overcome them. Rather, we look at them and renew our conviction that they have been overcome in Christ. We stand before these evils in a stance of victory and say, "You no longer have any place here! Your kingdom has been overcome! We work with courage to change this world and to apply the victory of life that has already been won!"

. . . .

Twenty-Eighth Sunday of Ordinary Time, Year C

Readings: 2 Kings 5:14–17 • 2 Timothy 2:8–13 • Luke 17:11–19

Life was difficult for lepers in the time of Jesus, not simply because of their disease but because of the ostracism they suffered. Leviticus 13:45–46 tells us that lepers were to wear torn clothes, let their hair be disheveled, and live outside the camp. They were to cry, "Unclean, unclean!" when a person without leprosy approached them. Lepers had no right to even speak to Jesus. Moreover, in the ancient Mediterranean world, touching a leper was a radical act.

In Mark 1:40 we read of another encounter of a leper with Jesus. Most English translations of the New Testament say that Jesus was "moved with pity" when he encountered the leper. However, the *Revised English Bible* says that Jesus was "moved to anger." If so, his anger was not at the leper but rather at the system that excluded certain people.

In his ministry, Christ consistently sought out those whom society oppressed and rejected. He broke down the false barriers that people set up among themselves, instead acknowledging the human dignity of every individual. Hence we see him reach out to children (Matthew 19:13–15). to tax collectors and sinners (Mark 2:16), to the blind (Matthew 20:29–34), to a foreign woman (John 4), to gentiles (Matthew 21:41–46), and to lepers (Luke 17:11–19). When it comes to human dignity, Christ erases distinctions.

St. Paul declares, "There is neither Jew nor Greek, there is neither slave nor free person, there is not male and female; for you are all one in Christ Jesus" (Galatians 3:28). Similarly, any distinction between the value of the born and that of the unborn is contrary to all that Scripture teaches. The unborn are the segment of our society that is most neglected and discriminated against today. Christ surely has a special love for them. Will you be his hands, his voice, to save them?

. . . .

Twenty-Ninth Sunday of Ordinary Time, Year C

Readings: Exodus 17:8–13 • 2 Timothy 3:14–4:2 • Luke 18:1–8

Today's readings are focused not only on the efficacy of prayer but more specifically on the efficacy of prayer amid battle and conflict. In the first reading, it is a battle for the very survival of God's people against fierce enemies. In the Gospel, it is a legal battle for justice. These themes of justice, deliverance, and securing rights apply to the protection of the unborn and vulnerable.

As for prayer in the midst of conflict, the connection with the pro-life movement is clear. In The Gospel of Life, Pope St. John Paul II wrote,

It is possible to speak in a certain sense of a war of the powerful against the weak: a life which would require greater acceptance, love and care is considered useless, or held to be an intolerable burden, and is therefore rejected in one way or another. A person who, because of illness, handicap or, more simply, just by existing, compromises the well-being or life-style of those who are more favored tends to be looked upon as an enemy to be resisted or eliminated. In this way a kind of "conspiracy against life" is unleashed. This conspiracy involves not only individuals in their personal, family or group relationships, but goes far beyond, to the point of damaging and distorting, at the international level, relations between peoples and States.[103]

The efforts of those who build a culture of life must be sustained by prayer but not limited to prayer. Moses's hands raised in prayer were essential to victory, but the Israelites also had to fight (first reading). Likewise, we must pray for an end to abortion, but we must also speak, organize, lobby, vote, protest, and intervene.

Finally, this homily can provide an opportunity to invite people to join in the daily prayer campaign to end abortion. There is information about this at PrayerCampaign.org.

- - - - - - - - - -
Thirtieth Sunday of Ordinary Time, Year C

Readings: Sirach 35:12–14, 16–18 • 2 Timothy 4:6–8, 16–18 • Luke 18:9–14

The story in the Gospel passage for today proves the point of the first reading: "The prayer of the lowly pierces the clouds."

But the lesson is not just about the efficacy of prayer. It's about God's love for the smallest, the outcast, the poor. The latter refers to more than the materially deprived. More fundamentally, the poor are those who have no help but God. "The Lord hears the cry of the poor." These cry to him because they don't have access to any of the power structures of this world. Those who should protect them don't.

It belongs to God's very nature to hear the cry of the poor. He is, as the first reading proclaims, "a God of justice." Justice, a powerful theme in Scripture, refers to the intervention of God to rescue the helpless. The fundamental act of intervention in the Old Testament is the Exodus. It foreshadows the supreme act of justice in Jesus Christ, who rescues us from the kingdom of death and hell by his death and resurrection.

All of this points to God's concern for the poorest of the poor. Surely among these are the most helpless of all, the children still in the womb. The power structures of this nation have officially deprived them of their rights of personhood. No group of human beings is more victimized, or in greater numbers, than children in the first nine months after conception.

The God of justice requires his people to "do justice," that is, to "hear the cry of the oppressed," as he does. The unborn child is indeed "the orphan," abandoned by mother and father. Many mothers of the unborn face the plight of the "widow" in Scripture. Half of those who have abortions say that they can't go forward with their pregnancy due to lack of support from the father of the child.

We are called to intervene, to reach those tempted to abort and strengthen them to do what is right. We also must speak out and take action to restore protection to the unborn. The Lord hears the cry of the poor, and so must we. He hears our cry too.

· · · · · · · · · · ·

Thirty-First Sunday of Ordinary Time, Year C

Readings: Wisdom 11:22–12:2 • 2 Thessalonians 1:11–2:2 • Luke 19:1–10

The Gospel story today shows our Lord's eagerness to seek out those whom others disparage. Zacchaeus would have been lost in the crowd because of his small stature had he not climbed the tree. People looked down on him also because of his role as chief tax collector. But Jesus sought him out. He noticed him and even went to dine at his house.

Jesus breaks down the false barriers we place between people. He goes first to those who are pushed aside or ignored by the crowd. The Church, through which Jesus continues to carry out his mission today, does the same thing. We speak up for those pushed aside by the world, including the smallest of the small, the unborn.

The lives of these small ones, like our lives, are the handiwork of God and a continuous proof of his love. The first reading reminds us that, at every moment, God sustains each one of us with the breath of life. We would fall back into nothingness at once if God did not have his love focused on us in an uninterrupted way. To snuff out a life, therefore, whether of the born or the unborn, is a direct contradiction to God's loving will.

On the other hand, we cooperate with the life-giving love of God each time we reach out to those around us who may be unsure about how to handle their pregnancy. We serve God when we give mothers and fathers the strength to love their unborn children. We do likewise when we strengthen those who care for the vulnerable, the disabled, and the dying.

By helping one another grow in love for the weakest in the human family, we and they become more like God. For "how could a thing remain, unless you willed it, or be preserved, had it not been called forth by you?" (first reading).

· · · · · · · · · · ·
Thirty-Second Sunday of Ordinary Time, Year C
· ·

Readings: 2 Maccabees 7:1–2, 9–14 • 2 Thessalonians 2:16–3:5
Luke 20:27–38 or 20:27, 34–38

Today's readings are about the victory of life over death, of fidelity over circumstances. The clear affirmation that God will raise the dead shows that death cannot and will not have the last word in the human story. God is in the business of destroying death, as Isaiah foretold:

He will destroy
the veil that veils all people,
the web that is woven over all nations;
he will destroy death forever. (Isaiah 25:7)

To stand with God is to stand with life; to stand with life is to stand against whatever destroys it. We who work to transform a culture of death into a culture of life begin with this affirmation: God has already won the victory over death! We do not wonder if we will be successful in overcoming abortion, euthanasia, and other forms of violence. Rather, we declare these evils defeated. We strive to bring all society into line with this victory already obtained.

The theme of fidelity in difficult circumstances, such as the Jews in the first reading faced, provides a context for the help we give to those in difficult pregnancies. By our faithfulness to what is right, even if it seems we are going to lose our own lives in the process (literally or figuratively), we end up with the fullness of life.

Martyrdom is exactly the opposite of suicide. In suicide, one declares oneself to be the owner and disposer of one's life. In martyrdom, one declares that God alone is owner and disposer of one's life. We can neither take life nor hold on to it, lest we betray him.

. . . .
Thirty-Third Sunday of Ordinary Time, Year C
. . . .
Readings: Malachi 3:19–20 • 2 Thessalonians 3:7–12 • Luke 21:5–19

The liturgical readings in these days point us toward the end of time, the culmination of salvation history. Themes about the Second Coming in these final Sundays of the liturgical year blend smoothly with the first part of Advent.

The readings of today convey conflict on many levels: within oneself, in families and communities, between Church and state, between nations, and in the heavens. Although God is almighty, he allows good and evil to conflict and allows his people to choose sides. Once we choose, we fight for what we have chosen. Even when we are on God's side, the fight will not be easy. There is a price to pay for doing what is right.

This is the context in which we need to see the Church's defense of human life and our own acknowledgement of the sanctity of life. It is never enough to acknowledge the beauty of life and even present that beauty to others. We are engaged in a full-scale war for the sanctity of life in our day.

Pope St. John Paul II's encyclical *Evangelium Vitae* makes it clear that nobody is exempt from this war. Some pay a high price for their conscientious objection to the forces of death—for example, medical professionals who refuse to take or endanger the lives they are committed to serve.[104] Our suffering, on the other hand, may simply be the ridicule or misunderstanding of family, friends, or fellow Christians when we take a strong stand against abortion.

We have to be ready to fight, both as individuals and as a Church community. We have to be fearless in the face of laws and public policies that contradict the gospel of life, and we must challenge those laws. In the end, the Gospel today tells us, "Not a hair on your head will be destroyed." Indeed, "for you who fear my name, there will arise the sun of justice with its healing rays" (first reading).

· · · · · · · · · · ·

Solemnity of Christ the King
(Thirty-Fourth or Last Sunday of the Year), Year C

· ·

Readings: 2 Samuel 5:1–3 • Colossians 1:12–20 • Luke 23:35–43

Jesus Christ is King of the universe. This feast reminds us that we are accountable to him not only as individuals but also as nations, as societies. It is not only personal, individual actions for which we are accountable; we also must answer to Christ the King for the social policies, cultural mores, and organizational structures on every level of society. These realities are the result of the accumulated actions of many people over long periods of time. Sin is always personal, but there are "structures of sin" that embody the wrong choices individuals have made.

The Church has much to say in this regard. At the heart of her social teaching is the dignity of the human person.

> The Church receives from the Gospel the full revelation of the truth about man. When she fulfills her mission of proclaiming the Gospel, she bears witness to man, in the name of Christ, to his dignity and his vocation to the communion of persons. (*CCC* 2419)

We see in the first reading Israel's acknowledgment of David as her king. Yet the people recognize that it is the Lord who made him their king. "The Lord said to you, 'You shall shepherd my people Israel and shall be commander of Israel.'" Both the people and their king belong to the Lord.

The Gospel shows kingship in another way. Earthly authority made a terrible mistake in crucifying Jesus, and one of the criminals realized that mistake. Jesus is the one with the real power, even while on the cross. He accepts the criminal's acknowledgment that he has a kingdom and asserts that he is the way into paradise.

Jesus's kingship is based on his identity as God and on his redemptive act of suffering, dying, and rising. It is also based on the fact, which comes through clearly in the second reading, that he is Creator. Although we normally attribute this role to the Father, what any person of the Trinity does outside the Trinity is done by all three.

In the passage we read today from Colossians 1, Paul comments on the first words of the Bible, "In the beginning,...God created." He indicates that this "beginning" is none other than Jesus Christ. He is "the beginning" because he is "firstborn of all creation," the one through whom all else was made, the one in whom "all things hold together."

Everything in creation deserves a measure of reverence, for all came through Christ, and all exist for Christ. To stand with Christ is to stand with life. He is King because he is at the very heart of all that is, including the supreme gift of human life.

SOLEMNITIES AND FEASTS SOMETIMES OBSERVED

ON SUNDAYS

· · · · · · · · · · ·

February 2: Feast of the Presentation of the Lord

· ·

Readings: Malachi 3:1–4 • Hebrews 2:14–18 • Luke 2:22–40 or 2:22–32

Today's celebration brings forward several themes that illumine in a particular way the Church's dedication to building the culture of life. The presentation of Jesus in the temple emphasizes, for one thing, the fact that he was like us in all things but sin. This child shared the journey each human being makes through his or her mother's womb. Jesus was an embryo, a fetus, a newborn, and so on. By assuming all the stages of our human journey, he also redeemed them.

This is closely related to a second key theme: We belong to God. In Jesus's case, this is true in a particular way, because he is God's only begotten Son. Yet we all belong to the Father, as do the poor, the sick, the marginalized, the oppressed, and the unborn. Human life cannot be owned by other human beings or by the state. It belongs only to God.

Mary and Joseph recognized that this child entrusted to their care belonged to the Father. Celebrating the presentation gives each of us the privilege of proclaiming, celebrating, and serving the life entrusted to our care, not our ownership.

The candles blessed on this day represent the "light for revelation to the Gentiles" that Simeon recognizes in Christ. Processions with lighted candles commemorate the entry of this light into the temple. Today we shine the light of truth in a dark culture of death. The glory of God, which Christ shines forth to the world, is a glory reflected in every human life.

. . . .
June 24: Solemnity of the Birth of St. John the Baptist
. . . .

Readings:

Vigil Mass

Jeremiah 1:4–10 • 1 Peter 1:8–12 • Luke 1:5–17

Mass during the Day

Isaiah 49:1–6 • Acts 13:22–26 • Luke 1:57–66, 80

To proclaim the culture of life, we must be prophetic. We realize, as the first readings from the Vigil Mass and the Mass during the day tell us, that God gives us the message we proclaim and the motive for which we proclaim it. These messages do not derive from us.

This is a key point of our pro-life stance. Pro-choice activists think that we proclaim our own opinion and that, in doing so, we are setting ourselves up as superior to others. But nothing could be further from the truth. The message we have is the Lord's, and the authority we have to proclaim it is precisely his command and his will to save humanity.

John the Baptist, as the Gospel passages from both Masses make clear, was chosen by God to announce the Lord's coming. His ministry was completely focused on Jesus, as is ours. The proclamation of the gospel of life is the proclamation of a person who by his life and death conquered the kingdom of death. It is by introducing others to the person of Christ that we bring them solidly into the culture of life.

Moreover, coming to Christ requires repentance, which is why John baptized. Integral to repentance is accepting God's dominion over human life and rejecting the idea that life is disposable. One cannot be Christian and pro-choice; this is inherently contradictory. The fruit of repentance is a clear and uncompromising commitment to defend the sanctity of every human life, on both a personal and a societal level.

June 29: Solemnity of Sts. Peter and Paul

Readings:

Vigil Mass:

Acts 3:1–10 • Galatians 1:11–20 • John 21:15–19

Mass during the Day:

Acts 12:1–11 • 2 Timothy 4:6–8, 17–18 • Matthew 16:13–19

We pray on this feast that we will be faithful to the teaching and grace handed down from the apostles. At the heart of that "catholic and apostolic faith" (Eucharistic Prayer 1) is the teaching on the sanctity of life. The fact that God cares for human life is the basis of all he does for us; the fact that he has entrusted us to the care of each other is the basis of all we do for each other.

Also strong among today's themes is that of battle. Peter and Paul had to fight off many enemies and rely on the Lord's power to rescue and sustain them. And what was true for them is true for the Church throughout the ages. We will endure many storms. Yet "the gates of the netherworld shall not prevail." These words apply well to the battles to defend a culture of life against a culture of death.

Yet when we hear about the gates of hell not prevailing, we often forget that it is evil that is on the defense. Gates do not run out onto a battlefield to attack the enemy. Rather, their role is to protect the city from the enemy attacking it. The Church storms the gates of hell. She is on the initiative to advance the kingdom of God and reclaim territory lost to the kingdom of darkness!

Hence today's feast issues a rallying cry for the faithful to build a culture of life, faithful to the teaching handed down from Peter and Paul. We are confident that the gates of sin will melt in the presence of saving grace. The gates of falsehood will flee in the presence of truth. The gates of death will fall in the presence of the people of life.

· · · · · · · · · · ·
August 6: Feast of the Transfiguration
· ·

Readings: Daniel 7:9–10, 13–14 • 2 Peter 1:16–19

Year A: Matthew 17:1–9; Year B: Mark 9:2–10; Year C: Luke 9:28b–36

Christ allowed some of his apostles to see him transfigured, precisely to strengthen them for the coming crucifixion and for the suffering they would endure for proclaiming his name. Today, we too can strengthen people for the trials of their lives by reflecting on who Christ is. He is the one who calls them and accompanies them each day of their lives.

If we think of Christ just as a role model or teacher, we will get some inspiration, but it will not be sufficient to sustain us for the sacrifices that fidelity requires. It is only when we see him in the light of the Transfiguration that we are truly empowered. With an understanding of his identity as God, we begin to understand that our strength comes from his living presence among us and within us. He lives in us; he loves through us.

In the second reading, Peter tells us to be attentive to the Gospel, "as to a lamp shining in a dark place." We might expect him to say that we keep our eyes on the lamp until the morning star rises to give light. But he says, "The morning star rises in your hearts." The image has shifted to the internal world.

But perhaps it hasn't shifted that much. The rising of the morning star in our hearts represents our faith in Christ transfigured—the Christ of glory. This light given to our hearts, our minds, our every choice, indeed enlightens the world. We see creation and circumstances more clearly because we know who Christ is and what he calls us to do.

This presence of Christ strengthens us for sacrifice. It helps us meet the challenges we face and the sacrifices we have to make in order to say yes to life.

· · · · · · · · · · ·
August 15: Feast of the Assumption of Mary
· ·

Readings:
Vigil Mass
1 Chronicles 15:3–4, 15, 16; 16:1–2 • 1 Corinthians 15:54b–57
Luke 11:27–28
Mass during the Day
Revelation 11:19a; 12:1–6a, 10ab • 1 Corinthians 15:20–26 • Luke 1:39–56

Today's feast is a perfect opportunity to preach about the Christian truth of the victory of life over death. Christ is life, and he shares his victory over death with all the members of his body, the Church. "In Christ shall all be brought to life" (second reading). Mary, who was and is closer to him than anyone else, is the first to share, body and soul, in this victory.

Mary's bodily assumption reminds us that human beings are not disembodied souls but rather a unity of body and soul. This is a critically important truth to emphasize in the culture of life. The culture of death so often relies on a dualism that says that it's the spirit (good intentions and love) that matters, while what we do with our bodies is of little consequence. This dualism degrades sexual relations and justifies the destruction of the body by abortion and euthanasia. But the truth is that the body is just as much an aspect of the person as is the soul. To attack the body is to attack the person.

Finally, the assumption reminds us that in God's plan for life, mother and child go together. In bringing Mary to bodily glory with him, Jesus shows that there can be no closer human bond than that between a mother and her child. The pro-life movement stands with both the mother and the child. We ask, "Why can't we love them both?"

September 14: Feast of the Exaltation of the Cross

Readings: Numbers 21:4b–9 • Philippians 2:6–11 • John 3:13–17

This feast ties in easily with pro-life themes. For the cross is the antidote to the perversion of autonomy that lies at the heart of the culture of death.

Pro-choice is an exaltation of self; the cross is the denial of self. Pro-choice is the assertion of oneself; the cross is the emptying of oneself. Pro-choice says we can lift ourselves up; the cross says that we are obedient and that God lifts us up.

The war between the culture of life and the culture of death did not begin with *Roe v. Wade*, although it did enter a new chapter at that point. It is a cosmic struggle, with its origins at the dawn of human history and, in fact, in the history of the angels. In Revelation 12:7 we read, "War broke out in heaven."

War is a terrible thing on earth. What must it mean to have war break out in heaven? This war involved some angels who rebelled against God and became devils. What would cause an angel to become a devil? What was the devils' mistake?

In Isaiah 14, we read a rebuke to the king of Babylon. The passage has a deeper spiritual meaning; it is a glimpse into the thinking of the evil one.

> How you have fallen from the heavens,
>> O Morning Star ["Lucifer" in the Vulgate translation]…!
> In your heart you said:
>> "I will scale the heavens;
> Above the stars of God
>> I will set up my throne….
> I will ascend above the tops of the clouds;
>> I will be like the Most High!" (Isaiah 14:12, 13, 14)

There is the devil's mistake. He thought that he could be God! The angels who fought him in heaven were led by one named Michael, which means "Who is like God?"

Michael and his angels won, but the war did not end there. Satan and his legion were "thrown down to the earth" (Revelations 12:9), and our troubles began.

The solution to the thinking of the evil one is the thinking of the Holy One. As Isaiah lifted the veil to show us the mind of Lucifer, so St. Paul, in today's second reading, lifts the veil to show us the mind of Christ:

> Christ Jesus, who, though he was in the form of God,
> did not regard equality with God something to be grasped.
> Rather, he emptied himself,
> taking the form of a slave…
> He humbled himself.…
> Because of this God greatly exalted him.

This attitude, which St. Paul says must be ours, counters the attitude in which we exalt ourselves by our own choices. Our true exaltation, our true freedom, and our fulfillment come from a humble acceptance of and obedience to a truth that we did not create. True freedom is the power to choose what is right and to love as Christ did. We find it in embracing the cross and giving ourselves away for the good of others.

. . . .

November 1: Feast of All Saints

Readings: Revelation 7:2–4, 9–14 • 1 John 3:1–3 • Matthew 5:1–12a

One could say that this is a feast of perspective. It is a day to renew our focus on what really matters. Our human way of thinking is not God's way. The eschatological perspective provided by the first reading, the second reading's words on the essence of holiness, and the lesson of the Beatitudes, reminding us how we usually get things upside down—all point to this.

It is not just a matter of how we see things but of where our passion is, as the psalm response makes clear. We are "the people that longs to see" God's face (Psalm 24). That's the driving force behind our worship, our daily activities, and the manner in which we handle our daily trials.

When we have the perspective of the saints, we see that people are more important than things and that the most neglected of people are most worthy of our attention and service. The saints lived the Beatitudes, first of all by weeping over the evils in themselves and in the world. Have we wept for the oppressed? Have we shed tears for the unborn? Have we allowed our hearts to be broken open so that God can pour into them the compassion and love necessary to meet our neighbors' needs?

The saints thirsted for holiness (for themselves) and for justice (for others). They did precisely what the Church does today in speaking up for the helpless. It's not simply a political agenda but rather part of this longing to see God. We see his face in the poor, the oppressed, the forgotten, the unborn. We serve our neighbor there, and we proclaim to others that God is there. And if we are faithful in doing that, we will see God face-to-face for all eternity.

· · · · · · · · · · ·
November 2: Feast of All Souls
· ·

Readings each year are chosen from among the Masses for the dead.

"In him the hope of blessed resurrection has dawned, that those saddened by the certainty of dying might be consoled by the promise of immortality to come," says Preface 1 for the Dead. This declaration of the Church's liturgy sheds light on her commitment to building a culture of life. The gospel of life is ultimately about life eternal, a precondition of which is natural life.

In our struggle against the forces of death, we must feel its sorrow and pain. To fail to do so is to fail to be human and to fail to love. When we lose a loved one, we weep because we love that person. We grieve just as Jesus did at Lazarus's death (see John 11:35–36). Yet we are not overwhelmed by sorrow, nor are we caught in despair. We grieve with hope, because we know that death does not have the final word. We know that the farewell is a temporary one. We will be reunited with our loved one in the resurrection.

As we confront the culture of death and in particular the holocaust of abortion, we grieve and weep. Yet we do so with hope. Ours is the unshakeable confidence that the kingdom of death has already been destroyed. We continue our pro-life work with confidence and joy.

· · · · · · · · · ·

November 9: Feast of the Dedication of the Lateran Basilica in Rome

· ·

Readings: Ezekiel 47:1–2, 8–9, 12 • 1 Corinthians 3:9c–11, 16–17
John 2:13–22

On this feast, the liturgy focuses on the unity of the Church throughout the world as the living body of Christ and temple of the Holy Spirit. That unity implies solidarity and the obligation to care for one another's lives. God has entrusted us to the care of each other.

The second reading points out that we are each a dwelling place of the Holy Spirit. It draws the conclusion that one who destroys a human life destroys God's dwelling. This recalls some striking lines in Pope St. John Paul II's *Evangelium Vitae*:

> Life, especially human life, belongs only to God: for this reason whoever attacks human life in some way attacks God himself.[105]

And:

> It is precisely in the "flesh" of every person that Christ continues
> to reveal himself and to enter into fellowship with us, so that rejec-
> tion of human life, in whatever form that rejection takes, is really
> a rejection of Christ.[106]

The Church is the sign and stimulus of the unity of the human family. The supernatural unity expressed so strongly by today's feast presupposes and fosters the more basic unity on a purely human level—starting with the respect and vigorous defense of everyone's right to life.

The waters of life in the first reading reinforce this reflection. These waters make the sea fresh. And wherever they flow, "every sort of living creature that can multiply shall live." These waters "gladden the city of God, the holy dwelling of the Most High!" (Psalm 46). Our God is the God of life.

1. U.S. Conference of Catholic Bishops, Resolution on Abortion, November 7, 1989.

2. See statistics on abortion from 1975 to 2015, www.gallup.com/poll/1576/abortion.aspx.

3. See Lydia Saad, "Americans' Abortion Views Steady Amid Gosnell Trial," May 10, 2013, www.gallup.com.

4. See William Robert Johnston, "Reasons Given for Having Abortions in the United States," August 26, 2012, http://www.johnstonsarchive.net.

5. Pope St. John Paul II, *Evangelium Vitae*, 99.

6. "Among the 42 areas that reported the number of previous abortions for 2008, the majority of women (55.6%) had not previously had an abortion; 36.4% and 8.0%, respectively, had previously had either one to two abortions, or three or more abortions." See Karen Pazol et al., Division of Reproductive Health, National Center for Chronic Disease Prevention and Health Promotion, "Abortion Surveillance—United States, 2008," www.cdc. gov.

7. Pontifical Council for the Family, *The Truth and Meaning of Human Sexuality: Guidelines for Education within the Family*, 137.

8. Guttmacher Institute, "Fact Sheet: Induced Abortion in the United States," July 2014, www.guttmacher.org.

9. See Dr. Philip Ney, "A Consideration of Abortion Survivors," posted September 28, 2006, www.messengers2.com.

10. Vatican II, Decree on the Apostolate of Lay People, 12, in Austin Flannery, *The Conciliar and Post Conciliar Documents*, vol. 1, *Vatican Council II* (New York: Costello, 1998), 781.

11. *Evangelium Vitae*, 2.

12. See *Sing a Little Louder*, a movie inspired by the memories of an elderly man who in his youth witnessed the horrors of the Jewish Holocaust from the pews of his church. (Catholic Witnesses, 2014), http://singloudermovie. com.

13. Memorial Acclamation, Order of the Mass.

14. Dr. Bernard Nathanson, *Archdiocese of New York, Respect Life Clergy Days 1990 Audiocassettes* (Pleasantville, NY: Mustard Seed, 1990).

15. Cardinal Joseph Bernardin, "A Consistent Ethic of Life: Continuing the Dialogue," lecture delivered at St. Louis University, March 11, 1984.

16. Cardinal Joseph Bernardin, address at Seattle University, March 2, 1986.

17. U.S. Conference of Catholic Bishops, "Pastoral Plan for Pro-Life Activities: A Campaign in Support of Life" (Washington, D.C.: USCCB, 2001).

18. See Bernard Nathanson, *Aborting America* (New York: Pinnacle, 1979).

19. See Carol Everett, *Blood Money: Getting Rich Off a Woman's Right to Choose* (Colorado Springs: Multnomah, 1992).
20. See Michael Medved, *Hollywood vs. America: Popular Culture and the War on Tradition* (New York: Harper Perennial, 1993).
21. *General Instruction of the Roman Missal (GIRM)*, 65, www.usccb.org.
22. Opinion delivered by Justice Blackmun, *Roe v. Wade* (1973), No. 70–18, IX, B, caselaw.findlaw.com.
23. *Evangelium Vitae*, 76.
24. Carol Everett and Jack Shaw, *The Scarlet Lady: Confessions of a Successful Abortionist* (Brentwood, Tenn.: Wolgemuth and Hyatt, 1991), 101.
25. Nathanson, *Aborting America*, 193.
26. See Vatican II, *Gaudium et Spes*, 22, in Flannery, 922.
27. Homily of John Paul II, Holy Mass at Yankee Stadium, New York, October 2, 1979.
28. Pope St. John Paul II, *Veritatis Splendor*, 35.
29. Justice Anthony Kennedy, *Planned Parenthood v. Casey*, 1992, [505 U.S.833, 851].
30. Pope St. John Paul II, Homily at World Youth Day, 5 (1993), www.vatican.va.
31. Vatican II, *Lumen Gentium*, 11, in Flannery, 362.
32. Sacramentary, Common Preface III.
33. See Athanasios Moulakis, *Simone Weil and the Politics of Self-Denial* (Columbia, Mo.: University of Missouri, 1998), 206.
34. Sacrament of Penance, Prayer of Absolution.
35. U.S. Bishops, "Pastoral Plan for Pro-Life Activities."
36. Cardinal Joseph Bernardin, "The Consistent Ethic of Life and Health Care Systems," Foster McGaw Triennial Conference (Loyola University of Chicago, May 8, 1985), p. 4, www.paxjoliet.org. See more quotes at www.priestsforlife.org/ConsistentEthic.
37. U.S. Bishops, Resolution on Abortion, 1989.
38. Office of General Counsel, U.S. Catholic Bishops, Political Activity and Lobbying Guidelines for Catholic Organizations, March 1, 2015, p. 19, www.usccb.org.
39. Bob Dufford, S.J., "Be Not Afraid," St. Louis Jesuits.
40. Lectionary, 93.
41. *Gaudium et Spes*, 39, in Flannery, 938.
42. John Philip Sullivan, trans., "O Holy Night," 1855.
43. *Gaudium et Spes*, 22.
44. *Evangelium Vitae*, 9.
45. *Evangelium Vitae*, 104.
46. *Evangelium Vitae*, 1.
47. Order of the Mass, priest's prayer between the Our Father and the Sign of Peace.

48. St. Athanasius, quoted in Michael E. Molloy, *Champion of Truth: The Life of Saint Athanasius* (New York: Alba, 2003), 10.

49. *Evangelium Vitae*, 79.

50. See *Evangelium Vitae*, 78–101.

51. Pope John Paul II refers to the "people of life" repeatedly in *Evangelium Vitae*. See section 79 of this encyclical for a fuller explanation.

52. Renewal of Baptismal Promises, Easter Liturgy.

53. *Evangelium Vitae*, 34.

54. *Evangelium Vitae*, 30.

55. Helen Prejean, *Dead Man Walking: The Eyewitness Account of the Death Penalty That Sparked a National Debate* (New York: Vintage, 1994), 195.

56. *Evangelium Vitae*, 51.

57. *Evangelium Vitae*, 104.

58. See SilentNoMore.com and RecallAbortion.com.

59. *Evangelium Vitae*, 1, 2, quoting Vatican II, *Gaudium et Spes*, 22.

60. *Evangelium Vitae*, 79.

61. Fr. Seraphim Michalenko, "Wombs of Mercy," *Marian Helpers Bulletin*, Summer 1995, 13. See St. Faustina's diary, *Divine Mercy in My Soul*, 474.

62. See Susan Donaldson James, "Down Syndrome Births Are Down in U.S.," November 2, 2009, abcnews.go.com.

63. *Lumen Gentium*, 11.

64. See Pope Benedict XVI, *Ubicumque et semper*.

65. *Evangelium Vitae*, 1.

66. William Brennan, *Dehumanizing the Vulnerable: When Word Games Take Lives* (Chicago: Loyola University Press, 1995).

67. St. Augustine, *Confessions*, bk. 1, chap. 1.

68. See U.S. Catholic Bishops, "Living the Gospel of Life: A Challenge to American Catholics," 4.

69. Congregation for the Doctrine of the Faith, "Doctrinal Note on Some Questions Regarding the Participation of Catholics in Political Life," 2. See *Evangelium Vitae*, 22.

70. *Gaudium et Spes*, 22.

71. *Evangelium Vitae*, 62. See Pope Paul VI, *Humanae Vitae*, 14.

72. *Evangelium Vitae*, 34.

73. Moulakis, 206.

74. *Evangelium Vitae*, 76.

75. *Evangelium Vitae*, 8.

76. *Evangelium Vitae*, 92.

77. *Evangelium Vitae*, 9.

78. Diane Gianelli, interview with Dr. James McMahon, *American Medical News*, July 5, 1993.

79. Gianelli, interview with Dr. James McMahon.

80. See Pontifical Council for Justice and Peace, *Compendium of the Social Doctrine of the Church*, www.vatican.va.
81. *Evangelium Vitae*, 99.
82. Pope Benedict XVI, *Caritas in Veritate*, 76.
83. *Caritas in Veritate*, 79.
84. Pope Benedict XVI, Meeting with Roman Clergy, Hall of Blessings, March 2, 2006, www.vatican.va.
85. See *Compendium of the Social Doctrine of the Church*.
86. Blackmun, IX, A.
87. *Evangelium Vitae*, 9, 104.
88. *Evangelium Vitae*, 91.
89. See U.S. Bishops, "Pastoral Plan for Pro-life Activities."
90. Memorial Acclamation.
91. Communion Rite, 125.
92. Eucharistic Prayer III.
93. Preface, Feast of Christ the King.
94. Gianelli, interview with Dr. James McMahon.
95. Pope Paul VI, *Evangelii Nuntiandi*, 76.
96. *Evangelium Vitae*, 2.
97. Preface, Feast of Christ the King.
98. Mother Teresa of Calcutta, "Whatsoever You Do...," speech to the National Prayer Breakfast, Washington, D.C., February 3, 1994. See transcript at www.priestsforlife.org.
99. Dr. Martin Luther King Jr., "I've Been to the Mountaintop" speech, Memphis, Tenn., April 3, 1968, www.americanrhetoric.com.
100. See Dr. Philip Ney, "Wanted or Welcomed: The Real Choice That Decides Which Child Survives," *Free Republic*, December 1998, www.freerepublic.com.
101. Terry Beresford, "Abortion: Securing Women's Rights, Ensuring Women's Health," National Abortion Federation, Seventeenth Annual Meeting, April 25–28, 1993, Loews L'Enfant Plaza Hotel, Washington, D. C., Spirituality and Abortion Providers Workshop, Tape 5-937.
102. Rose Marie, "Come Forth," December 1979, private correspondence with the author.
103. *Evangelium Vitae*, 12.
104. See *Evangelium Vitae*, 73–74.
105. *Evangelium Vitae*, 9.
106. *Evangelium Vitae*, 104.

ABOUT THE AUTHOR

Fr. Frank Pavone is the national director for Priests for Life, the largest pro-life ministry in the Catholic Church, and is one of the most prominent pro-life leaders in the world. Originally from New York, Fr. Pavone was ordained in 1988 by Cardinal John O'Connor, and since 1993 has served full-time in pro-life leadership with his bishops' permission. He is also the president of the National Pro-Life Religious Council and the national pastoral director of the Silent No More Awareness Campaign and of Rachel's Vineyard, the world's largest ministry of post-abortion healing.